CENSORED

The master of
ceremonies (Anton
Walbrook) in Max
Ophuls's *La Ronde*
(1950).

CENSORED

TOM DEWE MATHEWS

CHATTO & WINDUS

LONDON

First published 1994

5 7 9 10 8 6

First published in the United Kingdom in 1994 by
Chatto & Windus Ltd
Random House, 20 Vauxhall Bridge Road,
London SW1V 2SA

Random House Australia (Pty) Limited
20 Alfred Street, Milson's Point, Sydney,
New South Wales 2061, Australia

Random House New Zealand Limited
18 Poland Road, Glenfield
Auckland 10, New Zealand

Random House South Africa (Pty) Limited
PO Box 337, Bergvlei, South Africa

Random House UK Limited Reg. No. 954009

A CIP catalogue record for this book
is available from the British Library

ISBN 0 7011 3873 4

Designed by Margaret Sadler

Printed in Great Britain by Butler & Tanner Ltd,
Frome , Somerset

CONTENTS

INTRODUCTION ✂

Today, Britain possesses the most rigorous film censorship system in the western world. Yet from the emergence of cinema at the turn of the century when the upper and middle classes already scented danger, from the 'new excitement' through until today when sex and violence on the screen are still treated warily, the British political establishment has always stood to one side while the public received films with open arms.

Throughout its lifespan censorship has varied with the social mores of the day – slowly becoming more liberal but always influenced by what the social historian Geoffrey Pearson has called our 'respectable fears'. For censorship as a way of filtering culture lies at the core of English custom. Traditionally we have been and still are a coercive society. Just over two centuries ago London magistrates banned such games as skittles from being played outside the capital's pubs. Fifty years later buskers, football players and street traders were outlawed from the streets. By 1870 music halls were threatened with withdrawal of their licences if performers included material 'offensive' to magistrates, police or politicians. And sixteen years after its birth in 1896, cinema was caught in the same net.

But the practice of censorship as a means of blanking out what we do not want to witness has not been an arbitrary vendetta against precocious voices. It is, in fact, a systematic process which chooses its victims with care. The direction and intensity of censorship is determined by the popularity of a new medium. Thus film was censored in Britain more than any of the other media until cinema was superseded by television as the primary mass medium in the fifties. From then on censorship of film relaxed until its offspring, video, proved to be popular in the eighties and so the spotlight of censorship turned to film once more. So how did we come to accept this vigorous intervention in what the Italian director Federico Fellini called 'the tenth muse'?

Dickens once remarked that the British have supine natures because we are 'habitually consenting parties to the miserable imbecilities into which we have fallen'. Apart from such questions of national character, more specifically our allegiance to a self-restrictive cinema is largely due to the unbending structure of a class system which demands that 'them' be separated from 'us'.

The historian A. J. P. Taylor has pointed out that cinema-going was the 'essential habit' of the Edwardian age, yet 'highly educated people saw in it only vulgarity and the end of Old England'. This fear of the effects of a mass medium on a mass audience has never left us. Presumably the political establishment really did believe that the working class would revolt if given the opportunity of seeing Russian propagandist films such as *Battleship Potemkin*, and so the genre was assiduously censored in the 1920s. Equally the censor of the fifties was convinced that middle-class property would be destroyed if working-class youth were allowed to witness – and therefore emulate – Marlon Brando's leather-clad 'leader of the pack' in *The Wild One*. For, then as now, film censorship was not governed by the actual content of films; it was more concerned with their effect. Thus the censor's long-serving, silently spoken rubric: the larger the audience, the lower the moral mass resistance to suggestion.

But fear of political consequences has also determined that film censorship has remained shrouded in secrecy. This was especially the case in the inter-war years when any accurate presentation of the working classes was either not made, or, if it was produced, such a film did not gain a general release for fear of damaging an already fragile social status quo. To remain covert, however, this form of censorship necessitated the silence of the censored. Fortunately for the censors the promoters of the nascent film industry colluded in the unpublicised pact because they wished to gain respectability, without which they could not have won the vital patronage of middle-class customers. And once the industry had been drawn into this mutually supportive system the distributors and the exhibitors had to reinforce it, as exposure of their partnership would – and occasionally did – bring down abuse and ridicule upon their heads as well as on those of the actual censors. So the power of such a vetting system can be measured by its current ability to withstand exposure and examination, and consequently the censorship of British cinema still remains covert. Today it is possible to find out if a film has been censored, but the censors are still not obliged to reveal by how much, or for what reason.

It is not surprising, therefore, that the censor's priestly dependence on mystery has also affected the contents of this particular book. It has to be admitted at the outset, though, that the first difficulty in this survey was not caused by British censors. It was, in fact, a consequence of a *Luftwaffe* bomb which in 1941 destroyed the Board of Censors' offices along with nearly all the papers dealing with the examination of individual films from before that date. As a result the Board's treatment of pre-war films, as described here, is largely based on sources from outside the British Board of Film Censors.

The second stumbling-block, however, can be laid firmly at the door of the BBFC and the present head censor's insistence that BBFC examination papers dated after 1975 must remain secret because of 'the examiners' need for confidentiality'. In spite of considerable assistance from James Ferman, the current

Director of the BBFC, I felt that this history would be incomplete without the contribution of other censors who had been examining films since the cut-off date. In order, therefore, to draw the fullest possible picture of present-day attitudes towards the control of cinema and its contents I interviewed examiners who have censored films from 1969 to the present day, but, although they were prepared to speak out freely, their words have to remain anonymous.

Of course this examination of the meeting ground between politics and film where censorship exists has also been circumscribed by intentional barriers. In order to concentrate on the ways in which films and scripts have been specifically altered by 'approved' censors, I have left to one side wider and more general attitudes within the film world which also play their part in deciding whether one film is made while another never sees the studio. Apart from these external dictates, I have tried to allow the nature of Britain's film censorship to guide the contents of *Censored*.

Britain's censors have cast their net far and wide, catching forgotten 'B' movies, skinflicks, dry documentaries, as well as the classics of the cinema. I have therefore treated films not so much in terms of their cinematic merit but more according to the reaction, or alternatively the striking lack of reaction, that they provoked from the censor. This has meant, in turn, that some film subjects, such as sex in the early cinema, have had to double back in the overall chronology of the book to their origins.

The very nature of censorship in this country has dictated that a history of censorship is also a history of its censors. The influence of the individual censors themselves has ebbed and flowed, being especially strong during the thirties and the eighties when the censorship system became centralised almost to the extent of becoming an arm of the government. At these times the character of such censors as Sir William Joynson-Hicks, the anti-Semitic Home Secretary who banned Eisenstein's *Potemkin*, or that of the current head censor James Ferman, who has described himself as a 'better feminist than women', has affected policy as well as censorship style. But this is not to say that the system has been monolithic; on the contrary, there have been disparate sources of intervention and a changing cast of external players in the roundelay of Britain's film censorship. Many have shoved their way to the front so effectively that they cannot be ignored; but other equally concerned but more thoughtful voices are also heard.

Overall, my personal aim in writing this book is to throw some much-needed light into the murky processes and opaque aims of Britain's film censorship. I began this project believing that a centralised system of delegated censorship was not too high a price to pay in order to protect those too young to discriminate for themselves. However, after a lengthy look at the currency involved, I now doubt its value. Just like all the other media – books, theatre, the visual arts – films should find their audience in the market-place without intervention, and be subject only to the laws of the land. While these laws may not be to everyone's liking, at least they are open to public debate.

Undoubtedly the abolition of an officially approved intermediary between the cinema and its audience would not win the support of the British film industry, as it would encourage court cases; but once films have settled into democratically agreed terms under the law they could be freed from the ever-contentious question of whether they should be released or banned and open to the more appropriate and more public discussion of their merits or lack thereof. For as the essayist William Hazlitt wrote in defence of the theatre, when that medium was under attack for its own irredeemable immediacy: 'The stage not only refines the manners, but it is the best teacher of morals, for it is the truest and most intelligible picture of life.' The screen has succeeded to that claim of universality and it should now claim the same freedom.

ACKNOWLEDGEMENTS

No history of film in Btitain could be written without recourse to the work of various scholars and commentators. In the arena of film censorship this dependency on the groundwork of others is doubly true and my first debt is to the writings of Annette Kuhn, James C. Robertson, Jeffrey Richards, Jeremy Croft, Nicholas Pronay, Derek Hill, Paul O'Higgins and Alexander Walker.

Throughout this project's lengthy gestation and birth I have been indebted to the encouragement and advice of Marina Warner. Since then I have benefited from long, fruitful conversations with Philip Dodd and Neil Norman and I am especially grateful to Mark Kermode for his scrutiny of the last three chapters of the book and his ready availability to discuss the finer points of film censorship whether he was far or near from his home.

My thanks also go to Kerry Kohler, Rene Eyre, Tony Morris, Richard Strange, Tim Rayner, Ticker and Chrissie Blunt and Judy Breakell for the use of their books and for help with the manuscript. I am especially grateful to George Melly, Philip French, Kevin Brownlow, Stephen Woolley, Nigel Floyd, Pete Dean, Alan Bryce and the late Derek Jarman for making themselves available for interviews and for pointing me in the direction of lost nuggets of censorship.

I would also like to acknowledge the help of the Director of the BBFC, James Ferman, for granting me many lengthy interviews and of his secretary, Xandra Barry, for her immediate response to the constant requests for the verification of multiple as well as single facts. My thanks are also due to the Deputy Director Margaret Ford and the Principal Examiner Guy Phelps for their explanations of the censorship system and to my copy-editor Betty Palmer.

I owe an incalculable debt to those examiners who have made themselves available for interviews. Without their comments this book would have had to stop short in 1975; yet those views have been given at considerable risk to their own careers and livelihoods. I hope this book reflects their unanimous belief that Britain's film censorship should be more open to the public.

To my publisher at Chatto & Windus, Jonathan Burnham, I owe a special thanks. His sense of organisation helped shape a book dependent on chronological structure and his unerring eye for contradictions saved me from embarrassments too numerous to mention. From my editor, Rowena Skelton-Wallace, I have also benefited from a diligent eye, but even more importantly, at times when curiosity was tempted to give way to torpor, I am grateful for her infectious enthusiasm.

I am also indebted to the patience and skill of Peggy Sadler whose design of the book exceeded my hopes, and to the long hours of picture research put in by the staff of the Ronald Grant Archive.

A huge debt of gratitude is owed to Peter Dewe Mathews for generosity way beyond the call of brotherly love.

Lastly, and most of all, I would like to thank – and seek redemption – from Louisa Buck for whom my never-ending question, 'Can you check this?' became the only confirmation of my presence for too many years.

BRIDGET SERVED THE SALAD UNDRESSED

The first film to be censored in Britain did not possess a star. It could not even boast a human cast. Instead it featured a piece of cheese – a slice of Stilton, to be precise. The blue-veined English cheese was filmed through a microscope by the film pioneer and experimental colourist Charles Urban in 1898. However, the prospect of customers gazing at the intricacies of bacterial movement magnified over a hundred times on to a wall-sized screen spurred the British cheese industry into virulent protest and the ninety-second film was withdrawn.

Such realistic drama, albeit microscopic, was not the usual fare on offer to Britain's first cinema-goers. The smash hit of 1896 was less than two minutes of *Girl Climbing a Tree*, only to be outgrossed in the following year by ninety seconds of *How Bridget Served the Salad Undressed*. This modest little tale was described in a Biograph catalogue of the 1890s as 'an old and always popular story. Bridget of course brings in the salad in a state of déshabillé hardly allowable in polite society.'

Nevertheless, it is appropriate that Britain's first film censorship was instigated by the American-born Charles Urban. Urban managed the English interests of Thomas R. Edison. After inventing the gramophone and the light bulb, 'the wizard of Menlo Park' had created the Kinetoscope, or peepshow, in 1891. Within a decade Edison's peepshows were to be eclipsed by projected film, but not before they had indelibly tainted the early cinema with a reputation for sleaze. It was not the content of the short peepshow tableaux such as 'Beware My Husband Comes', 'Love in a Hammock', or, most famously, 'What the Butler Saw' that aroused the ire of the Edwardian church and courts – the only provocative thing about these little scenarios was their titles; what gave the 'peeps' a bad name was the people who watched them.

It was the working classes who peered into the little black boxes to see more of 'What the Curate Really Did' and their obvious enjoyment created a mixture of envy and distaste amongst the upper echelons. But there was very little that the 'nicer class of person' could do to curb this instrument of mass appeal. The sheer novelty of the invention placed it in a legal vacuum. Showmen at funfairs and amusement arcades didn't need a licence to operate Kinetoscopes. And even more importantly, this loophole also applied to the other great cinematic invention of the time: projected film.

A butler's eye view of Esme Collings's 'Victorian Lady at Her Boudoir' (1896). A rare shot from an end-of-the-pier Kinetoscope in the year film was invented.

Power abhors a vacuum and the local councils of Edwardian Britain came to resent their lack of influence over this burgeoning new industry. By the beginning of 1909 this frustration had reached fever pitch. The Home Secretary was bombarded by a volley of petitions issued by indignant local bodies. The rallying cry became public safety: venues for viewing Kinetoscope and celluloid were deemed to be a fire risk and therefore had to be brought under official control. The government responded with the Cinematograph Act of 1909 which invested local authorities with the power to grant or veto licences to both the peepshow arcades and the new purpose-built picture palaces. But under the cloak of safety, censorship would be smuggled in.

Public safety became the Trojan horse through which the myriad controls were ushered in under the cover of the new cinema licensing laws. It was not long before the councils and other local authorities such as magistrates and the police were able to determine not only how films should be shown but also what should be shown in them. From such questionable democratic origins the cinema licensing system thus became the sole legal foundation of film censorship in Britain, and it has remained so until today.

The passing of the Cinematograph Act was, in fact, the price that cinema had to pay for its runaway success. By 1909 this success had been coupled with a new aura of respectability; and it was this new status that turned the cinema into a bureaucratic object of desire. The stages by which this evolution from working man's pastime to middle-class recreation occurred reveal the attitudes which lay behind early censorship and which led up to its first legal enshrinement.

With the turn of the century working people drifted away from the rows of peepshow machines to cram together in converted shops for the exhibition of the very first films of waves breaking or trains rushing towards them from the new big screen. These 'pennygaffs' were not furnished with discreet sidelights; the films were projected in total darkness. To counter the reports of 'misconduct' amongst the packed audiences which immediately appeared in contemporary newspapers, many penny-gaff owners foisted daylight projection on to their audiences. The idea behind this early intervention was that if the screen was placed in a darkened alcove the rest of the room could be fully illuminated. But imposed morality did not pay. 'I have tried the light and the dark halls,' one showman complained, 'and find the public prefer the latter, especially the young couples, who like to see the pictures and have a canoodle at the same time. I found that I lost nearly all the courters – the biggest portion of my patrons – by adopting the lighting principle, and soon went back to the old principle.'

If contemporary moral reformers were worried that the cinema might become a popular site for youthful lust, Edwardian social reformers were more concerned about the health hazard presented by cinemas. It was not uncommon for some members of film audiences at this time to be so transfixed by moving images they would relieve themselves while they remained seated rather than use a toilet outside the auditorium. Consequently, many penny gaffs smelt of urine and disinfectant.

Moral reformers, on the other hand, were more disturbed by the size of the 'wall-sized monster' being projected on to walls. For moralists on both sides of the Atlantic bigger now meant worse. In *The Kiss* of 1896, 'neither of the participants' according to the Chicago publisher Herbert S. Stone, 'was physically attractive and the prolonged pasturing on each other's lips was hard to bear . . . magnified to Gargantuan proportions and repeated three times over it is absolutely disgusting.' The newspaperman issued a 'call for police interference'.

As the screen size increased so did the obsession of film-makers and their audiences to see how anything and everything would look once it was placed in front of a camera. This innocent curiosity often had grisly results: contemporary taste, as one exhibitor put it, ran towards 'the hot and strong'. Human operations could be seen in all their gory detail as well as attacks on animals including bulls, foxes, and two lions killing an elephant. Cinematic curiosity even inspired a continental film-maker to force a horse over a cliff so that he could photograph the results as the animal was dashed on the rocks below. Yet

The beheading of Chinese bandits at Mukden from a 1901 newsreel produced by Charles Urban.

it is indicative of Edwardian attitudes to animal rights that out of all these films the only one that attracted any adverse comment was the death of the elephant, and that was because a citizen of Burnley disapproved of 'the natives' dancing around the carcass.

It is not altogether surprising therefore that the snuff movie also had its origins in this era. Real-life executions were particularly popular, a special favourite being the beheading of half a dozen 'bandits' by the Chinese army outside Mukden, the ancient capital of Manchuria, which was shown in the same programme as the hanging of a cattle rustler amidst a huge crowd in Missouri. Across the Channel it was the withdrawal of a newsreel showing four Frenchmen being guillotined at Béthune that became the first official instance of French film censorship in 1909.

The same unconscious lack of taste seeped into the melodramatic plots of fiction films once they started to be produced after the turn of the century. Innocent or not, it's doubtful whether these films would be passed by censors today. A letter to a 1909 issue of *Kinematograph & Lantern Weekly* picks out a particularly brash example in the threadbare plot of *The Black Hand* (1908):

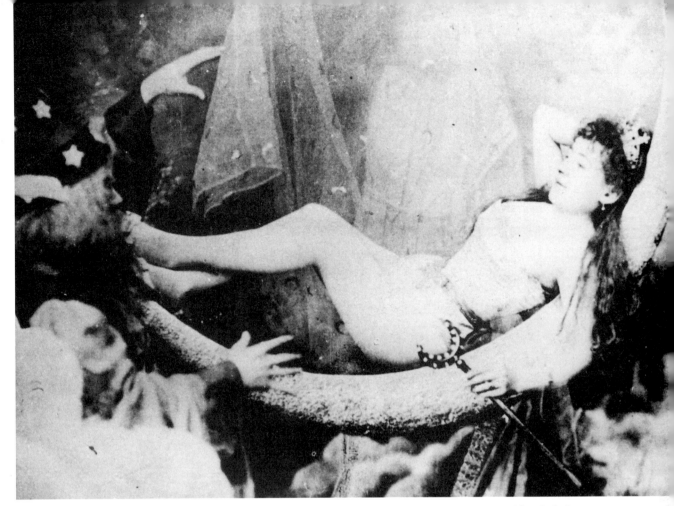

How high the moon
– early cheesecake
from an unknown
Méliès film (c.1900).

'two ruffians enter a bedroom where a little child is sleeping in its cot while its mother is doing some sewing. These two men are seen to take this young child out of its bed, tie a rope around its neck, pass the rope over a peg behind the door, and actually pull the young innocent up by the neck until its feet are two or three feet from the floor whilst the mother is kept at bay.'

Whereas gratuitous violence was common on the early screen, nudity was rare. Early French cheesecake like Méliès's tableau 'Le Tub' (1901) and many versions of the notorious 'Danse du Ventre' or belly dance – one of which was viewed by Anton Chekhov when he visited Paris in 1897 – were a rarity in Britain. Instead the home-grown industry provided even more insipid British variations of the already tepid tableaux 'vues un peu de déshabillés'.

Yet in spite of their innocuous content, these early films still managed to outrage fragile sensibilities. The celebrated court case of Dodsworth v. Spencer of 1899 was initiated by a country parson who contracted a travelling showman to put on a film show for his parishioners in the local church hall. The parson objected to a short sequence entitled *Courtship* in which a robust-looking lady is sitting on a park bench when a moustache-twirling gentleman sneaks up from behind and plants a kiss on her cheek. The judge ruled that the parson was within his rights not to pay the showman.

In the years leading up to the milestone Cinematograph Act of 1909 it was parsons, along with teachers, the moral purity movements and other like-minded guardians of public morals, who assumed the role that was subsequently to be assigned to local authorities. The clergy, in particular, were often the bane of an exhibitor's existence as the film pioneer Cecil Hepworth discovered during his early days as a travelling showman. He describes how a 'dear old' parson took issue with a hand-coloured version of the famous *Serpentine Dance* starring Loie Fuller. Hepworth was reluctant to leave out his best film: 'This was the last picture but one on the spool. There was no earthly means of getting rid of it except by running it through in darkness and I didn't think that the little flock would stand for that.' Hepworth's solution would not be lost on future film-makers trying to get round the censor. 'I announced the film as *Salome Dancing Before Herod*. Everyone was delighted. Especially the parson . . . he thought it was a particularly nice idea to introduce a little touch of Biblical history into an otherwise wholly secular entertainment.'

Curiously, it was to be Loie Fuller's sister who would instigate the most incongruous effect of censorship to be witnessed on the early screen. Loie's younger sister performed in front of the camera under the name of Fatima, and her 'danse du ventre' appeared in two different versions. The uncensored one for peepshow viewing showed her generously clad body in sinuous rhythm, but once Fatima was transferred to the big cinematograph screen a local American censor superimposed what can only be described as two separated strips of white fencing which partially but not completely obscured the bust and groin area of the ex-Coney Island belly dancer. This solution, which was released in Britain, left Miss Fuller's undulating midriff naked to the gaze of the public; and for the first time, but not the last, a film censor trying to subdue the sexual passions of the audience only succeeded in arousing them even more. Contemporary reports state that Fatima's fans, in an endearing testament to the power of the moving image, gathered round the bottom of the screen. There they gazed upwards in the expectation of being able to see behind the divided fence.

Patrons of a different kind of establishment from the cinema were able to see more than just a midriff. Cecil Hepworth reports that at the end of the decade 'there came a small but growing quantity of short films which were said to be intended for "smoking-room" exhibition. There were only a few at first but like the small black cloud . . . they seemed to some of us to be ominous.' History proved him right. In fact sexually explicit films had been made before the arrival of the twentieth century and they could soon be seen in London's 'smoking-rooms' and brothels. Of course they weren't censored because they were never publicly exhibited, and since there is no record of the

British police confiscating 'stag' films from brothels in the Edwardian era it would seem that the authorities turned a blind eye so long as the films were projected in front of a selected audience.

Part of the responsibility for the creation of blue movies can once again be laid at the feet of Thomas R. Edison. A group of adventurous Brazilians are known to have bought one of the first cameras manufactured by the great inventor. By 1904 Brazil was supplying not only London's smoking-rooms but also the Parisian brothels, and by 1910 South America had almost cornered the world market in hardcore films. In that same year the American playwright Eugene O'Neill gives an account of seeing 'the stags' in Buenos Aires. 'Those pictures were mighty rough stuff. Nothing was left to the imagination. Every form of perversity was enacted and, of course the sailors flocked to see them.'

Meanwhile the ordinary British cinema-goer had to be satisfied with a close-up of an ankle, as in Edwin Porter's *The Gay Shoe Clerk* of 1904, and, not surprisingly, this caused frustration. 'I heard a man at the recent Cambourne Fair,' a letter informed the *Kinematograph & Lantern Weekly* of 20 June 1907, 'insinuating that it would be advisable to "step up and see a suppressed film of Paris high life – one of the naughtiest pictures ever taken. No children permitted." I naturally paid my 6d for a reserved seat, only to find ballet girls on screen and a mild flirtation scene which disappointed the audience.'

Even rabid moral reform groups of the time like the Manchester Purity League displayed very little concern about contemporary film content. They did, however, believe that a proletarian film audience was especially susceptible to any outside influence and therefore prone to disruptive, immoral and even criminal behaviour. From a middle-class point of view the cinema in its first years was at best vulgar entertainment, at worst a threat to social order; and in the years directly preceding the Cinematograph Act of 1909 this sentiment was to gather momentum in an atmosphere of moral and political paranoia. Moreover, this inhospitable climate was given extra impetus by the very nature of the film industry itself.

Like any totally new industry the film business was ruled by anarchy. It was undeveloped and up for grabs. Unlike today when films are rented, the first films were sold outright for 6d a foot, regardless of content. Producers therefore had no incentive to publicise particular films and what's more they dumped poorly lit or badly edited footage on to the exhibitors. The exhibitors themselves ignored conventional business methods, as the pioneer distributor A. C. Bromhead testified: 'A representative meeting a showman who was behind with his accounts was immediately invited to "come and collect it yourself on the roundabouts . . . in tuppences".'

The film-makers, for their part, stole each other's plots. Edwin Porter, who is acknowledged as the creator of the first narrative film, *The Great Train Robbery* of 1904, was first employed by the Edison Company to study

13

imported films for easily adaptable story ideas. Some producers were too lazy even to do that. They stole whole films and put them out again under their own names. In response companies printed their insignia on the title cards; but this was ineffectual since the pirates could cut out the titles and splice in new ones. Finally, in a measure which must have dampened the naturalism of early films, producers printed their company logo on the scenery and painted back-drops.

Such get-rich-quick schemes may have exhilarated the film pioneers, but they didn't help the reputation of early cinema. Along with the legacy of peepshows, this lack of quality control not only discouraged British banks from investing in the picture business (at a time when American financiers saw a golden opportunity); it also furnished the trade with the kind of tone which did not entice the middle classes into becoming patrons of the local 'kine-matographic emporium'. As the ex-patriate film director, Alfred Hitchcock, later observed, 'no well-bred English person would be seen going into the cin-ema; it simply wasn't done'.

But if the cinema was to survive it had to tap in to this culturally as well as commercially valuable audience. So in the early years of the twentieth century the film industry desperately tried to clean up its image. One of its first lunges towards respectability involved the industry shifting the exhibition site of films from squalid penny gaffs into ornate music halls. But the short films shown between stage acts looked so close to what would now be described as home movies that the theatre business referred to them as 'chasers' – which meant that they were used to chase customers out of the auditorium so that new patrons could come in to take their place for the next performance. J. B. Priestley presumably followed the crowd; he writes in *The Edwardians* that 'like most other people I spent very little time looking at films which were so much prolonged "Bioscope" and for that reason I shall spend no more time here, leaving them to flicker away, a final disregarded item in the great gaudy programmes of the music hall.'

Other ploys to tempt the bourgeoisie into the music hall, such as 'a dainty cup of tea with an animated display', were offered to the uninterested middle classes. But it wasn't until the showmen started to rent theatres for the exclu-sive showing of films that the custom of the 'bon ton' crowd was finally won. Despite initial economic doubts this step pointed the way to the construction of specially built picture palaces: whitewashed walls were replaced by veined marble and bevelled mirrors, bare floorboards by fitted carpets, and the loud-mouthed barkers were transformed into courteous uniformed attendants. The penny gaff had been replaced by the 'Bijou'.

The new Empires, Majestics and Jewels were literally an overnight success. They practically doubled year by year from 250 in 1907 to nearly 4,000 in 1911 and with the provision of so many 'high-class rendezvous' the industry

The Picture Playhouse in Aberdeen. As the century turned, cinema ushers were dressed up in finery in an attempt to win the custom of the *bon ton* crowd.

wasn't slow to disclaim its low birth. 'Separate entrances and exits,' recommended *The Bioscope*, 'must be provided for the cheapest people.' An irate ratepayer complained to his local council that the less well off didn't seem to know their place. They were swarming into a picture palace in his area and, 'when the riff-raff of the surrounding neighbourhoods are drawn into a quiet residential locality nothing but wholesale depreciation can result.'

In spite of these attempts to censor the audience, cinema had come of age by the end of the decade. Everybody from all walks of life went to the picture palace. The Kensington upper classes slummed it at the Electric on Hammersmith Road, while Edinburgh's hoi polloi patronised the Palace on Princess Street, and the ultimate seal of approval was set in 1911 when the Prime Minister, Herbert Asquith, 'for the first time in his life entered the portals of a cinematograph theatre'. He even 'laughed heartily and continually made witty comments about the pictures'. Sadly, history doesn't relate which pictures these were.

Inevitably, the cinema's eventual popularity with the bourgeoisie gave it a different social dimension; it had become an institution, but one which was

15

The Granada in Woolwich, one of the first purpose-built picture palaces. The cinema finally won middle-class respectability with the introduction of such ornate, 'romantic' surroundings.

still outside anybody's power. Its independent status only added to the desire of local councils to have a stake in the control of cinemas. By 1909, London alone had more than 300 music halls and picture palaces free from official inspection and free therefore from social and political intervention. 'At present,' pointed out Walter Reynolds of the London County Council, 'we have no authority over clubs and entertainments where music licences are not taken out. A bioscope performance, for instance, does not need a music licence though an electric piano may play. As long as no money is taken at the doors we cannot, as the law stands, take action against any Sunday performance. If we get the parliamentary powers we seek, by which we shall be able to control every branch of amusement, every entertainment caterer will have to take out a licence.'

With the desire for official control escalating, councils increasingly began to take the law into their own hands. A cinema in Sheffield was forced by the local authorities to install a fireman in the projection booth on permanent standby and councils employed a variety of regulations to close cinemas which they deemed to be in unsuitable areas. By February 1909 the Metropolitan

Police Commissioner had lent his weight to the municipal cause, with a public declaration urging the Home Office to initiate legislative control because of the fire risk presented by inflammable film.

In the face of official censure the film industry offered no resistance. Apart from a few bleats in the trade press it caved in before the charges and allowed a one-sided campaign to be conducted through scare stories in the popular press.

Despite there being scant evidence of any link between fires and the showing of films the government surrendered to the public safety lobby. The Trojan horse had been wheeled into place and the Home Secretary, Herbert Gladstone, undoubtedly recognised that many forms of social control would be concealed within its belly. Nevertheless he introduced the Cinematograph Act into Parliament under a private member's bill which passed – with minimal opposition – on to the statute book in November 1909. This easy progress from private member's bill to an Act of Parliament must have seemed curious at the time, but the Act's increasing importance for Gladstone and the Home Office is explained by the wider context in which the Labour Party was emerging, unemployment was rising and the cinema had continuing popularity with the working classes.

The film trade showed great naïvety in not opposing the move, for should a Parliamentary Act give powers to a local authority to license cinemas, the danger was there for all to see that those authorities might attempt to improve upon Home Office regulations. Furthermore, another rousing speech from the LCC's Walter Reynolds should have provided the industry with an obvious clue of what was to come. 'Will the power given to the Council enable it to control the nature of the entertainments given?' the councillor blandly asked, and then answered himself in the affirmative. 'It is the duty of the police to stop any entertainments of a doubtful character, but certainly the Council would have the power when the licence came up for renewal once in twelve months, to refuse to license places which had presented undesirable shows. The knowledge that it possessed that power would be another powerful factor in securing a high class of entertainment, to the general good of the trade.'

Reynolds was true to his word. On the day that the Cinematograph Act came into effect the LCC announced that cinema licences would not be extended to Sunday film performances – a measure which was almost immediately adopted by other councils throughout the country. Too late, London's cinema managers protested in court that, in the words of the Home Secretary, the Act's 'intention was simply to secure safety in the construction of buildings in which inflammable films are exhibited', and therefore the LCC was acting outside the law. The Divisional Court dismissed the plea, stating that the Act conferred discretionary powers upon the county councils, 'so long as these conditions are not unreasonable'. The local authorities didn't need to hear any more. Chorley outlawed barkers, unaccompanied children were not allowed into Liverpool cinemas after 9 pm, and Accrington refused to grant a licence to one prospective cinema manager because councillors considered that their area already had enough 'emporiums'.

The LCC can claim the dubious honour of officially censoring a film for the first time in Britain. On 12 July 1910 the Council declared that, 'the public exhibition of pictures representing the recent prize fight in the United States of America is undesirable; and that the proprietors of cinematograph performances be so informed.' The fight had been for the heavyweight championship of the world between Jack Johnson and James J. Jeffries, and indeed it was a long, bloody battle lasting over forty rounds with the champion spending most of them bludgeoning the challenger into the canvas. But the reason why the film provoked so much 'agitation' might have had more to do with the indisputable fact that the champion 'Big' Jack Johnson was black while the loser, James Jeffries, was white.

The British film industry by this time was in a not dissimilar state to James J. Jeffries. Wherever it looked either its films or its cinemas were being browbeaten by officialdom. In October 1911, Blackburn Council ordered cinema owners to 'submit their programmes to the Chief Constable on the Friday before they were presented', other grievances included the popularity of American slang in subtitles which 'would bring ruin upon the English language', and the standard of film posters was claimed to be worse than the advertising for 'the most plebeian play in the vilest and most poverty-stricken purlieus frequented by the veriest riff-raff of the amusement-going public'. According to a consensus of council critics the films themselves were full of 'obscenity', 'cruelty' and 'lunacy'; what's more, they 'caused blindness'.

In spite of being the cause of so much supposed depravity, celluloid did possess one undeniable point in its own favour. Even the councils conceded that it stopped people from drinking. Contemporary figures confirm that the location of working-class social life moved in the Edwardian area from the pub to the cinema, and the film trade seized upon one of the few arguments that would hold sway with pontificating magistrates or proselytising preachers. In a rare display of support from that quarter, a prison chaplain from the North even declared that the shortage of prisoners in his particular jail could be attributed to the number of cinemas in the area.

But contemporary statistics also showed that a large part of the film audiences was made up of working-class children, and the self-same children cited the new medium as the cause of their delinquency. Over the Edwardian decade a vision of these working-class children looking for something or somebody to attack after a night spent at the movies was transformed by the middle class from fantasy into fact. Not surprisingly, juvenile criminals were quick to step into their expected role. Facing the magistrate, many a young burglar claimed that he had learnt how to thieve from watching the 'flicks'; and in case the bench hadn't got the message the adolescent outlaw would insist that he now stole for film-money not sweet-money.

The accusation that films caused juvenile delinquency accompanied the birth of cinema and it has put the industry on the defensive ever since. Films which today are classified 'PG' still have to show that a life of crime is a life full of misery and pain rather than luxury and largesse. Edwardian exhibitors and distributors had no defence against the charge that crime on the screen provoked crime in the street except the unstated one that they would lose a lot of their income if children under a certain age were barred from their cinemas. Each adopted the attitude that his own films were harmless and that it was a selfish minority who were exposing the nation's youth to moral corruption.

But shifting the blame didn't minimise the concern of teachers who were noticing more and more gaps in their classrooms from children 'playing wag' at the local picture palace. Maybe in an effort to reverse this journey and get truants out of the cinema and back to their desks the president of the National Union of Teachers suggested that British producers abandon their current film schedules and substitute instead 'clean, healthy plays and pictures of the beauty spots of our isles and empire together with pictures representing the great industries of the country'.

In an age when there was a consensus that social ills could be cured by social legislation, such advice could not be taken lightly. Maligned by preachers, teachers and magistrates, and with revenue being lost due to different councils imposing different decisions about the same film, the industry was already paying a substantial price for its new middle-class clientèle. But it would have to sacrifice even more if it wanted to maintain credibility in the face of such influential criticism. To free themselves from the mercy of arbitrary authorities film producers would therefore have to relinquish control over the content of their own films. They recognised that the key to their survival lay in not only accepting but actually proposing a state system of film censorship. The British film industry therefore conceived its own controller, the British Board of Film Censors.

The inception of Britain's film censorship began in the first month of 1912 when the film-maker Cecil Hepworth initiated an overture to the Home Office. There, with a group of exhibitors and fellow producers, he suggested the formation of a Board of Film Censors. The Board would be set up by the industry itself; it would be financed by the fees paid by producers seeking a 'Certificate' from the Board, thereby avoiding the need for public funds; but the Board would be under the leadership of a Home Office-appointed chief censor who in turn would act as an arbiter between the new Board and film-makers unwilling to accept its decisions. The deputation also conceded that the chief censor's rulings would be final and, even more crucially, that there would be no means of appeal against his decisions.

This system of paying for the means of your own control has its roots in the papal 'Index' of censorship, formalised by the Vatican secretariat during the sixteenth century to repel the Protestant reformation and it is not altogether surprising that the Home Secretary, Reginald McKenna, approved of it; but he

The audience of the Mile End Palladium waits for the film to begin (c.1910).

only approved in principle, not in practice. 'It is a project which smiles upon me,' he regally replied to the industry delegation and then neatly sidestepped the all-important issue of institutionalising a uniform system of censorship with the consent of all local councils by refusing to grant official Home Office support. 'I could not act as a censor,' he said, because it would require special legislation and 'that would raise such controversy in a crowded session it would be useless for me to hold out any hope for you.'

The actual reason for McKenna's reluctance to become a censor only became apparent from a Home Office circular sent out to local councils eight years later. Being official, such a censorship system would be answerable to Parliament and therefore potentially 'embarrassing to the Minister responsible' for answering MPs' questions as to why a particular film had been censored or banned. At the time, McKenna attempted to shift responsibility by calling the meeting to an end with a suggestion that the deputation solicit the help of the LCC. But when faced with the actuality of administering film censorship the LCC adopted the same hands-off policy. 'Not one single complaint,' they insisted, 'had been sent to the Theatres Committee of any film or representation put before the people of London.'

The downcast deputation took what was an increasingly hot political potato to a poorly attended trade meeting in Birmingham where they introduced a motion that 'a censorship is necessary and advisable'. But still no government official was willing to step forward and acknowledge the role of father to the Board. The industry hurriedly announced the event in the trade papers anyway, and so the illegitimate child called British film censorship was born.

But before a single film could be considered the British Board of Film Censors had to choose a chief censor whose past would win approval from the Home Office, yet whose future would not antagonise the film industry. They found the appropriate compromise in George Redford.

Redford had recently retired from the position of Chief Examiner of Plays under the Lord Chamberlain, a post viewed with some ambivalence by the most celebrated playwright of the day, George Bernard Shaw. 'Mr Redford cannot help himself: a censorship cannot work in any other way, until a censor can be found greater than the greatest dramatists. That being impossible he is doomed . . .' But then with characteristic acerbity, Shaw dismissed the Examiner with the words, 'George Alexander Redford, said to have been a bank clerk, but not ascertained to have been anything except lucky enough to obtain a place at court.'

In spite of his humble beginnings and, more importantly, his lack of experience in movie production or distribution, the British film industry welcomed Mr Redford. Maybe they knew that they had no cause for concern. On his appointment as President of the Board Redford was already sixty-six years old

Opposite The exterior of the Mile End Palladium was one of the music halls that began to double up as a cinema (c.1910).

and within weeks he became so ill that he was President in name alone. The actual job of chief censor fell to the BBFC Secretary, Joseph Brooke Wilkinson. He had been a journalist with the Northcliffe press when Cecil Hepworth first met him and recommended him as a liaison between the industry and the putative Board. Currently he was Secretary of the Cinematograph Exhibitors Association, so at least he had a knowledge of the business that Redford lacked.

Hepworth described the Board's new Secretary as 'a dapper little man' with a pleasant but rather bland demeanour. Yet however inconsequential his personality Wilkinson would require the diplomatic resilience of a statesman in order to ensure the very survival of the BBFC in the years ahead. Not only would he have to put into effect the military's insistence that no films be made about the First World War, from the political right he would have to defend the Board from local council criticisms of being too liberal and from the left he would have to deflect the communist exhortations which permeated the powerful Russian films released after the 1917 Revolution. Also, Wilkinson would have to withstand this opposition and place the Board on a firm footing while he suffered from an affliction which was particularly unfortunate for a man in his position. 'Brookie' Wilkinson was going blind.

The BBFC opened its doors for business at 75 Shaftesbury Avenue on 1 January 1913. The narrow neo-classical building was within the nascent British film industry in Soho, although the top two floors which the Board occupied were so cramped that only one room could be set aside for the examination of films. There four censors sat simultaneously watching two films being projected alongside each other, the only ill-effect apparently of this visual overload being the requirement for one censor of 'green-tinted spectacles'. On the occasions that the examiners disagreed they officially referred the decision to the President, but owing to the ill health of G. A. Redford the fate of a contentious film was usually decided by the partially sighted Secretary of the Board, Brooke Wilkinson.

Just as the British constitution does not exist on paper the Board had no written code; nevertheless it did start with two specific rules – no materialisation of Christ and no nudity – as well as with two specific classifications: 'U' for general exhibition and 'A' which was an advisory, but not compulsory, restriction to those over sixteen. Unlike the American film censorship system a code never would be drawn up, but the number of rules would multiply. In the first year of the Board 166 films were caught in the rapidly expanding net, 144 of them being cut and the rest banned. The reasons given in the BBFC's 1913 Annual Report extend from the aforementioned representation of Christ to 'indecorous dancing', 'confinements', 'native customs in foreign lands abhorrent to British ideas', in addition to a catch-all restriction which rejected any 'scenes tending to disparage public characters and institutions'.

This severity surprised British film distributors who had expected greater leniency from an institution which they themselves had created to act on their behalf. The Board's resolve also had an unintended effect: its draconian approach to film censorship was swiftly seized upon and imitated by local authorities. Amongst others, Leeds, Liverpool and Leicester responded to the BBFC's example by installing their own censors to re-cut, unban, or ban such films as the Italian epic, *Dante's Inferno* (1912), which featured glimpses of male genitalia, or the Victoria Knight melodrama *Five Nights* (1914), a tale of passion and unrequited love which had been passed by the Board in 1915.

Not surprisingly the film trade despaired. The only reason why they had created a censorship board was to neutralise the 'faddists' on local councils, and now every crank on the country's 688 local authorities was threatening to take up cudgels against them. And to make matters worse, by the end of 1915 the film industry's supposed champion George Redford had permanently retired to the sickroom.

Acknowledging that the BBFC was being undermined and eclipsed by local censors, the trade journal *Bioscope* pointed out the need for the film industry to have a centralised censor with just one voice: 'The trade has got to make a move . . . to obtain Government approval and recognition of an Official Censor Board. Let us call upon the Government to give Mr Redford official powers, that no LCC or borough councils can question.' But the government did not take up the challenge. It was content with a situation in which it could 'advise' through Home Office memos and circulars and yet, because those letters were not made public, not be seen to advise.

Paradoxically, although they wanted to retain their own licensing powers over cinemas, the local authorities also agreed with the film trade's demand for centralised censorship: they wanted it both ways. Thus the state's control over released material would be doubly tight. The local councils assumed that a state censor would be stricter than the BBFC; and Britain's Chief Constables, who were a crucial voice within local authorities, particularly felt that a state censor would be tougher than the BBFC. A recurring worry amongst the constabulary was the apparent link between the cinema and juvenile crime; they believed that stronger film censorship would have a direct impact on recently released statistics showing a sharp upsurge in juvenile delinquency. 'The establishment of a central Government censor of cinematograph films is essential,' declared the annual Chief Constables' report of 1916, 'and will conduce to the reduction of juvenile crime in the country.'

Before the end of 1916 both the film industry and the local councils had found a powerful ally in their crusade for official film censorship in the new Home Secretary, Herbert Samuel. With the consent of twenty urban local authorities Samuel proposed in December that a new Board of Censors should become part of the Home Office and if any film producer or distributor attempted to bypass the Government Censor the relevant cinema would be prosecuted. The new rules were drawn up by the Home Office and immediately circulated to all the local authorities. State censorship of films, said Samuel, would start on 1 January 1917.

Although he was now nearly at death's door, George Redford rallied to the defence of the BBFC at this critical moment; and he was soon to be joined by the British film industry. A month earlier, the government had committed a major tactical blunder in its negotiations with the film trade. A permanent official at the Home Office informed the Cinematograph Exhibitors Association's chairman, Anthony Newbould, that it was not possible for the government to take away the censorship powers of local authorities without resorting to parliamentary legislation; and that was impossible because the government had told parliament that while the war lasted it would not introduce 'controversial' legislation. According to this ruling there would therefore now be central government film censorship as well as that by local councils. Newbould protested that this would open up the industry even more to the vagaries of local opinion and demanded that the film trade 'be safeguarded against bureaucrats, cranks and extremists. What we want,' he protested, 'is to place ourselves in the hands of sane, rational, reasonable people.'

Ignoring this outburst the Home Office official then outlined the implications of state censorship for the British film industry; Newbould must have been deeply worried because he left the meeting concluding that the government 'would exclude every film of a dramatic or sensational nature, every film which had the slightest allusion to sex, every film dealing with crime even when incidental to the subject.' That didn't leave much over – Newbould calculated that 75 per cent of films would be banned. But that was not all. Such was the contemporary prejudice of the governing classes against the vastly popular new mass medium that far from conceding the disastrous effects for the film industry of this kind of censorship, the Home Office official then revealed that the government was taking the short step from censoring films to censoring film-goers. Home Office circulars had been issued to all councils advising them to adopt a clause excluding all children under fourteen from cinemas.

The government presumably thought that the film industry would strike the same attitude that it did in 1909 and the white flag would be raised. But the industry had gained confidence from the respectability which it had won from the middle classes during the pre-war years, and Newbould immediately responded with a strongly worded letter to the Home Secretary. No reply exists in the records, but an internal Home Office minute commented: 'This letter suggests war.'

But just when government censorship of films seemed to be actually on the point of being carried out, two events occurred. On 10 November 1916, George Alexander Redford died. Within a fortnight the film industry had chosen a successor and from their point of view they chose well. According to a later censor, T. P. O'Connor 'had all the makings of a television personality, if he had lived at the right time'. Aside from that loss, the 'colourful' O'Connor was already in his late sixties when he became President of the BBFC but this Catholic, Liberal MP, journalist, biographer, publisher and editor of political magazines, and ex-President of the CEA, was a robust and relentless expert in the art of bureaucratic conciliation. Even more importantly for the BBFC, O'Connor's oleagenous expertise in public relations was backed up by familiarity with the corridors of power. As well as numbering amongst his friends all the leading politicians of the day, including Lloyd George, Ramsay MacDonald and Winston Churchill, the President was later appointed Privy Councillor, giving him access to all confidential government information.

The other benchmark event occurred less than a month later, when Asquith's Liberal government fell to the Lloyd George coalition and Herbert Samuel was replaced by Sir George Cave. The new Home Secretary did not like the cinema and he was apparently appalled at the prospect of having to be the ultimate judge of a film's suitability. State censorship fell by the wayside; but the danger was postponed rather than averted. Cave was incensed by the industry's antagonistic attitude to his predecessor's plans, and in a double-barrelled blast aimed at the BBFC he advised the local licensing authorities to 'exercise to the full extent the powers of control which they possess'. Then he fired off a second round by recommending that the government endorse an enquiry into the cinema 'with special reference to young people' which was due to be held the following spring by the collective organisation for British moral reform groups, the National Council of Public Morals.

Whether they were precocious cineastes or conservative politicians, all interested parties agreed that the conclusions of this commission would decide the future of film censorship. Unfortunately for the film industry, the NCPM encompassed nearly all the known enemies of early cinema from Purity Leagues and Watch Committees to the Ragged School Union; and this brew was made all the more potent by the addition of such influential figures as Marie Stopes and Sir Robert Baden-Powell, who had been appointed to sit on its Commission. Opposite them in the first row of the audience, reported Lady Henriques, a committee member, 'sat a phalanx of clergymen with their eyes firmly shut'. The forty-seven witnesses, who included a doctor, a hygienist and a probation officer as well as Brooke Wilkinson and T. P. O'Connor, provide us with the first detailed record of what British people actually wanted and did not want to see in films. Much of the evidence in the 400-page survey can be summed up in one bald statement from John Percival, the Chief Constable of Wigan: 'The cinema is responsible for the increase in juvenile crime.'

Of course, every generation thinks that it knows why juveniles commit crime. In nineteenth-century Britain, for example, it was the appearance amongst the lower orders of the 'penny dreadful' and then the 'shilling shocker' that had been held responsible for increases in juvenile delinquency. It is therefore not altogether surprising that it was now the turn of the latest medium of mass appeal: films. The general view, quaintly expressed in the Commission's report was that the 'flickers' encouraged 'a penchant for pilfering'; but, significantly, many of the complaints to the 1917 Commission give the impression that it was the kinetic power of films rather than their content that concerned the middle classes. 'The cinema is too exciting,' said a Miss Vickers, a voluntary worker from Hatton Garden. 'It should be more normal.' Miss Margery Fox of the Head Mistresses' Conference was disturbed by the magnitude of faces. 'You can see the pores of the skin,' she pointed out, and when she was asked if it was 'the very impressiveness of the cinema that aggravates the danger of it to the child?' she replied, 'Certainly; the better it is the worse it is.'

Other complaints about the link between delinquency and films were more specific. When asked by the Bishop of Birmingham what films he liked, one Bethnal Green schoolboy replied, 'All about thieves.' Another anonymous East End boy said he liked mysteries and when the Bishop asked him what he meant by this term, the young Cockney replied, 'Where stolen goods are hidden away in vaults so that the police can't get them.' Asked what was the 'nicest film' that he had ever seen, the boy replied, 'A picture about the death of a boy's mother,' then added, 'and he revenges her.' And had these 'crook films ever made you wish to go and do the same thing?' 'Yes,' came the monosyllabic reply.

Such evidence must have left the cinema managers with the feeling that they were about to lose half their audience. But more than one of the witnesses who actually worked amongst the urban poor pointed out that a more likely reason for the increase in juvenile crime was the World War.

With fathers away at the front and mothers having to go out to work there was more likelihood of children being picked up on the street by the police on the newly created charge of 'wandering without proper guardianship'. This meant that cinemas could now have a positive social function: keeping children off the streets; and the industry found an unlikely champion in John Massey, a probation officer in the East End, who suggested that his job would be made that much more difficult by the suppression of the cinema. He insisted that the children in his district could learn very little, 'if anything' from crook films. 'They see and learn very much more in their miserable so-called homes. For a few hours at the picture house at the corner they can find breathing space, warmth, music, and the pictures, where they can have a real laugh, a cheer and sometimes a shout . . .To be able to make the poor pinch-faced, half-clad and half-nourished boys and girls in the crowded slums in cities forget their pain and misery and their sad lot is a great thing, and the pictures do it.'

Leaving aside heartfelt pleas, what really saved the cinema's standing at the Commission hearings was the stark but very positive statement denying the link between juvenile crime and cinema that was given by Roderick Ross, the Chief Constable of Edinburgh. 'I am unable,' he said, 'to find a single case where any juvenile set out to steal for this one purpose,' and he concluded that the cinema, 'has had little or no effect on the crime committed by children and young persons'; even more surprising than this evidence was the revelation that, in spite of a few vociferous individuals, a large majority of the country's Chief Constables agreed with it.

It was, in fact, a compound of police evidence together with the affirmative statements of teachers and welfare officials from working-class areas that swayed the NCPM Commission not to recommend the exclusion of children from cinemas or the banning of crime films. But the question of whether films cause delinquency did not lie down and die. It was to resurface in the thirties, and again in the fifties, when rock and roll films allegedly incited the slashing of cinema seats; and more recently it reappeared when the 'video nasty' was blamed for an upsurge in violent crime during the early part of the eighties.

Nevertheless, the conclusions of the 1917 Commission have never been improved upon. Responsibility for juvenile crime could not be laid at the door of the cinema. 'The problem is far too complex,' their report concluded, 'to be solved by laying stress on only one factor and that probably a subordinate one, among all the contributing conditions.' With unexpected foresight they recognised 'the superfluous energy of youth, and its spirit of adventure, which are often deprived of lawful and useful outlets'. The problem, the Commission realised, was a question of nature rather than copy-cat behaviour. 'The cinema,' they concluded, 'suggests the form of activity rather than provides the impulse to it.'

The film industry therefore had been granted a relatively clean bill of health, albeit with provisos, and although the Commission recommended government censorship of films, it was the report's favourable conclusions on the work of the BBFC under the energetic leadership of T. P. O'Connor which took the heat out of the censorship issue for the remainder of the First World War. So the Board had survived not just its tumultuous birth but also its first major battle against the whippers-in of morality; and more significant to its future it had also come to an accommodation with successive governments who, each in turn, would discover the advantages of an extra-legal system to control the content of this vast, pervasive, new medium; but in the meantime the Board had to ensure its continued existence by consolidating its reputation for severity.

The First World War itself initially presented the newly born BBFC with an insurmountable problem. The government would not allow any films to be made on the subject. Within weeks of the outbreak of war, however, the War Office relented because of the obvious propaganda value to be gained from feature films depicting vicious Huns attacking friendly Tommies. The public was desperate for information on the war itself, yet in spite of the increasing clamour in British homes for details about life in the trenches the government remained obdurate in its refusal to allow filming at the front line. Not until three years after hostilities had broken out did the selfsame Charles Urban, who had instigated British film censorship in 1898, persuade the British High Command to permit cameras to film the massive British offensive in the spring of 1917.

The resulting documentary, *Somme*, actually conveys very little sense of the famous battle. Events usually occur offscreen – 'Twenty minutes after these pictures were taken,' the subtitles informed the audience, 'these men came under heavy machine gun fire,' – and anybody seeing the film would find it difficult to believe that the Battle of the Somme was the most disastrous military engagement experienced by the British in their whole history. On the first day alone 57,470 men were killed – two for every yard gained.

Even the one action scene that does show the British infantry going over the top has since been discovered to be a fake. It was filmed at a battery school behind the lines. The film historian Kevin Brownlow, who uncovered these mocked-up shots, has pointed out that although the film is a sanitised version of reality, no other scene in *Somme* is staged. For such a scene to be reconstructed, he suggests that War Office censorship actually demanded it.

Nevertheless when the film, on its release, was compared to previous flag-waving features it emerged as a great success on the Home Front. Audiences praised its realism and evidently there was some truth in such a reaction because *Somme* was banned in British Columbia in case it discouraged potential recruits from joining up. The film also worried exhibitors who thought that the British public would be disgusted by the prevalence of death in the trenches. W. Jefferson Woods, the manager of the Broadway cinema in Hammersmith, put up a notice announcing his intention not to show *Somme*: 'This is a Place of Amusement, not a Chamber of Horrors.' When a reporter from the *Evening Standard* asked Mr Woods to explain his decision the exhibitor remarked, 'I don't think it is suitable for those who have lost relatives. I think it is harrowing and distressing.'

'But it is historical,' pointed out the reporter.

'I was at the Trade Show,' Woods replied, 'and one man gave a shriek and said, "Let me out. I feel so bad. I have just lost a brother."'

'But the public can stand seeing what the boys go through,' persisted the journalist, only to be rebuffed by the response:

Previous pages
The decimation of
the First World War
– filming at the front
was forbidden for
the first two years of
the War.

32

'The papers are full of it every morning. We see for ourselves the wounded walking about our streets . . . and another point,' added Woods, in a premonition of the way modern media is asked to treat enemy wounded, 'in the film you see stretcher after stretcher coming in with wounded Germans. I think it is likely to create pity for the brutes. It is possible for people to say "Poor devils!" It is likely to create pity for the enemy.'

But overall the BBFC had an easy war. Before 1914 Britain produced barely a quarter of the films shown in its own cinemas and, due to blockades and severed trade links, it now became virtually impossible to obtain imported European and American films. British producers tried to fill the gap but the BBFC still had comparatively little to censor.

Another reason for the BBFC's inactivity was that prestigious American and European productions which were likely to fall foul of their rules were simply not submitted. But this did not mean that such films were not exhibited. Showcase cinemas like the Theatre Royal, Drury Lane, sometimes ignored the censorship system and went ahead with exclusive screenings of the big new fourteen-reelers now coming in from abroad.

Provincial cinema-goers were usually denied these ground-breaking films but they caused an impact nevertheless; none more so than Abel Gance's anti-war epic, *J'Accuse!* It was probably inevitable that in 1918 a film in which dead troops return to ask whether their loss was justified, would have caused apoplexy in government circles as well as amongst the BBFC's examiners. For that reason the British release was postponed, but when the French film did finally come to London two years later, in May 1920, it proved a success in spite of the fact that it was uncertificated and could only be seen at one cinema.

In the middle of those drawn-out hostilities it would have been equally foolhardy for the American director Thomas Ince to have submitted his own pacifist epic *Civilization* (1916) to the British censor. In a God-fearing country which believed that its struggle was blessed by divine providence, a film portraying Christ as an anti-war agitator would have done more than raise eyebrows. Ince was sufficiently aware of British attitudes to send a shortened version of his film to London at the beginning of 1917 under an expanded title, *Civilization: What Every True Briton is Fighting For*. However this ploy to mollify the British trade was only partially successful because cinema managers were afraid that any exhibition of the full-length version would bring with it accusations of treachery. And unfortunately for Ince, by the time *Civilization* did gain a limited release in London during the latter half of 1917, the public had become more interested in another even more notorious film which had also bypassed the censor.

David Wark Griffith's *Intolerance* of 1916 not only represented Christ; more shockingly, it featured bare-breasted temple maidens. The dancing

33

acolytes in the sumptuous Babylonian sequence had been inserted at the insistence of Griffith's New York producers who felt that the most expensive film ever made – and probably that ever will be made – 'ought to have more sex in it'. But even though the BBFC had admitted at the 1917 Commission that they 'objected to nude statuary when we have seen it in certain positions', the censors would probably have been more agitated by the scenes of industrial unrest shown in *Intolerance*'s modern sequence. These posed a much more direct threat to the status quo at a time of increasing social unrest in Britain.

In 1915, the year before Griffith's great episodic film was released, there had been strikes in the Welsh coal mines and the Asquith administration had been forced to accede to the miners' demands. George Redford, still the BBFC's President at the time, had responded to the government's enemy within by introducing a new restriction in the BBFC's 1915 annual report. Rule No. 16 banned all references to 'Relations between Capital and Labour', by which was meant the screening of anything which suggested conflict between employers and the employed. Griffith's film obviously fell within this catch-all category, so it was fortunate for contemporary film-goers that this ambitious epic was released when the censorship system had not yet been fully established, was still permeable and therefore could still be safely ignored.

If British film distributors and American producers felt that they could ignore the BBFC, the Board now decided to return the compliment by snubbing some of their films. The films singled out for special inattention were the new genre of so-called social 'propaganda films' which were described by T. P. O'Connor in 1919 as being 'produced for the purpose of enlisting public opinion, or enlisting sympathy, on certain subjects. Such films have included the effects of certain diseases, contracted and hereditary, illegal operations (abortion), white slavery (prostitution), race suicide (birth control) etc.'

But whatever the Catholic President of the BBFC personally felt about these issues, 'propaganda' films were being produced in direct response to increasingly obvious social facts: in 1917 there were 60,000 prostitutes in London, two-thirds of them refugees from France and Belgium; one in four officers was returning from the War with VD; and because another one in four of those officers would never return from the front, social welfare groups were disturbed by the subsequent decline in the middle-class population. Moreover, instead of the lower classes it was the less populous well-to-do who were practising birth control. In a situation already aggravated by the pressures of war, progressive liberals, as well as moral reformers and organisations like the Eugenics Society, felt that the social fabric was in danger of being torn apart by an over-populated proletariat.

Propaganda film-makers were aware of the delicacy with which these issues were discussed at the time, so they usually submerged any educational message within a conventional love story. In *Damaged Goods*, for instance, in 1919, the hero contracts VD after spending a night with a prostitute – which is indicated by a solitary static shot of Piccadilly Circus. Yet before the film ends his wife has shelved her divorce proceedings against her hapless husband and the couple are reunited in a happy ending which repeatedly emphasises the sanctity of marriage.

Nevertheless the BBFC was not satisfied by even this coy approach to sexually transmitted diseases. It was the subject itself that the Board disapproved of, not the way in which it was treated, and they therefore refused to classify *Damaged Goods*. The film was eventually exhibited at one or two cinemas in Britain, but so much footage was removed a film historian has commented that the cut version comes 'dangerously close to being a series of subtitles'. There was also a bizarre footnote to the saga: in Belfast, the local authorities imposed a unique proviso – *Damaged Goods* could only be shown if the audience was segregated, with men on one side and women on the other and the aisle in between.

Opposite
Intolerance (1916). D. W. Griffith's producers insisted on the inclusion of this Babylonian orgy scene, and that is probably why the great epic was never submitted for British censorship.

35

Richard Bennet in *Damaged Goods* (1919), a film considered so inflammatory that Belfast film-goers were segregated according to their sex.

In the changing social climate after the war the BBFC still continued to deny certificates to a wide range of propaganda films such as *White Slave Traffic* (1919), in which women were advised not to go overseas; the anti-abortion melodrama *Where Are My Children?* (1916); the anti-drug exposé *Human Wreckage* (1923), which Brooke Wilkinson condemned as the most dangerous film ever made; and *Night Patrol* (1934), a British film championed by George Bernard Shaw for its exposure of prostitution in London. This last was banned because the Board's President claimed it would only discourage girls from coming to London where they were sorely needed to fill domestic vacancies.

Back at the 1917 Commission, O'Connor had been asked to explain the Board's blanket ban and his response was significant because it sums up the inter-war role of the BBFC as the watchdog of the entertainment industry, not the information industry. 'We exist mainly, almost exclusively, for the cinema theatre alone,' stated the chief censor, 'for the amusement of the public and for the profit of the proprietor or the owner of the film. I would not bring educational films under our Board, as I think they are entirely outside our skill. They are for the educational authorities to decide and not for us.'

The fact that O'Connor could not impose this definition of cinema was largely due to the efforts of one woman. Marie Stopes, the birth control pio-

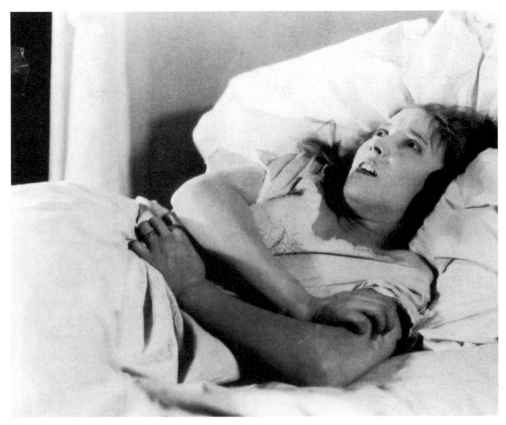

Bessie Love as the drug-addicted mother in *Human Wreckage* (1923). Branded by the BBFC's Secretary Brooke Wilkinson as the most dangerous film to have ever come before the Board.

neer, was adamant that her own propaganda film would not be shunted out of the cinema into a school hall; while the attempt to censor it illustrates the changing post-war strategy of the BBFC and highlights the nature of the Board's own propaganda.

Stopes had written the screen version of her influential best seller *Married Love* in 1922, and as her central theme of birth control was carried through from page to screen the film would normally have been rejected out of hand by the Board. But Marie Stopes had a worldwide reputation as a social reformer and O'Connor could not merely cast her work aside. At the same time though, as a Roman Catholic, he was particularly appalled by the film's theme. So he decided to adopt a more subtle strategy. If he could not censor the film he would censor its author.

Marie Stopes's screenplay actually bore no relationship to the non-fictional plea for marital sexual harmony within her book. The film is a romantic drama revolving around its heroine, Maisie, a parlourmaid who is hesitant to marry her fireman boyfriend, Dick. This is because Maisie comes from a large South London family and she is afraid that she and Dick will emulate her parents' procreative urges.

The film eventually comes to its interventionary crux when Maisie's redoubtable employer Mrs Sterling explains to her charge that marriage need not necessarily lead to an oversized family. This piece of home-help is illustrated first by a bedraggled, overgrown rosebush sprouting wilting flowers which is superimposed over the earnest employer's face; that is then intercut with a healthy plant sporting upright blooms and a title card bearing the motto of the prudent Mrs Sterling: 'armed with knowledge he pruned his trees carefully.' Forewarned and presumably forearmed, Maisie is soon afterwards reunited with the estranged Dick when he saves her from Mrs Sterling's burning home.

In spite of several promptings from the picture's producers at G.B. Samuelson, the BBFC took over six weeks to come to a decision on how to censor *Married Love*. Finally in mid-May 1923, after the film had been examined four times, O'Connor himself viewed it together with a group from the London County Council and a young official from the Home Office called Sidney Harris (who would become President of the BBFC in 1947). O'Connor and Harris both favoured a ban, but the LCC wanted to pass the complete film. This put O'Connor in a difficult position since he had to have such a powerful council as the LCC on his side if he was to achieve censorship uniformity. So he retreated and asked for a few minor cuts which the LCC quickly agreed to.

O'Connor's deletions from the film itself were inconsequential – for instance, Maisie could no longer live in Camberwell, instead residing in generic 'Slumland'. But the Board's President was especially insistent on one cut: the title of the film itself, which now became *Maisie's Marriage*; and in a further attempt to stop the prurient from making any connection between the film and Marie Stopes's name, O'Connor also insisted that posters, and any other advertising, must not carry the title of the book.

But the censors could not completely eradicate the troublesome association between author and work, since the following title card opened the film:

> G.B. Samuelson presents
> *MAISIE'S MARRIAGE*
> A Story specially written for the Screen
> by DR MARIE STOPES DSc PhD
> in collaboration with
> Captain Walter Sommers

In a further twist O'Connor's devious tactics also rebounded because cinema managers not only ignored the BBFC's rulings by showing uncut versions of the film, they also featured the scriptwriter's name on posters outside their cinemas in lettering almost the size of the film's original title, *Married Love*. The government was so alarmed by this development that it resorted to state censorship, issuing a confidential circular memo to all the licensing authorities warning them to carry out the BBFC's conditions for showing the film. But Stopes found out about the memo and because she had not agreed to O'Connor's conditions she threatened to take the Home Office to court. Suddenly a meeting was arranged between Stopes and the Home Secretary. He assured her that there had never been any intention of removing her name from the film or from its advertising and although he refused to withdraw his department's memo its effect was negligible.

Marie Stopes had won a significant victory over the combined forces of the BBFC and the government. Without her intervention even fewer films that strayed outside the BBFC's boundary of entertainment would have reached the British screens in the silent era.

Unfortunately for cinema-goers, *Maisie's Marriage* was an exception to the increasing hegemony of the BBFC. By the end of the 1920s it had become virtually impossible to see banned films in Britain's cinemas; first, because more and more local authorities were coming into line with BBFC decisions and second, and even more crucially, because the Cinematograph Exhibitors Association entered into individual agreements with its members in 1929 to rent out only films which had received certificates from the Board.

Propaganda films, however, posed a specific problem to all censor-appeasing institutions. They were supported by influential middle-class reform groups who were determined to improve the physical and moral standards of the cinema-going public. On the other hand the film industry resented this intrusion because they knew that there was very little profit to be gained from the exhibition of propaganda films. The official attitude of the CEA was summed up in the trade journal *Kinematograph & Lantern Weekly* in the latter part of 1924: 'It is no part of the duty of the exhibitor to act as a purveyor of pornography masquerading as propaganda.'

The battle lines between propaganda and entertainment became even more fuzzy when the government reversed its previous fence-straddling policy and started to support the BBFC covertly in the mid-twenties. The Home Office assumed that cinema-goers, being mostly working class and therefore, in the words of *The Times*, 'less intelligent and educated', would misunderstand the morally uplifting message within propaganda films. For the Home Office the commercial success of *Maisie's Marriage* merely confirmed this assumption and from 1924 onwards they bombarded the local authorities with circulars in support of the BBFC's blanket ban of all propaganda films.

But the social reformers enjoyed the support of the liberal intelligentsia, who recognised that double standards were being applied. 'When I find an official,' declared an irate Shaw, 'allowing unlimited liberty to pornography and absolutely refusing to allow honest and decent welfare films to be exhibited, then I appeal to public opinion to sweep that official and his powers and department into the dustbin.'

Leaving aside his opinions about what constituted pornography, what must have appeared strange to social reformers like Shaw was the BBFC's opposition to films which were trying to improve the moral behaviour of cinema audiences. But what the reformers and their supporters had not taken account of was that these films dealt with sexual subjects and were therefore bound to be controversial; and for an institution that was still obsessed by its own survival this over-riding fact breached a cardinal tenet of political bureaucracy: namely that controversy brings wounding blows whereas silent assent leads to an increase in power.

A policy of imposed quietude was therefore applied by the BBFC in the face of the next likely cause of controversy: the great Russian propagandist films of the twenties. O'Connor had signalled his intentions early on when he told the 1917 Commission that he had drawn up a list of forty-three rules for excluding films. Known as 'O'Connor's 43' they were regarded as sacrosanct within the BBFC. Thirty-five of them dealt with moral or religious issues, but seven were overtly political, including 'Scenes holding up the King's uniform to contempt and ridicule', 'Scenes tending to disparage public characters and institutions' and 'References to controversial politics', as well as the retention of 'Relations of Capital and Labour'. The President of the Board also informed the Commission that he thought it was 'necessary to keep, not only in touch with, but in the friendliest relations with the Home Office'. This bond, forged in the battle against the social reformers, would now try to hold the political status quo against the openly pro-revolutionary films arriving from the Soviet Union which were lighting up a beacon for swelling numbers of unemployed.

Opposing the BBFC was the Film Society, which had been formed in 1925 by the communist aristocrat Ivor Montagu in order to show imported films which were unlikely to receive a general release. The Society's roll call of members covered nearly every aspect of intellectual life in the twenties, including Bertrand Russell, Julian Huxley, John Maynard Keynes, G. B. Shaw, Roger Fry and Ellen Terry. Their rallying cry was provided by H. G. Wells: 'We cannot allow ourselves to be ruled by a gang of mystery men.' And the bloodiest battleground upon which these two film adversaries would face each other in their ongoing war was provided by the most dynamic and exciting call for armed struggle that the cinema had ever produced – Eisenstein's classic agit-prop film of 1926, *Battleship Potemkin*.

Potemkin not only contains the most famous scene in silent film, the Odessa steps sequence, in which Tsarist troops relentlessly advance downwards firing upon the townspeople; the whole film employs the revolutionary cinematic technique of colliding successive images, in order to whip up the audience's emotional response. Eisenstein's use of 'montage' continues to exhilarate cineastes everywhere and the film is still a regular fixture on critics' 'Top Ten'

A still from the
famous Odessa steps
sequence of
Battleship Potemkin
(1926). Banned until
1954 – the second
longest running ban
in British cinema.

lists, but at the time it was *Potemkin*'s depiction of a successful rebellion against political authority that over-excited the world's censors. The French police burned every copy they could find, in Pennsylvania it was banned on the grounds that it 'gives American sailors a blue-print as to how to conduct a mutiny', and in Europe one censor tied a knot in Eisenstein's Marxist dialectic with a sinister warning to any would-be revolutionaries: every scene that occurred after the Odessa steps sequence was cut.

In Britain the provocative film could not have arrived at a worse time. The General Strike of May 1926 had collapsed within nine days, but the fear of working-class insurrection continued to dominate the newly elected Conservative government under the leadership of Stanley Baldwin. The incoming Home Secretary, Sir William Joynson-Hicks, disliked films in general and radical films in particular and it was upon his command that *Potemkin* was summarily banned by the BBFC in September, four months after the defeat of the unions.

There matters rested until 1928, when Ivor Montagu tried to sidestep the BBFC by submitting the film to the LCC. This manoeuvre failed, however, because the Conservative-run council confirmed the initial ban. Apparently Montagu then intended to apply to other local authorities, but before he could do so *Potemkin*'s distributor, Film Booking Offices, was visited by Scotland Yard officers in February 1929. Although there is only Montagu's word for

41

Sergei Eisenstein at the helm of *Battleship Potemkin* (1926).

this action by the police, it can be no coincidence that the distributors suddenly refused to supply prints of the film to the Film Society or for any other private performance without Joynson-Hicks's written permission – which not surprisingly was never given.

It is a compliment to Eisenstein's skill in the editing room that his film received a blanket ban which denied access even to middle-class intellectuals. Presumably Baldwin's government really did believe that the film would cause an uprising; yet however paranoid their beliefs the 'mystery men' achieved their objectives. *Battleship Potemkin* was kept out of Britain's cinemas until 1954, by which time the exhibition of silent films was no longer profitable. One of the few to protest against the compulsorily enforced darkness imposed on what is widely acknowledged to be the most astounding film of its time was the Marxist critic Winifred Ellerman (Bryher), who gave colourful vent to her imagination in 1930: 'One can visualize a high-spirited youth kidnapping the censors responsible for the prohibition and forcing them to witness the film four or five times over until they cheered the Red Flag in order to get released.'

Eisenstein himself also tried to have his film unbanned when he visited London in 1930, but to no avail. He took a bitter-sweet revenge, however, in his memoirs with a satirical description of Britain's censors: 'One of them is blind and probably deals with the silent films; another one is deaf and so gets the sound films; the third one chose to die during the period that I was in London.' And, as one film historian has pointed out, death probably did not 'preclude him from continuing to censor films'.

Back in 1926 another homage to the Bolsheviks had moved into the fray. In many ways Pudovkin's *Mother* (1926) is even more pro-revolutionary than *Potemkin* and its exclusion from the audience it was intended for throws a light on the increasing co-operation between the BBFC and local councils when they were agreed upon a common aim. *Mother*'s plot is simple and direct: first, the factory-worker hero is beaten up by strike-breakers; then, after he has regained consciousness he is shot dead by the Tsar's cavalry. But before he expires he passes on the union flag to his mother who wraps it around her body before being crushed under the hooves of the Tsarist horses.

After examining this film, which he inexplicably viewed within the privacy

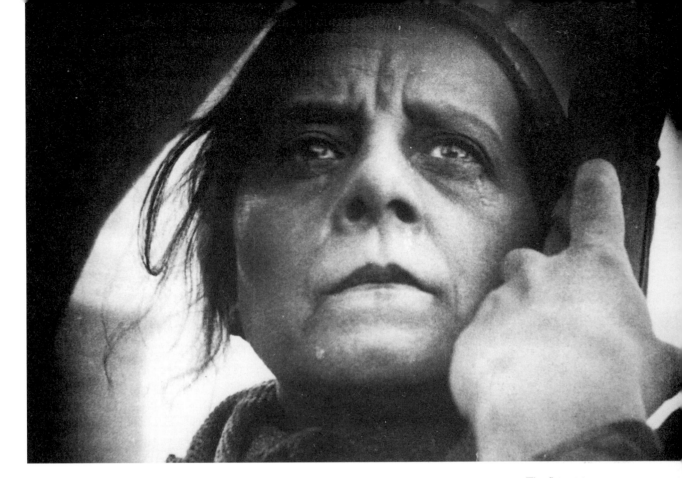

of his flat, T. P. O'Connor astonishingly misread Pudovkin's unsubtle plot to the extent that he thought *Mother* contributed towards a better understanding of Russian conditions. The Baldwin government, however, was more perceptive and the Home Office immediately brought pressure to bear on O'Connor to veto the film. Within days the President of the BBFC had carried out their wishes and Pudovkin's film has rarely been seen since.

However, one distinguished agitator was not prepared to accept this decision. The philosopher Bertrand Russell took action by arranging for a secret screening of *Mother* at the Film Society. Following his example, the newly established workers' film society, the Masses Stage and Film Guild, applied for permission from the LCC at the end of 1929 to see *Mother*, along with other outstanding banned Russian films. Among them were Eisenstein's *October* (which had already been pre-censored – all appearances of the disgraced Trotsky having been removed by a nervous Eisenstein) *Strike* (1924) and *Battleship Potemkin*, Pudovkin's *Storm Over Asia* (1928) and Trauberg and Kozintsev's extraordinary *New Babylon* (1929) which had been refused by the Board earlier that year because of its 'constant alternation of brutality and bloodshed and its scenes of licence and in many cases indecency'.

The following March, at a public meeting in London's County Hall, a letter from the BBFC was read out to the LCC's entertainments committee stating that the films would cause a breach of the peace if they were shown either privately or publicly. In reply the Labour MP George Strauss pertinently pointed out that since the middle-class Film Society had already gained permission to show these films, not allowing a workers' film society to see the same thing was 'nothing else but pure class bias and predjudice'.

A comic satire set in the Paris Commune of 1871, Trauberg and Kozintsev's *New Babylon* (1929) was banned for its 'constant alternation of brutality and bloodshed'.

But in an echo of the prevailing mood of anti-Bolshevism, the Conservative chairman of the committee, Miss Rosamund Smith, refused the application. 'I do not think anyone could be more opposed to political censorship than I am,' Miss Smith insisted. 'But I think we are up against something quite different in these Russian films. I feel that Communism is a great deal more than the doctrine of a political party, and I am not prepared to give the authors of these films any right to publish their propaganda in this country ... I do not think we should give any preference to people whom we thoroughly distrust.' Shouts were then heard from the gallery of, 'That is political.' 'It is not a political thing at all.' 'Yes it is,' said a spectator. 'Everybody knows,' riposted the lady councillor, 'that Communism is a great deal more than politics.'

A month later the Labour council at West Ham extended this somewhat quixotic definition of politics when it granted permission for a screening of *Mother*. This provoked an immediate response from the LCC, who decreed that henceforth the annual subscription of workers' film societies would be increased tenfold to ten shillings (50p) – a considerable sum in the depression years. And in order to tighten up any other loopholes, the LCC then instructed all film societies that they were not allowed to show any film which had been banned by the BBFC.

It was still legal for film societies to show films that had not been submitted to the BBFC. However, such films were open to other forms of harassment – especially if the intended audience was working class, and therefore 'susceptible'. For instance, an attempt by the police to stop the screening of *Potemkin* at a miners' hall in Jarrow led in 1934 to the foundation of the National Council of Civil Liberties.

The police would usually prevent workers' film society performances through the use of safety regulations; failing that, they would interrupt them to conduct on the spot 'inflammability tests'. Because a cinema was threatened with the withdrawal of its licence if it showed a film on inflammable stock, local authorities would often demand that propagandist films prove their resis-

Robert Wiene's *The Cabinet of Dr Caligari* (1919) is now remembered for its extraordinary Expressionist sets, but the BBFC wanted it banned so as not to distress the relatives of the insane.

tance to fire. This culminated in a notorious incident at the Manchester Labour Hall in August 1933 when the police raided a showing of the pro-revolutionary American documentary *The Road to Hell* (1931). The secretary of the society passed a burning match under a strip cut from this film, but the police were not satisfied. They insisted that the whole reel be laid on an open fire for at least half an hour. When this order was carried out the film still did not burst into flames; however it had become too distorted to pass through the projector.

Of course, the producers of social welfare and Russian propagandist films were not the only film-makers to suffer at the hands of the censors during this period. German Expressionist films of the twenties were particularly prone to the peccadilloes of the BBFC. Fritz Lang's *Metropolis* (1926) was so heavily cut that H. G. Wells declared it to be 'incomprehensible' and Robert Wiene's *The Cabinet of Dr Caligari* (1919) was nearly rejected because the Board argued that the asylum scenes would upset people in the cinema audience who had relatives in mental hospitals.

Other great Expressionist directors also suffered. Nobody outside the BBFC was even apparently aware at the time that F. W. Murnau's *Nosferatu* (1922)

Louise Brooks – all things to both men and women – has an uncomfortable encounter with her new husband in G. W. Pabst's *Pandora's Box* (1929). The BBFC deleted this famous Sapphic-waltz sequence from the British version.

had been banned in 1922, and the Czech-born auteur G.W. Pabst seems to have been especially singled out for attention. His first film with Louise Brooks, *Diary of a Lost Girl* (1929), was heavily cut, as was *Joyless Street* (1925), the last European film of Greta Garbo, while his other more famous and acclaimed production, *Pandora's Box* (1929), with Louise Brooks was rendered virtually meaningless by censorship.

Pandora's Box presents the fall from grace of Lulu, a femme fatale endowed with 'animal beauty and erotic power' but lacking in moral sense. The film had already been given a more elevated ending by its Berlin production company for the British release version in which, instead of being stabbed to death by Jack the Ripper, Lulu is saved, morally as well as physically, by the Salvation Army. Yet even after this self-imposed absolution the BBFC then chopped out one of the main characters, the lesbian Countess Geschwitz. As the critic and novelist Angela Carter has observed in her essay 'Femmes Fatales' from *Nothing Sacred*, whereas all the male characters ruthlessly exploit the heroine's expressive sexuality the Countess is the only figure to allow herself to be exploited by Lulu. In fact Pabst had already toned down the more explicit manifestations of the Countess's homosexuality, and Carter points out that this directorial act of self-censorship reinstated the very sexual hierarchies that the film was originally trying to undermine. Thus a film which dared to suggest that sexual desire can cross conventional boundaries was censored threefold.

In spite of the European contribution of these classic silent films, nearly 90 per cent of what was seen on British screens in the 1920s came from America. And nearly all mainstream silent American films enjoyed immunity from the BBFC because their innocuous content came within O'Connor's definition of cinema as a place for entertainment. Successful but also daring Hollywood movies of the time like Rudolph Valentino's *The Sheik* (1921), Raoul Walsh's *Sadie Thompson* (1928) with Gloria Swanson, or King Vidor's ambitious epic *The Big Parade* (1926) were also difficult to censor because their popularity sustained the British film industry. As a trade-sponsored body, the BBFC would obviously not want to censor the very films that kept them and their film-industry colleagues in their jobs. But the overriding reason why American films were largely left unscathed was simply because they were not politically controversial.

By the time silent film gave way to sound in 1928, the BBFC had ensured that the power of the moving image would not be employed to shock the British public. Of course, anybody could make a film about anything they wished, but unless it conformed to conventional beliefs within the status quo the BBFC, with the help of distributors and local authorities, could be absolutely sure that such a film would not reach a mass audience. The BBFC had proved to the government that state censorship of film was not needed because other means of control had rendered it unnecessary. The BBFC, in other words, had done enough to set Britain's film censorship system in place.

Four years later, in 1932, the Board was to cut the following line by Bertolt Brecht from Pabst's first talkie, *The Threepenny Opera* (1930): 'The rich have hard hearts but sensitive nerves.' As the BBFC prepared itself for sound, these words provide a testimonial to the Board's ability to silence so many outstanding silent films.

THE SOUND OF SILENCE 4 ✂

The BBFC was not prepared for the advent of sound films. Presumably the censors thought that the talkies would be a passing fad, because, for nearly three years after the Warner Bros Vitaphone system had been in operation, they did not even bother to acquire sound equipment. Instead the examiners would watch a film while someone else read the script out loud. Whether this caused confusion when the usual BBFC practice of watching two films at the same time was followed is not known. Once the equipment did arrive at the end of January 1930 the Board discovered that, whereas cutting silent films was a simple matter of wielding scissors, cutting dialogue from a sound film re-aligned the synchronisation between word and action and thereby destroyed all subsequent continuity. While they continued to unravel these technical mysteries the Board, however, devised a simple stop-gap solution: under the new system a film was either passed intact, or – if it required a cut of any kind – it was banned outright.

While they were discovering how to cut talkies the BBFC suffered a temporary setback. In November 1929 their President, T. P. O'Connor died at the age of eighty-one. Although 'T. P.' had been incapable of examining films during the latter part of his Presidency, as partial paralysis prevented him from mounting the stairs to the Board's projection room, it was nevertheless due to O'Connor's political dexterity that the BBFC had consolidated its power and fended off the advances of the state. Not only had he balanced the conflicting interests of the film industry, the local authorities and the central government; more significantly, O'Connor had recognised that the apex of this institutional triangle was occupied by the government. In the early, crucial, years of the Board, when the Home Office had yet to make up its mind whether to adopt state censorship or an industry-sponsored system or a combination of both, O'Connor had ably demonstrated to the government of the day the advantages of a censorship system that was not answerable to Parliament.

It was in recognition of that service that O'Connor was appointed a Privy Councillor in 1924. The position was not merely honorary; O'Connor had to sign the Official Secrets Act, which meant that he could be trusted with confidential information. Thus he no longer had to second-guess government intentions which in turn meant that the BBFC could function with

Opposite The script of *The Lives of a Bengal Lancer* (1934) was reluctantly approved by the BBFC's scenario censor Colonel Hanna – who was appalled by Hollywood's Americanised image of the British Raj.

49

greater efficiency as a front for government decisions on the cinema.

Luckily for the BBFC, O'Connor's successor as third President of the Board also understood the hierarchy of power within British film censorship. Indeed, Sir Edward Shortt had been Home Secretary in the Lloyd George coalition when in 1921 he and O'Connor had secured an agreement with many of the major local authorities that they abide by BBFC decisions. But Shortt had no direct experience of the film industry and upon his appointment as President the monocled barrister confessed that he personally disliked the new talkies. This might explain the sudden increase in the number of banned films during Shortt's six-year reign as head of the Board until 1935. Where O'Connor would ameliorate, Shortt tended to ride roughshod. Yet the arrival of the talkies would provide Shortt and the BBFC with the means to extend their control over the film industry. From 1930 onwards they would not only decide which films could be seen, but would also have a role in deciding what films could actually be made.

Throughout the 1920s the BBFC had requested film producers to submit their scripts to the Board prior to production. To begin with the producers ignored the invitation, but with the coming of sound at the end of the decade they began to recognise the financial advantage in avoiding the risk of having to re-shoot scenes to which the censors might object. And once the scripts of popular but potentially troublesome pictures such as colonial dramas like *Clive of India* (1934) or historical films like *The Private Life of Henry VIII* (1933) were submitted at the beginning of the thirties the BBFC's influence vastly increased. The censors no longer had to act after the event. They could now pre-censor films before they were even produced as well as post-censor the finished product.

The scenario reports from 1930 to 1939 give a rare insight into the pre-war attitudes of the newly empowered BBFC and, in particular, they highlight the personalities of the two supervisors responsible for judging a script's suitability. The principal examiner was Colonel J. C. Hanna, an artillery officer who had served in India, then in France where he was awarded the Croix de Guerre, and finally in Ireland until he joined the BBFC in 1922. He was already a mature sixty-three when he became chief script supervisor in 1930, but four years later a more youthful note was provided by the arrival of his assistant Miss N. Shortt, the daughter of Sir Edward.

The comments of these two examiners leave no doubt as to their colourful and wayward prejudices. With an obsession for military procedure, Hanna would ignore plots and instead make such comments as: 'There is a point which must be watched. It would be absolutely against all Guards' etiquette to drive about shopping in a taxi in full dress kit. Better make the occasion khaki' or 'N.B., the command "Right by Twos" should read "Move to the Right in File".' Naturally, the Colonel's expertise on army life extended to India, as he volunteered in a criticism of the 1934 Gary Cooper vehicle, *Lives of a Bengal Lancer*. After pointing out that 'Swords are never drawn in the orderly room,' the Colonel seems almost resigned to the fact that 'The author's Hindustani does not appear to extend to the difference between a punkah and a punkah-wallah.'

Miss Shortt left battle-dress order in scripts to her brusque supervisor; however she was constantly on the lookout for any possible transgression of her own hobby-horse. This was the defamation of any profession or institution – especially doctors: 'Delete "these poor people afraid of hospitals",' she instructed the producers of *The Amazing Quest of Ernest Bliss* (1936); and a year earlier she remarked of the 1935 British detective drama *Malice Aforethought*: 'Apart from the fact that a member of the medical profession is shown as the murderer the whole story is thoroughly sordid,' and therefore 'quite prohibitive'. On the other hand, 'The nationality of Sartoris the villain doctor,' in the 1936 thriller *Juggernaut*, 'is not expressed and therefore I do not think any medical authorities should take exception.'

Miss Shortt's concerns, however, did not stop with doctors, they extended from bell ringers, the BBC, and London Transport to mines and fisheries; and if the reputation of any one of these bodies came into question this script examiner always knew that any judgement would have to wait upon the opinion of the relevant institution. After Colonel Hanna points out that a police sergeant in a 1934 screen adaptation of Edgar Wallace's *The Crimson Circle* would never address a senior officer as 'Inspector', 'they would say "Sir"', Miss Shortt concedes that 'the story is suitable for production if there is nothing in it to which Scotland Yard would take exception.'

Later on in the decade, Miss Shortt became Mrs Crouzet but the daughter of the Board's President always gives the impression that she led a sheltered existence. She did not know what the word 'twerp' or the expression 'gives me the heebs' meant and the appearance of 'sex harmones' (sic) in a script elicited the sorry remark, 'I do not know what they are but would like to draw your attention to the expression which seems quite an unnecessary one.' Yet this sensitive censor who shrunk from anything 'nasty' was prepared to pull rank. On the proposed 1936 remake of Robert Wiene's *The Cabinet of Dr Caligari*, she wrote, 'My father has given his views on horror films and he agrees that it is quite prohibitive to show any version of this story.' She also felt no hesitancy in recommending the refusal of a script on the hearsay of her friends. Following an unspecific criticism of a projected 1936 British remake of D.W. Griffith's *Broken Blossoms*, being 'a sordid horrible story', she reports, 'I know the silent version drew numbers of people but my own experience was that my friends who saw it said to me "it is horrible, don't go".'

Unfortunately the consequences of such remarks were not confined to the offices of the BBFC. In spite of their evident anti-American snobbery Hanna and Shortt would usually pass Hollywood scripts with a few suggested cuts because they knew that the British film industry was totally dependent on the American studios. Home-grown films, however, were within the reach of these two eccentric censors. Thus Herbert Wilcox's proposed picture *The Hanging Judge*, on the life of the infamous eighteenth-century jurist Judge Jeffreys, was abandoned in 1934 because Hanna insisted that 'no reflection on the administration of British justice at any period could be permitted'. But then a different set of critical criteria would be applied to hard-hitting American films on a similar theme, such as Mervyn Le Roy's prison drama *I Am a Fugitive from a Chain Gang* (1932) starring Paul Muni. The only line that was cut from Le Roy's condemnation of judicial brutality was the request from a convict on a work gang to a warder as to whether he could 'go into the bushes for a moment?'

Yet even if they passed American social protest films like *Fugitive from a Chain Gang*, this did not mean that Hanna and Shortt approved of their potential effect upon cinema-goers. Indeed, the BBFC was worried that British audiences would draw moral conclusions from these films and then apply them closer to home. Any inflammatory danger therefore had to be dampened down with a message emphasising their foreign setting. So the British versions

The BBFC tagged on a written preface to Mervyn Le Roy's *I Am a Fugitive from a Chain Gang* (1932) stating that such conditions did not exist in British gaols.

of American 1930s prison dramas such as *Each Dawn I Die* (1939) with James Cagney, or *Fugitive from a Chain Gang* carried a preface assuring the audience that 'Prison conditions revealed here could never exist in Great Britain.'

If the effect of American crime films could be distanced from the cinema audience, this was not so easy to accomplish with scripts that were set in contemporary Britain. For instance Walter Greenwood's celebrated play about unemployment, *Love on the Dole*, which was submitted to the Board at script stage in March 1936, was set in Salford. In this case it was the very directness of Greenwood's treatment of his subject that set Hanna and Shortt's antennae bristling. With her usual protectiveness towards the political establishment, Miss Shortt pointed to what she saw as the heart of the problem by noting, 'I do not consider this play suitable for production as a film. There is too much of the tragic and sordid side of poverty.' Doubtless she saw the danger of working-class audiences recognising their own circumstances in the proposed film and being spurred to take action to better them.

The kind of attitude to unemployment that Miss Shortt desired from a scenario could be found in a 1934 Gaumont British production, *Red Ensign*. Instead of *Love on the Dole*'s heroine leading a stone-throwing mob against the police, Michael Powell's *Red Ensign* features a managing director hero who not only persuades his dockworker employees to give up their strike but also convinces them, 'for the good of the country', to work for nothing. Not surprisingly the script was passed with the single comment, 'Quite a good story with a strong patriotic note.'

Throughout the 1930s, however, over three-quarters of the films shown in British cinemas were American. In turn, Britain provided the American studios with nearly half of their international sales and Hollywood acknowledged that economic fact with the production of movies designed specifically for the British market, such as Dickens adaptations or British Empire eulogies like *The Lives of a Bengal Lancer*. Because the uncomfortable truth was, British people did not like run-of-the-mill British films.

The censors were eager to keep the spectre of industrial unrest at bay – and accordingly approved of *Red Ensign* (1934). Here, managing director Leslie Banks pacifies agitation led by Percy Parsons.

All too often they were either placid domestic dramas such as Victor Saville's *Storm in a Teacup* (1937) or patronising class-ridden cinema-fodder like the comedy *While Parents Sleep* of 1935. As one London cinema manager reported in 1936, 'British pictures are disliked because the acting is wooden, because the actors and actresses talk "society fashion" and because they are too slow.'

Outside the cinema, the popularity of American pictures engendered resentment of various kinds: from the apoplectic jingoism of Colonel Hanna who had to pass 'an even worse parody of the British officer' from Hollywood every year, to the serious charge from British industrialists that 'trade is following the American film' in the world market. Even more fundamentally, many social workers, teachers and church leaders were recognising that the power to project national dreams through the use of film had been snatched, not by Britain, but by America. Such people were at a loss as to what to do; so instead of asking why British studios were under-capitalised, some of them took an easier path: they descended into racism.

In 1931 the Methodist Church's 'cinema expert', the Reverend H. Carter, observed that, 'A little group of men of Southern European birth with no Anglo-Saxon standards of culture and morality have seized hold of the motion picture industry of the USA and it is their type of thinking which is going out to the nations and into local cinemas.'

A year later, this kind of euphemistic anti-Semitism was taken to its most extreme in a book called *The Devil's Camera* by two journalists, R. G. Burnett and E. D. Martell. After its dedication to 'the ultimate sanity of the white races' and under such chapter headings as 'Hollywood: The Triumph of Disraeli', 'Sex Ten Feet Square', and 'Elstree – The Way of Death', Burnett and Martell propounded the theory that 'sex-mad cynical financiers' who were 'mainly Jewish' were submitting Britain's film-goers to 'squandermania, promiscuity, crime and idleness'. Finally in a *crie de coeur* which foreshadows General Ripper's supposedly Soviet-induced loss of 'essential fluids' in Stanley Kubrick's *Dr Strangelove*, the authors despair that 'our national strength is being sapped, our capacity to triumph over adversity undermined. This sinister weapon, in its celluloid self so flimsy and trivial, is robbing us of the qualities we most need for survival.'

Unfortunately, inchoate fascism of this kind, which would be pushed to its logical conclusion a decade later in German concentration camps, was echoed in renewed calls for government censorship from moral reform groups. Giving evidence to one of the numerous enquiries set up in the thirties to investigate films and film-goers, Sidney Dark, editor of the *Church Times*, summarised the feelings of the anti-cinema lobby: 'This vast army of the least intelligent and least morally equipped members of society were allowed to have all kinds of intellectual and moral poison pumped into them without any kind of interference . . . In this complex age it was race suicide to allow foreigners to impregnate falsehood into the lifeblood of this nation.'

In the meantime, 20 million Britons with 'untrained judgement' kept going to see American movies every week. In fact there was very little concern amongst the general public about the content of films, be they American or not. In 1931 only 21 of the 603 local licensing authorities told the Home

Opposite 'Kept women, petting parties, French studio life, cocktails, sneers at virtue and shooting galore – guns, guns, guns!' In an attempt to stave off the effects of this kind of 'prostitution' from Hollywood on British film-goers *The Devil's Camera* married moralism to racism.

The DEVIL'S CAMERA

R·G·BURNETT & E·D·MARTELL

Office that they had received complaints in the previous three years about the films shown in their area. More significantly, 586 of the authorities stated that they no longer banned films which had been passed by the BBFC.

This is a measure of the Board's increasing public credibility. Yet mavericks still existed. One Cornish borough solemnly banned films throughout the thirties despite the inconvenient fact that there were no cinemas within its jurisdiction. Upon the initiative of its Bishop, Croydon Council set up its own censorship committee and by October 1934 proudly claimed that in two years it had stopped 200 films from being shown, and Beckenham Council even set up its own Board of Censors in 1933 which created a new certificate, 'Passed under Protest'.

In a short life of notoriety Beckenham's upright Board banned nine BBFC-passed films including two archetypal gangster movies. Howard Hughes's *Scarface* (1932) featured Paul Muni as Tony Camonte, a hoodlum based on Al Capone, whose moral philosophy was summed up in the line, 'There's only one law – do it first, do it yourself and keep doing it.' William Wellman's *The Public Enemy* was refused admission to Beckenham auditoriums a year earlier in spite of the BBFC's prior removal of the notorious scene in which James Cagney reaches over the breakfast table to push a grapefruit into the face of his wife (Mae Clarke). The council also eviscerated officially approved films and replaced 'U' certificates with 'A's, as in the case of the Ritz Brothers' over-active horror comedy *The Gorilla* (1938), which it considered to be 'too full of growls' for exhibition to children. The local Kent populace, however, refused to go and see cut films and as a result of falling trade Beckenham cinema own-

Paul Muni (**below right**) in *Scarface* (1932) and James Cagney (**below left**) in *The Public Enemy* (1931) – both banned in Beckenham!

ers refused to pay their rates; after only nine months of existence the council was forced to dissolve its censorship board.

For the BBFC itself, the decade could be viewed as one of overwhelming success. Thanks to the pre-censorship winnowing of script outlines and then full-blown scripts by Colonel Hanna and Miss Shortt and the rigorous application of ever-expanding restrictions during post-censorship, almost every British film produced before 1939 qualified for the Colonel's highest approbation: 'quite harmless'. At the end of the decade the British film director Victor Saville summed up the effect of all these constraints when he complained that if he abided by the BBFC's rules he wouldn't even be able to film *Cinderella*.

Hollywood movies also became less contentious as the decade progressed because of the increasing co-operation between the BBFC and their American counterparts at the Motion Picture Producers Association, which under the aggressively sentimental leadership of Will H. Hays became known as the Hays Office. The purpose of this self-regulating body was the 'establishment and maintenance of the highest moral and artistic standards in motion picture production' and, indeed, it is true that whereas film censorship in Britain at this time was inconsistent, wilful and prim, it was still predominantly political. American film censorship, on the other hand, was largely moral.

Due to their ideological beliefs and the lack of profit incentive, the Hollywood moguls did not want to make politically adventurous movies anyway. Also, as the Hays Office tightened its grip on the studios in the thirties through its own use of script supervision and the threat of a $25,000 fine,

57

which could be imposed upon any studio that released a picture without a certificate, it became common practice in America for any possibility of potential trouble to be removed at source by the censors.

Yet the BBFC's victory over film producers and directors cannot be solely accounted for by the intervention of the Hays Office and, thereafter, by recourse to blue pencils and scissors. Unfortunately, all the pre-war BBFC papers which would have recorded individual decisions as to why particular films were cut or banned and who took those decisions were lost during the night of 10–11 May 1941, when the Board's Wren-designed building in Carlisle Street, Soho, was destroyed by a *Luftwaffe* bomb. In order therefore to gain a more reliable picture of what the censor wanted from the cinema, it is necessary to supplement the incomplete and often misleading documentation that did survive the Blitz with a close examination of the censors themselves. Who were these shadowy guardians of the country's pre-war cinema?

The Board's existing scenario reports contain numerous comments which can now be seen as the blusterings of bumbling eccentrics. The upper echelons of the BBFC, however, were staffed by experts in the manipulation of mass media. Far from displaying any hint of unrestrained idiocy, the employment record of the Board's leading personnel betrays a canny understanding not only of how images are disseminated, but also how they can be twisted so that they lodge in an audience's mind.

The administrative head of the Board, Joseph 'Brookie' Wilkinson had been in charge of the government department for Film Propaganda to Neutral Nations during the First World War. This post meant that he would have overseen the production of fake newsreels portraying atrocities perpetrated on Belgian nuns by German soldiers. And, in spite of his blimpish obsession with military procedure, before he became the Board's chief film censor and later its vice-president, Colonel Hanna had held the position of Deputy Chief of Intelligence in Ireland during 'The Troubles'. There he would have gained a familiarity with Sinn Fein propaganda along with an even more intimate knowledge of British counter-propaganda.

This expertise in the art of disinformation at the censor's office was considerably strengthened in 1929 when Edward Shortt assumed the BBFC presidency. Shortt was not just a practitioner of counter-propaganda, which would have helped him to interpret the ideology behind particular films; the ex-MP was also the government's chief expert in the even more delicate task of counter-subversion. As Chief Secretary of Ireland in 1918–19, he had honed his skills in counter-insurgency against the Irish nationalists. He adapted the lessons which had been learnt from the use of British concentration camps in South Africa during the Boer War to order wholesale arrests in specific areas of Ireland, thereby cutting off mass support for Sinn Fein.

When Shortt was recalled to London in 1919 by Lloyd George he was given the sensitive Cabinet post of Home Secretary during a period of increasing internal dissent. Again, in this delicate climate when the government had to keep its nerve, Shortt demonstrated his precision in counter-subversion. First he took overall command in the suppression of mutinies in the army, then he broke up strikes in the police force and on the 'Red Clyde' and he followed that up with the drawing up of contingency plans in case of a General Strike – which were successfully adopted in 1926. It is consistent with such a background that one of a few explanations which is still in existence for the banning of a film during the early thirties can be clarified: the French version of *The Threepenny Opera* was refused a certificate in 1932 because it included a scene in which an army of beggars breaks up the coronation of a British queen.

Rudolf Forster as Mac the Knife in G.W. Pabst's *The Threepenny Opera* (1931) – banned in the French-language version due to its disrespectful attitude towards the British monarchy.

Upon his death in 1935 Sir Edward Shortt was succeeded as President of the Board by Lord Tyrell of Avon. Unlike his predecessor, William Tyrell did at least like going to the cinema. Indeed he co-wrote the script of the 1938 box-office hit *Sixty Glorious Years*, a hagiographic account of Queen Victoria's reign starring Anna Neagle. Tyrell's connections, however, with the covert side of government were just as pervasive as Shortt's had been. Like O'Connor and Shortt before him he was made a Privy Councillor, a position which gave him access to ministers and government information, but unlike his predecessors Tyrell was not only a practitioner of propaganda policies, he also invented a completely new form of propaganda which had close ties to the cinema.

The BBFC's President from 1935 to 1947 was the father of British cultural propaganda, a subject he had pioneered at the Foreign Office before the First World War. He later headed the FO's Political Intelligence Department, from within which he created a News Department to propagate British culture and 'news' as a means of diplomacy. Unfortunately, after he became its permanent head, Tyrell's innovative career at the Foreign Office was cut short by a rumoured overfondness for the bottle. He took early retirement in 1934 but within a year he was offered the presidency of the BBFC, a post he would hold in conjunction with the chairmanship of the British Council. This articulate bon viveur therefore became responsible both for promotion of British culture

One of the few pre-war British films about the monarchy that was allowed to reach the screen – *Sixty Glorious Years* (1938), a hide-bound biopic of Queen Victoria which probably owed its certificate to the fact that William Tyrell, the President of the BBFC, co-wrote the script.

abroad and censorship of its major mass medium at home.

But the question then emerges: why would such high-powered officials want to concern themselves with a job that merely drew down opprobrium on its holder's head? Jack Vizzard, the Hollywood chief of the BBFC's American counterpart, the Hays Office, during the thirties, provided the answer when he emphasised that American film censorship before the war was a moral censorship whereas the British version was political. Inevitably the political prescription was enforced on the screen by the British film industry. But the person entrusted by the government of the day to steer the trade down that chosen path was the BBFC's President.

In theory, BBFC Presidents were chosen by the film industry in conjunction with the Home Office, but in practice the government of the day had to be sure that the job was held by a man who understood their political requirements from the cinema. Those included the prevention of films which opposed government policy, but more importantly still, as the film historian Nicholas Pronay has emphasised, they designated to the BBFC the primary task of stopping alternative visions and projected policies from reaching the screen.

Those were the two drumbeats that constantly punctuated the speeches that Tyrell and Shortt gave to the film industry throughout the thirties. 'The first tendency to which I would draw your attention,' Tyrell told a conference of British exhibitors in 1936, 'is the creeping of politics into films. From my past experience I consider this dangerous. I think you will agree that I am entitled to speak with some authority on the subject of politics.' The denizens of Wardour Street obviously concurred, and anyway, they would have taken this advice to heart because they had already been warned by Edward Shortt three years before that, 'There is no case on record of a film, after its rejection by the Board, proving a commercial success.'

But within a year Lord Tyrell had to remind his supposed employers that, 'We have a duty to perform, which is at times a very difficult task, and that is to prevent films being shown which are likely to give offence to the public and imperil the industry itself. In the carrying out of these duties I know that I shall have not only your sympathy but, when necessary, your co-operation.'

Just in case these words were too diplomatic for Britain's cash-conscious producers and distributors, Tyrell rammed the point home in his next BBFC report to the trade: 'The cinema needs continued repression of controversy in order to stave off disaster.' This time the British film industry must have got the message because at that year's conference in 1937 the ex-mandarin was able to congratulate the exhibitors: 'We may take pride in observing that there is not a single film showing in London today which deals with any of the burning questions of the day.'

The government and the BBFC may have rid British cinemas of 'offence', but that did not prevent the enemies of film censorship from firing into the flanks of the advancing Board. The ammunition was supplied by the BBFC itself; for its personnel not only lacked their leader's political finesse, their ignorance also provided a reliable source of mockery for journalists and the Board's opponents. The British film director Thorold Dickinson described the Board's membership as being made up of 'ex-colonels and maiden aunts in long flowered frocks'; one of the most notorious examples of their boorishness was contained in a BBFC rejection slip which became a prized possession of Ivor Montagu, the secretary of the Film Society during the 1930s. The rejection referred to Germaine Dulac's ciné-club hit of the thirties, the surrealist fantasy *Le Coquille et Le Clergyman* (1926). Dulac had already cut out the film's one nudity scene in which the clerical hero rips the clothing from a female confessor's breasts; nevertheless an examiner at the Board dismissed Madame Dulac's psychoanalytical exploration of sexual frustration with the words: 'This film is so cryptic as to be meaningless. If there is a meaning, it is doubtless objectionable.'

The BBFC also laid itself open to charges of nepotism. Leaving aside Miss Shortt, the Board also employed the seventy-five-year-old widow of its first President, George Redford, as the first female censor in 1922. In 1937 she was succeeded by another female adjudicator when the BBFC employed a Madge

The protagonist priest takes solace in the eponymous seashell from *Le Coquille et Le Clergyman* (1926), a surrealist fantasy about sexual desire which prompted the censor's catch-all comment: 'If there is a meaning it is doubtless objectionable.'

Kitchener as script reader. Miss Kitchener had no previous experience in the film industry. But (in keeping with the military bias of the Board) what undoubtedly had some bearing on her appointment was the fact that she was the niece of Lord Kitchener. However, not even family ties or regimental loyalty can explain the BBFC's recruitment of Major de Fonblanque Cox.

The Major, known to his friends as 'Cockie', was appointed at the age of eighty-one by Lord Tyrell to act as assistant reader of scripts. Upon his appointment in June 1936 he told the *Sunday Express*, 'I shall preserve a perfectly open mind but I will not countenance vulgarity. No, my boy, let us show clean films in the old country. I shall judge film stories as I would horse flesh or a dog. I shall look for clean lines.'

World Film News then looked the Major up in *Who's Who* where they discovered 'that he is a judge at the Crystal Palace, Birmingham, Crufts and all the principal dog shows and that he is a life member of the Garrick and Leander clubs. His publications include "Coursing", "Chasing and Racing", "A Sportsman at Large", "Yarns Without Yawns", "Fugleman the Foxhound", "Dogs, Dogs and I", "Dogs of Today" ... His musical publications include "Air Marshal" (March), "United Empire" (March), "For King and Country" (March) and "Wong" (Chinese Patrol). Plentiful references to his excellence as a judge of dogs (with a penchant for patriotic music) indeed exist; but no reference to his special competence as a judge of films can be traced.'

The film historian Jeffrey Richards has, however, more recently extended the search and discovered that, in addition to his sporting interests, Major Cox also held the more appropriate post of drama critic for *Vanity Fair* magazine, as well as being a prolific journalist on a variety of subjects. But Richards also unearthed another fact which is not so auspicious for the Major's reputation, or indeed that of the BBFC: apparently the elderly script examiner suffered from 'lethargica', a condition which renders its victims unconscious whenever they try to read anything.

In addition to such unforeseen obstacles obstructing their plans to rid the cinema of controversy, Tyrell and Shortt must have expected attacks on the BBFC's political exclusion zone from more conventional opponents. But organised resistance to the BBFC was surprisingly thin on the ground and the two Presidents managed, in conjunction with the Home Office, to keep the subject of film censorship off the parliamentary agenda and therefore out of the public eye until 1938. On 7 December of that year, however, the Liberal MP, Geoffrey Mander finally forced the issue out into the open when he instigated a debate in the House of Commons on the question of whether the BBFC was acting as a convenient front for the government.

Mander declared that 'the Board of Film Censors is supposed to deal with questions of morals only, but on many occasions, there has been political action.' He then asked the Home Secretary Sir Samuel Hoare the pertinent question, 'Who asked them to be political?' Hoare denied the charge, replying: 'I say categorically to the honourable member for East Wolverhampton that no pressure at all has been put upon the producers of these films, and the fact that this or that incident may have been deleted from a film is in no way due to government pressure. Any action that may have been taken, has been taken by the chairman of the Board of Film Censors on his own responsibility.' This exchange must have been embarrassing for the government, but more pressure would have been required to force the BBFC to open its files and the debate had little impact. So the subject of censorship was buried once again within the substrata of Home Office and BBFC memos and did not reappear in the pages of Hansard until well after the Second World War.

The BBFC must have also anticipated sustained opposition to their selective and politically-based judgements from a group who during the twenties and thirties had become their fiercest critics: the literary and film intelligentsia. But surprisingly this never occurred. One explanation is that the legal and executive branches of film censorship were – and still are – split between local councils and the BBFC, and therefore attacks on film censorship were, by necessity, fragmented. But more unexpectedly the Board's control of film content in the

A less well known side to George Bernard Shaw is to be found in his campaigns against film censorship. Here he 'does lunch' with Marion Davies, the mistress of William Randolph Hearst, at her bungalow on the MGM lot in Culver City in 1932; with, left to right, Charlie Chaplin, Louis B. Mayer the head of MGM, and Clark Gable.

thirties was never threatened because its hegemony was accepted by progressive elements within the industry itself. Britain's two most powerful producers of the era, Alexander Korda and Michael Balcon, who despite being autocrats were both liberally inclined, not only accepted the political status quo which underpinned the censorship system, but, for reasons of personal ambition, they repeatedly made films which sang the praises of class harmony and cheerful conformity.

Even more importantly, the role of the BBFC was never challenged because the supporters of radical cinema were divided and ambivalent in their aims. Ivor Montagu, the founder of the Film Society and the BBFC's most outspoken critic of the time, may have called himself a communist film-maker, but he was also élitist enough to agree with the BBFC that popular mainstream films required more stringent censorship than those intended for the enlightened few. Astonishingly, he was supported in his discriminatory sentiments by such supposedly progressive figures as Graham Greene, J. B. Priestley and Bertrand Russell.

Celebrated reformist authors whose work was adapted for the screen might also have been expected to launch articulate attacks upon the BBFC's selective principles. Unfortunately, they either fudged the issue by shooting themselves in the foot, as in the case of H. G. Wells who let it be known that he was not unhappy that *Island of Lost Souls* (1933) had been banned as the film version of his book embarrassed him; or they inadvertently bolstered up the BBFC, like George Bernard Shaw.

Out of all the prominent figures who worked in British films during the thirties, Shaw was the only one who consistently took on the Board. And he was the only person to defeat them. His insistence in 1938 upon retaining Eliza Doolittle's famous response, 'Not bloody likely', in his screenplay of *Pygmalion* (1938) was the first time that a specific recommendation for a deletion by the BBFC had been ignored, and the inclusion of that phrase in the final film therefore constituted a direct challenge to Tyrell's authority as a censor. Furthermore, because Shaw won, he opened up a path for others to walk along.

But the Irish playwright compromised that victory because he believed, along with other liberal opponents of the BBFC, that censorship was necessary for the uneducated majority if not for himself and his kind. And, of course, that played into the hands of the censors. Shortt and Tyrell were not concerned if adventurous films reached a select audience in film societies. What worried them was the thought that such films could be available to a wider public on general release.

While it must have been a pleasant surprise for the BBFC to discover that any opposition to them was so half-hearted, it must have been less comforting to realise that as the decade progressed the future of British film censorship would be decided in a very different arena from Parliament or even the Board's offices in Soho. By the end of the 1930s it had become plain that the content of most films shown in Britain would be determined, not in the United Kingdom at all but on the other side of the world in a city variously described by one contemporary British commentator as 'the crime-builder of the age', 'the desecrator of marriage and morality', 'that enthronement of lust' – Hollywood.

ANGLO-AMERICAN ATTITUDES 5 ✂

Sex brought them together, but sex also threatened to break up the relationship between Britain's and America's film censors. Other matters may have caused disharmony between the two bureaucratic suitors, but it was upon the ever-contentious issue of sexuality that the couple would, after a series of misunderstandings, rows and even break-ups eventually draw up their marriage contract and settle down into celibate bliss.

At the outset of Britain's film censorship in 1912 the Board's examiners were only issued with two rules to apply to the screen: no portrayal of Christ and no nudity. Yet for two decades it was the former proscription rather than the latter that restricted Hollywood film-makers – most notably applied to Cecil B. De Mille's popular biopic of Jesus, *King of Kings* (1927), which bypassed BBFC censorship and therefore received a restricted release. But from 1932 a number of American producers began to submit their scripts to the BBFC for approval and it was then that the Hollywood studios encountered Colonel Hanna and Miss Shortt's cinematic campaign for modesty and decorum.

In spite of being 'an absolute eye-opener' to the Colonel, he dismissed 'about 95 per cent of American criminal jargon' as 'objectionable' and it was therefore deleted; so was any mention of 'sex appeal', 'sexual degenerates' and 'nymphomania', as well as 'bawdy', 'belly', and 'bum' amongst hundreds of other words which would now be excised from the scripts.

Of course, this kind of propriety was also extended to British producers. For them such colloquialisms as 'tonight's the night', 'old cock', 'bottom's up Auntie', and even an affectionate plea from the 1933 comedy *Some Are Cruises*, 'I'd iron your knickers with my mitt', came under the blue pencil. American scriptwriters also discovered that as far as Colonel Hanna was concerned sex and the soldier did not fraternise in the same line. For an old campaigner like the Colonel a speech ending with 'us girls have to make hay while the sun shines, there won't always be a war', constituted an act of treachery and he duly cut it from a 1933 MGM comedy, *Wait For It*.

Often, however, it was deemed that politeness could only be maintained by the exclusion of a whole film due to its 'general air of loose living and immorality'. Hanna, in particular, would not let anything, even historical realism, stand in the way of his crusade to fillet impropriety from a script. When

Elsa Lanchester as Anne of Cleves with her husband Charles Laughton as Henry VIII in the scene the censors wanted to keep chaste – from Alexander Korda's *The Private Life of Henry VIII* (1933).

in 1933 the film mogul Alexander Korda submitted *The Private Life of Henry VIII*, the new Chief Censor found fault with the script, protesting that: 'The language may be true to the standards of that period but is far too outspoken and coarse for the present day. Delete any suggestion that intimacy took place and all indication that this marriage (to Anne of Cleves) was consummated.' Fortunately from the point of view of British film, Korda possessed enough courage and enough influence in political circles to be able to withstand this advice and a year later the rumbustious performance of Charles Laughton in the title role boosted the film's box-office returns beyond any other English film until *Chariots of Fire* in 1981.

In nine years of constant restraint, the nearest that this odd couple of censors came to an acknowledgement of sexuality in film was on 14 April 1936, when an adaptation of W. B. Maxwell's novel *Spinster of This Parish* arrived on their desk. Taken from a tale of thwarted love over a period of twenty-seven years, such abstinence almost, but not quite, overcame Miss Shortt's determination to preserve the good name of her favourite protégé, the medical profession. 'A story of a great and abiding love,' she enthused. 'There is nothing sordid about their story. But omit scenes of doctors in asylum.' Maybe coitus had to be interrupted for nearly three decades to win Miss Shortt's indulgence; but none the less a proscription of the lewd had remained the *sine qua non* of British film censorship ever since nudity was forbidden by the BBFC at the Board's creation back in 1913.

If sex on the page could be purged with a stroke of the pen, sex on celluloid was harder to eradicate. While specific scenes of lovemaking were invariably controlled, it proved more difficult for the Board to censor an idea: whereas the actuality of sex could be deleted, a suggestive atmosphere proved more elusive. British film-makers tended to discover sex – along with the poet Philip Larkin – in 1964, but American producers had emerged from the Victorian twilight when the century was still in its youth. For them sex went hand in hand with the discovery of the star system in 1915, and March of that year marked the arrival of sex as a fully fledged cinematic commodity when a five-foot-one-inch New York-based actress called Theodosia Goodman emerged, white-faced and languid, in front of a movie camera at the Astoria Studios in Long Island.

Hawked by her press agents Johnny Goldfrap and Al Selig as 'foreign, voluptuous and fatal', this tailor's daughter from Chillicothe, Ohio, transformed herself into Theda Bara, the original femme fatale of the screen in her film debut *A Fool There Was*. In this 1915 prototype of the vamp movie, not just one but two of Theda Bara's married lovers destroyed themselves: the first expires from drunken remorse in front of the man-eater who consoles him with a shower of petals flung in the face. After being seduced – 'Kiss me, my fool' – the second shoots himself in front of the diminutive vampire but merely receives a laugh for his efforts.

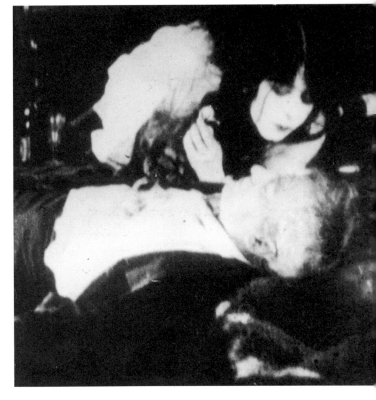

The first screen vamp, Theda Bara, lives up to her role in *A Fool There Was* (1915).

Two years after *A Fool There Was* arrived upon British shores the BBFC introduced a 'vamp clause' into its rules. But by then the sexual myth which whirled around Theda Bara had taken hold. Propelled by the information that Theda Bara was an anagram of Death Arab, journalists whipped up a chimera of the sexually dangerous and illicit, confiding to their readers that the star was, in fact, 'the daughter of a French painter and an Arab courtesan, raised on the banks of the Nile, suckled by crocodiles . . .' As a result both the public and the BBFC ignored the actual film, which is a series of studied poses, and instead swallowed the tall stories, with the inevitable consequence that the Board banned *A Fool There Was* in June 1916. Along with almost everyone else they had projected their fears and fantasies on to a single woman.

Because the Board was in a position to outlaw the celluloid existence of Theda Bara, it actually assisted in creating the fantasy of the sex symbol. The sexually illicit, the forbidden fruit, that essential component of the star system had been put into place by a compliant censor. The censor had, in effect, created what was censorable.

This paradoxical interdependency between censor and censored became more evident in the 1920s, when glimpses of female nudity in Cecil B. De Mille's biblical epics and the specially colour-tinted sequence of bare-breasted women in Fred Niblo's precociously camp *Ben Hur* (1925) were passed without comment by the Board. Even then, British distributors were dependent on the box-office success of such well publicised films. However there were limits. In the same year the Board's annual report registered a protest against gratuitous exposure of flesh, and censured 'The growing habit with actors of both sexes to divest themselves of their clothing on slight or no provocation. For instance, in what is a common scene when the heroine is assaulted by the villain, she almost invariably contrives to pull her dress well off the shoulders

A seragalio scene from what one critic has called 'Hollywood's greatest epic'. Surprisingly, the bare-breasted scenes in Fred Niblo's sumptuously excessive 1925 version of *Ben Hur* were passed uncut by the censor.

and this is done even by the leading actresses.' And the flesh wasn't always female. 'Equally, when there is a struggle between men,' the report observed, 'they tear their shirts to ribbons exposing their bodies to the waists.' The Board might disapprove of this 'unwholesome tendency', but throughout the twenties they nevertheless allowed the bare torsos of Fairbanks, Barrymore and Valentino – though not their female counterparts – to ripple across the silent screen.

Continental films tended to treat love-making with the same tentative touch as their British counterparts and in the rare instances when directors did include passion, such as Buñuel's *Un Chien andalou* and 'the scandalous' *Ecstasy*, which featured a close-up of Hedy Lamarr's face during cunnilingus as well as a more famous nude bathing sequence, they did not submit their films to British censorship. One exception to the celibate European silent screen which was viewed by the Board was Alexander Wolkov's 1927 biopic, *Casanova*. With the use of an overhead camera Wolkov not only employed every excuse to parade flesh in every possible scene, the director also introduced

a perverse element into a notorious post-coital sequence of cascading inter-twined bodies flowing from the great lover's massive bed. The camera moved down and then up the river of bodies to the bedhead where Casanova, lying like a horn of plenty giving birth to fruitful abundance, stretches out a beseeching arm in outrageous ennui for yet one more celebrant to mount his priapic altar. Quite how the distributor ever thought that this hymn to satiety would ever pass a British censor is not recorded; and the film was duly banned in 1929. As it has never been resubmitted to the BBFC, this ban remains in perpetuity.

While silent continental films were susceptible to interference from the British censor because of their lack of clout at the British box office, American movies, thanks to their profitability, were treated with more respect by the BBFC. Also the content of silent Hollywood films almost always remained within the parameters of good taste, so with that added assurance the BBFC rarely hesitated before passing the immediate successors to Theda Bara.

As the twenties progressed, however, the femme fatale gave way to a more sexually aware and independent woman who was less a fantasy and more an earthbound reality. This new species was first exemplified by Gloria Swanson in Cecil B. De Mille's marital comedies of the early 1920s, one of which boasted the then risqué line: 'Modern girls do not sit by the fire and knit.' Swanson was later joined by the 'Hot Jazz Baby' Clara Bow, the petulant Polish actress Pola Negri and finally by the 'Great Sphinx': Greta Garbo. But although the more suggestive scenes in their films were toned down with the occasional deletion of a line, the Board continued to grant certificates to Hollywood star vehicles, even if it meant, as in the case of Garbo's most erotic silent film, *Flesh and the Devil* (1926), that the running time was reduced by twenty-three minutes.

The BBFC was therefore at a moral disadvantage when the talkies brought an enhanced sexual presence to the screen. Again the problem lay outside the jurisdiction of the Board. In 1924 the Motion Picture Producers and Distributors of America – the Hays Office – drew up a code, based on various 'don'ts and be carefuls'. This eased the workload of the BBFC for the second half of the decade, with the result that the Board had relatively little to cut from Hollywood films. The studios, in fact, went out of their way to pacify British critics of Hollywood and the BBFC by re-editing many of the more con-tentious productions which they sent to Britain. But this useful relationship between the two censors was set to break down by the end of the twenties.

With the onset of the Depression in 1929 cinema attendances in America fell by over a third in the following two years. Competition between the Hollywood studios suddenly became cut-throat as they scrambled for subjects that would bring audiences back to the box office; and in the ensuing maul any restrictive advice issued from the Hays Office was virtually ignored. This free-

for-all in turn led to the appearance in Britain of the fully fuelled, wisecracking, cynical heroine of the 1930s who flaunts her body, enjoys the reaction and embraces the consequences.

The epitome of this modern-day woman was Jean Harlow. From 1912 to the present day no other actress has had as much footage winding its way on to the BBFC's floor as the 'blonde bombshell' from Kansas City. The first cut came from her first big role. The oil magnate Howard Hughes had looked at a screen test of Harlow in 1930 for his aerial combat epic *Hell's Angels* and commented, 'In my opinion she's nix.' But the vacillating millionaire hired her anyway and with her mother in close, protective attendance the eighteen-year-old platinum blonde actress announced her screen presence in a lazy slatternly style that had previously only been seen under a red light beside a kerb. Thrusting out a hip, she offered her body to the camera via various airmen and instantly and insistently shifted the male erotic gaze from the legs, where it had been in the twenties, to the breasts, where it has remained until today.

Sir Edward Shortt, the BBFC's President, examined *Hell's Angels* twice in the company of an Air Ministry official who was on the lookout for any infringement of military security. Even allowing for the potential loss of defence secrets the two men's attention must have been dragged back to the

A large part of *Flesh and the Devil* (1926) was made up of breathless clinches between Greta Garbo and John Gilbert. The censor responded by removing almost a quarter of it for British audiences.

73

The come-hither presence of Jean Harlow, here receiving the lips of Ben Lyon in *Hell's Angels* (1930), caused many a scissor-holding finger to twitch in the censor's office.

earth by Harlow's request to 'Excuse me while I slip into something more comfortable'; presumably for this reason Shortt only let the film out of his grasp after thirty-five minutes had been cut from its original length.

Harlow's British fans were to see even less of her a year later in 1931, when the BBFC took away almost her entire performance along with the first reel of Charlie Chaplin's *City Lights*. But, even if a few of Chaplin's adoring close-ups of Harlow escaped into the cinema from that film, nothing of the provocative, head-turning star's next production would be projected into light.

With a change of hair colour and at her most blatant, Harlow's *Red-Headed Woman* shamelessly plays up to the enticing myth of the femme fatale. Her grasping, gold-digger streetwalks through the film, stalking her boss, wrecking his happy marriage and finally discarding him when he cannot deliver the social acceptability she craves. Usually at this point in a Hays Office-approved film Harlow's character would return to the wrong side of the tracks to commit suicide or possibly enter a convent, but in *Red-Headed Woman* her life of sin pays off. She relocates to the Riviera in order to conduct a simultaneous affair in the final reel with both a sugar daddy and his chauffeur.

Yet again, this time without an air force officer, Shortt reserved the rights of censorship for himself with a personal examination of the film, and on 10 October 1933 he declared that nobody outside the BBFC would be allowed to see *Red-Headed Woman*. This is not altogether surprising since Harlow's character was probably the most amoral to be presented to the BBFC until the sexual revolution of the sixties. *Red-Headed Woman* was finally granted a certificate in 1965, but unfortunately by then the film had been forgotten and it has rarely been shown in a cinema or on television.

Although Harlow's other film of 1932, *Red Dust*, received extensive cuts (including her reply to the news from Clark Gable that the local climate around Saigon makes it hard to sleep – 'Guess I'm not used to sleeping nights anyway') it was passed a year later probably because the Board's attention had been diverted by the breathtaking screen debut of 'one of the finest women who ever walked the streets' – Mae West.

In its original form in the stage play *Diamond Lil*, Mae West's role as a San Francisco saloon keeper had landed her in jail for ten days; and when the subsequent film, *She Done Him Wrong* (1933), is judged against the frightened sexual attitudes dominating Britain at the time, the BBFC probably regretted that she was ever released. Paramount cut eight minutes out of the film before it was even submitted for British censorship and amongst that footage was a rare case of a proper name being censored – 'Lil' became 'Diamond Lou'. The BBFC then cut another six minutes; but although a lot of suggestive footage had been cut, a great deal more got through. Enough of Mae West's indolent innuendoes survived, enough winking asides in songs such as 'I Like a Man Who Takes His Time' and 'I Wonder Where My Easy Rider's Gone', and enough sashaying in sequins and feather boas remained for Miss West to be elected to that rare position in public life: a woman to whom everything is per-

Mae West strikes an hourglass attitude in *She Done Him Wrong* (1933). The voluptuous star's insatiable desire for satisfaction provided a delicious fantasy for many but a nightmare for the censor.

mitted because she remains at once womanly and one of the boys.

Except of course by the censor, who in its American guise at the Hays Office was especially afraid of the sassy way in which the languorous star linked a woman's desire to an uncomplicated urge for sexual fulfilment. In 1933 these fears were both underlined and exploited when the Catholic Legion of Decency came into being under the leadership of Bishop Shiel of Chicago to protest against Hollywood's 'betrayal of America'. In the following year the Legion with its ten million followers took to the streets and began a very effective boycott of America's 'greatest menace – the salacious moving picture'; and according to the Legionnaires the two most prominent examples of the genre were *Red-Headed Woman* and *She Done Him Wrong*.

Faced with such pressure the Hays Office, along with the rest of the American film industry, repented and promised to do better. The reputation of the cinema, said Hays, 'should be protected as we protect the integrity of our children' and this ex-postman, with the encouragement of his associates at the BBFC, immediately backed up his words by putting teeth into the MPPDA's 1924 Code. Among the new stipulations which affected American films from the mid-thirties up until the sixties were: 'No inside thigh of a female may be shown between the garter and the knickers', 'Miscegenation, sex-relationship between the black and white races is forbidden' and 'If two people are shown on a bed, they must have at least one foot on the floor'. Double beds were barred, 'God' and the 'Lord' could only be mentioned in church, and specific words like 'damn', 'hell', 'virgin', 'tart', 'broad', and even 'tom cat' and 'cripes' were all put on a forbidden list.

Sex had been shown the front door and although it made frequent attempts to clamber back through a side window, cinema audiences would not be permitted to look at bare flesh, hear loaded innuendo, or see sexual provocation of any sort in films again for almost thirty years. Towards the end of the decade when she made her last film, *Saratoga*, Jean Harlow was no longer allowed to seduce her co-star, Clark Gable. With her platinum blonde hair darkened she merely tempts him in a clearly enunciated accent more redolent of the sweet tones of a debutante than the wisecracking slang of a woman who wants to claim her man for sin and sex.

Because she died in 1937, Jean Harlow escaped the full rigours of the renewed Hays Code, but the forces for moral re-order then focused their fire on the fuller figure of Mae West. The languid star had followed *She Done Him Wrong* with her most successful picture, *I'm No Angel*, but a year later in 1934 the clamp-down began with her third feature, *It Ain't No Sin*. While the film was being shot, the Hays Office took the precaution of stationing a 'watchdog' on the set to monitor Miss West's on- and off-screen behaviour; and when billboards on Broadway proclaimed the imminent arrival of *It Ain't No Sin* flying pickets of priests from the Legion of Decency congregated in front of each poster with signs bearing the stark message, 'IT IS!'

Over the next few years the Hays Office continued to harass West and to oversee the humourless censorship of her scripts; none of their ploys diminished the commercial success of her films. In 1938, however, Will Hays arranged for the publication of a list of stars that exhibitors supposedly considered to be box-office poison. In reality Hays concocted the list with the aid of the right-wing publisher William Randolph Hearst, as an extra-legal means of ridding Hollywood of 'difficult' actors and writers who supported the trade unions' campaign against studio cutbacks during the Depression.

But Mae West's inclusion in this fabricated blacklist was solely due to the embarrassment her sexuality caused the American censor. More unfortunately still, the inclusion of her name on Hays's list led to the actress's betrayal by her producers at Paramount. In spite of the fact that the profits from *She Done Him Wrong* had saved the studio from bankruptcy in 1933, Paramount dropped West's contract in 1938 and after only two more films in which she had to mouth such pious sentiments as, 'Any time you take religion for a joke, the laugh's on you,' Mae West retired from films until her comeback in 1970 for *Myra Breckinridge*.

Because of her outrageous disregard for the censor Mae West had been hounded off the screen; and her sisters in celluloid sexuality were therefore in no position to ignore the more petty restrictions which were now being imposed upon them by the Hays Office. Marlene Dietrich's name featured on Hays's bogus blacklist and Paramount also refused to renew her contract in the late thirties. Even Garbo, the 'Queen of MGM' was affected. Her sexual mystery in films after 1933, such as *Anna Karenina* in 1935 and in the following year *Camille*, were clouded by sentimentality, and pressure from the Legion of Decency forced her studio in 1941 to insert an extra scene into *Two-Faced Woman* whereby Garbo's feigned adultery reverts somewhat undramatically to marital fidelity – which prompted one contemporary critic to retitle the film *One-Faced Woman*. Garbo herself found this kind of interference abhorrent and the fact that the incident contributed to her early retirement from the screen in 1941 marks the majestic Garbo as the most illustrious victim of Hollywood's rearmament against moral turpitude.

Britain's film censors no doubt heaved a sigh of relief as Hollywood re-buckled its chastity belt. Whether it was consciously acknowledged or not, the less savoury as well as the more obvious functions of censorship were now being carried out for them by the Hays Office and the working relationship between the two watchdogs was therefore resumed. Hays himself cemented the re-established partnership in 1936 with a visit to London, and the marriage continued to prosper for the next two decades.

However, while one problem was in the process of being resolved, Hollywood presented another dilemma to the BBFC in the form of a new film genre – horror. Not that the Board immediately recognised the danger posed by horror films. They had banned the genre's prototype, F. W. Murnau's *Nosferatu*, in 1922, but that was largely because Mrs Bram Stoker was indefatigable in her attempts to sue anyone who adapted her late husband's book *Dracula* for the stage or screen; so when the BBFC found out that Mrs Stoker was close on the trail of Murnau they avoided the danger of being dragged into court through a judicious refusal of a certificate to the film. They therefore passed the two most famous early examples of horror to come out of Hollywood. Todd Browning's *Dracula* in 1931 and in the following year

Above left The 1931 version of *Dracula* with Bela Lugosi as the legendary Count was cut by seven minutes before it was submitted for censorship and that is probably why it encountered no opposition from the Board.

Above right Originally, the monster twirled the little girl around his head before throwing her in the lake. Boris Karloff successfully suggested that the scene be replaced by floating flowers; nevertheless *Frankenstein* (1932) posed problems for the censor.

James Whale's *Frankenstein*, without much delay and with only minor cuts. Released under an 'A' certificate, *Frankenstein* could be seen by children accompanied by adults, and amongst other concerned groups the National Society for the Prevention of Cruelty to Children was especially wary of the menacing scene in which Boris Karloff's monster and a little girl from the local village float flowers upon a pond just before he strangles her off-screen.

This sequence – which had already been toned down at Karloff's suggestion – is in fact a testament to the vulnerability the English star brought to the role coupled with the newfound ability of talkies to create an atmosphere of terror through the use of sound effects and music, rather than an indictment of what was actually portrayed on the screen. Nevertheless the NSPCC complained to the Home Office, who recommended that the BBFC follow the advice of various local councils with the introduction of a special new certificate which would be designated 'H' for 'horrific'.

In spite of its apparent arbitrariness this suggestion demonstrated an acute sense of censorship strategy because, following the success of *Dracula* and *Frankenstein*, the Hollywood studios were producing more and more variations of the horror film and the BBFC did not know how to deal with them. In February 1932 the Board passed Rouben Mamoulian's *Dr Jekyll and Mr Hyde* (1931), but only after they had cut a quarter of it, the result being that Hyde's first victim (Miriam Hopkins) disappears before she is murdered. The following March a lurid *Murders in the Rue Morgue* (1932) was granted an 'A' certificate after minor cuts; but in July, Tod Browning's masterpiece *Freaks*, a circus tale of murder and the subsequent mutilation inflicted on the beautiful murderess by the slain midget's deformed friends – they turn her into a chicken – was refused any certificate. Browning's extraordinary allegory, as one critic has put it, 'of the antagonism between the beautiful and the damned' remained under a ban until 1963 when it was granted an 'X' certificate; and even then the sympathetic screen appearance of a real half-boy, a living torso and a troupe of pinheads caused considerable press criticism of the BBFC's belated tolerance.

Director Tod Browning with some of the cast from *Freaks*. Banned from 1932 until 1963 – the longest running ban in British cinema.

The Board continued to pass horror films throughout 1933, but they received constant complaints from local authorities who insisted that the 'H' classification be adopted as a means of excluding children from frightening films. Finally the Board complied in May when Carl Dreyer's *Vampyr* (1931) was released uncut as an 'H', with its extraordinary death scene in which the hero wakes up in a coffin; through a window cut in the lid we look out of his eyes as the vampire and her evil underling screw the lid down and, finally, see the sky and trees on our way to the grave.

Yet the BBFC never defined their terms for the new certificate. Such films as *King Kong* (1938) and Michael Curtiz's terrifying horror classic of 1933 *Mystery of the Wax Museum*, which was one of the first films to be shot in Technicolor, were given 'A' certificates, while Abel Gance's First World War pacifist epic, *J'Accuse*, which had been banned until 1933, was coupled with the Ritz Brothers' horror spoof *The Gorilla* under an 'H' certificate. However, at the same time the truly horrific *Island of Lost Souls*, with Charles Laughton as a surgeon who turns animals into a grotesque array of beast-men and tries to get his favourite creation, Lota the panther woman, to mate with the shipwrecked hero Richard Arlen, was refused a certificate altogether.

Nevertheless, by employing the 'H' certificate as a precursor of the 'X' certificate – which replaced it in 1951 – the BBFC was able to pass more than thirty films up to 1939 which would normally have been banned as too dangerous for children. But the Board did not always take advantage of this new system, and the most glaring example of their oversight is Fritz Lang's *M* (1931), a chilling account of a Dusseldorf child murderer starring Goebbels's favourite actor Peter Lorre.

If this film had been granted an 'H', then Lorre's incomparable performance as the schizoid serial killer would probably have been left largely intact. But

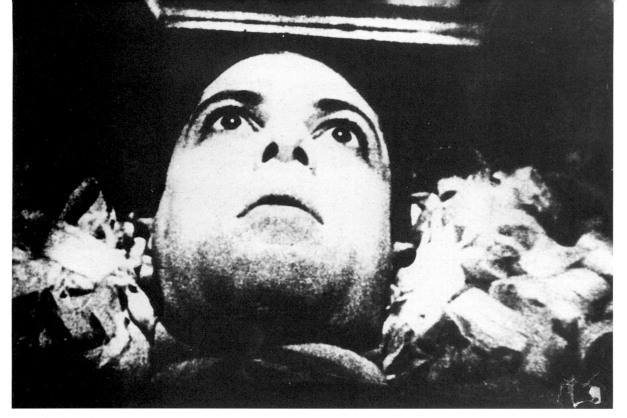

A window is cut into the coffin lid through which the ill-fated hero of Carl Dreyer's *Vampyr* (1931) looks – on the way to his own funeral. The film's release was delayed until the introduction of the 'H' (for horror) certificate in 1933.

because it was inexplicably released under an 'A' certificate, the censors cut most of the last scene which not only contains the very purpose of the film but also provides Lorre with one of the greatest speeches in cinema: the compulsive murderer, pursued by the ghosts of children and their mothers, cowers from his unforgiving accusers, the city's criminals and beggars. The ghosts never leave him, he insists, except when he kills. 'And afterwards I see those posters and I read what I've done . . . I read . . . and read . . . Did I do that? But I can't remember anything about it. But who will believe me? Who knows how it feels to be me? How I'm forced to act. [His eyes close in ecstasy.] How I must . . . Don't want to but must . . . must . . . Don't want to . . . must. And then a voice screams . . . I can't bear to hear it.'

The American censor Will Hays had come to London in 1936 not only to develop a common approach with the BBFC but also to improve communications between Hollywood studios and the Board. And not just for reasons of censorship. Unlike today, Britain in the thirties constituted the biggest market for American films outside the US and as President of the MPPDA it was part of Hays's job to make the entrance into that market as smooth as possible. In order to facilitate this commercial penetration Hays would have undoubtedly discussed the censorship of future Hollywood productions. Also, at the same time, the BBFC wanted the studios to submit more of their scripts for examination so that the Board's fingerprints would be less easy to discern on exhibited films; a film which shows the effect of this kind of international pre-

production censorship is Sam Goldwyn's 1937 thriller, *Dead End*.

In Sidney Kingsley's play the hero of *Dead End* is a well-meaning, moody cripple named Gimpty. An unemployed architect, he dreams of rebuilding his rundown Manhattan neighbourhood and then, with his conscience set at peace, he will escape from the slums. The play is set in motion by Baby Face Martin, a childhood friend of Gimpty's now turned gangster, when he returns to the neighbourhood to seek out his mother and his old flame, Francey, who has turned to prostitution.

Goldwyn's first edict to his scriptwriter, Lillian Hellman, was to turn Kingsley's hero into a suitable role for his contracted star, Joel McCrea. This meant that Gimpty metamorphosed into Dave Connell, an upright, broad-shouldered fighter for justice who instead of betraying his old chum Baby Face to the police, faces down the gangster himself. Then, at the insistence of the Hays Office, Baby Face was no longer to be repelled by Francey because she had contracted syphilis. He now discards her because she looks tired. When these instructions were combined and conveyed to Hellman, the renowned author and playwright recalled, 'Goldwyn said he wanted me to clean up the play. What he meant was, he wanted me to cut off its balls.'

But in spite of Hellman's misgivings her screenplay was submitted to the BBFC in June 1937, where it was not received with much enthusiasm by Colonel Hanna. 'Though the setting is squalid and many of the characters are not attractive,' the Colonel reported, 'I do not think we can say it is too sordid

The increasing collaboration between Hollywood and the BBFC during the thirties ensured that hard-hitting slum pictures like *Dead End* (1937) – with Joel McCrea and Humphrey Bogart – could be passed uncut.

for exhibition, unless of course the producer concentrates on getting sordid effects.' On the contrary, this was exactly the kind of effect that Sam Goldwyn wished to avoid. 'This set is filthy,' the movie mogul screamed just before the cameras began to turn on the first day of shooting. 'But Mr Goldwyn,' protested the director, William Wellman, 'this is supposed to be a slum. It's part of what we're saying in this picture.' Goldwyn however continued to pick up the carefully strewn rubbish, muttering to himself, 'There won't be any dirty slums – not in my picture.'

Sam Goldwyn found an ally of sorts in the BBFC's Miss Shortt, whose fastidious soul was always upset by the more overt signs of poverty in films. Amongst her own deletions from *Dead End* she sought the removal of the character 'T. B.', a member of the neighbourhood gang whose symptoms of tuberculosis disturbed Miss Shortt. 'He is always coughing,' she pointed out, and presumably as part of her continuing crusade to defend the reputation of doctors she therefore insisted that 'all mentions of spitting up blood' be excluded. She also had trouble with T. B.'s characterisation as 'a punk', which prompted the comment, 'I do not know what it means.'

For once, though, Miss Shortt did not get her own way. Goldwyn refused to make any more changes to a script which he had become proud of and to which he pinned his hopes of remaining independent of the major studios. Consequently some surprisingly radical dialogue remained in Hellman's final draft. 'What chance have they [the local kids]?' protests the hero in the last moments of the film. 'They've got to fight for a place to play, fight for a little extra something to eat, fight for everything. They get used to fighting. "Enemies of society", it says in the papers. Why not? What have they got to be so friendly about?' Such an outburst may sound mild today but Hellman's diatribe against city slums had an ominous resonance in the aftermath of Britain's depression.

On their part Hanna and Shortt must have felt that Hellman's liberal sentiments about slums would strike an uncomfortable chord in a paternalistic, class-structured society like Britain's, because they repeatedly recommended that the poverty of *Dead End* be glossed over. But their colleagues at the Hays Office knew that they could only make so many demands upon Goldwyn. The gruff producer did not own a major studio, but he had been at the meeting of Hollywood's founding fathers in 1922, when alongside Adolph Zukor, William Fox and Carl Laemmle, he offered Hays the job of 'Czar of the Movies'. Hollywood's chief censor, who possessed a keen political instinct (or as Kenneth Anger puts it 'Politics had taught Hays all he needed to know about hypocrisy'), would not have fought with a man who was capable of putting him back on the train to Washington.

Presumably when their criticisms met with no response, Hanna and Shortt were made aware of Hollywood's 'realpolitik'. But this underlying reason for their recommendations being stymied must have been especially galling to an anti-American, ex-colonial officer like Hanna. Because, in spite of the unspoken agreement between the Hays Office and the BBFC, for Hollywood Britain was just one more colony to be exploited; and even if it was an important market to which concessions had to be granted, it was rapidly becoming apparent to the BBFC that only so much interference in major American films would be tolerated. Because the Hollywood studios manufactured the films, they would decide what went into them and that is the reason why it was – and is – easier for the BBFC to censor British rather than American films.

Then, as now, power in a global industry like films lay not at the point of consumption or even at the point of distribution, but at the point of production. And this was a political and economic fact which had particular and potentially devastating consequences for a country that was dependent on an empire for its well-being. Slowly but surely the pragmatic truth dawned on the British establishment: the image of the white man that was being seen in the colonies had been coined by Hollywood rather than the Colonial Office. That image would therefore have to be closely invigilated. In fact it would have to be censored.

THE EMPIRICAL CENSOR 6 ✂

Opposite It's all in the eyes. Barbara Stanwyck as the smitten woman missionary with Nils Asther as her epicurean Chinese warlord captor in *The Bitter Tea of General Yen* (1932) – a Sino-American romance released in Britain but banned throughout the empire.

For as long as the British Empire still coloured a third of the globe in red, so the blue pencil followed. From the second decade of this century through until the end of the forties, censorship of films within the colonies had two distinct if not mutually exclusive objectives. The first dealt with the image of empire as it was presented to Britain's population, and the second with the perception of the empire from the perspective of those who were actually under British rule. These two images inevitably contradicted each other, because the home population needed, for the sake of their own moral equilibrium, to know that those who were ruled in their name were content with the status quo; while across the globe the subjects of this scrutiny had to be reminded that any alternative to the present order was delusory, impractical and therefore impossible.

Usually this dichotomy was veiled by religious proselytising or the education of a native middle-class élite who then acted as a buffer between the British and the rest of the population. But occasionally the disparity between imperial ideology and empirical reality became apparent through the selective use of film censorship. For example, in 1932 Frank Capra's *The Bitter Tea of General Yen* was passed by the BBFC for exhibition in Britain, but banned throughout the empire due to its depiction of miscegenation between an American missionary (Barbara Stanwyck) and a Chinese warlord (Nils Asther). Because, of course, what appeared to be an exotic romantic adventure to one audience might provide another set of cinema-goers with the sort of example the authorities did not want to see emulated.

The range of Britain's control over film censorship within the empire was bracketed by race. White-populated colonies such as Canada, Australia and New Zealand, which had all been granted dominion status before the invention of cinema, had set up independent censorship systems with boards operating within each state. Nevertheless, the 'mother country' still exerted some influence over the vetting of films even within Commonwealth countries. Upon the advice of the Foreign Office the Edith Cavell biopic *Dawn* (1928) was banned in several Canadian states as well as in Australia where it was deemed 'historically inaccurate'; and Pudovkin's *Storm Over Asia* (1928), which showed the crushing of a nationalist revolt in Mongolia by the British was suppressed, following a request from the Colonial Office, in Ontario and Australia.

Before 1939, both colonial and British censors agreed that the film treatment of politics and morality in whatever form had to be carefully controlled. In fact these shared conservative values were more assiduously pursued by censors in Canada and Australia than at the BBFC, and because those countries have federal censorship systems, individual examiners had the opportunity to indulge rabidly eccentric tastes. In the early days of sound one Australian censor begged for 'the occasional silences of everyday life . . . instead of filling up every moment with noise' and in 1926 the Manitoba State Board ruled that from then on any film which showed actors 'sitting down to dinner in bathing costumes' would be refused.

Britain did encourage campaigns such as Canada's to outlaw the American flag from early films unless the Union Jack (rather than the Canadian flag) was also waved in crowd scenes etc; and the government also backed the Australian High Commissioner's call in 1927 for all children within the empire 'to be marched to the cinema in the morning to see wholesome films depicting what was going on in the empire'. With one or two exceptions though, there was very little need for the British government to intervene directly in independently controlled colonial censorship. For, outside Russia, no country produced anti-imperialist films before 1939. Indeed, Britain did not even have to take the leading role in the cinematic glorification of its own empire. That task was largely left to Hollywood.

Whether British or not, films which banged the imperial drum were carefully vetted by the BBFC. Initially the framework of control was provided by two BBFC rules from 'O'Connor's 43': rule 21, rejecting 'scenes which held up the King's uniform to contempt and ridicule', and rule 22, concerning 'subjects dealing with India, in which British officers are seen in an odious light, and otherwise attempting to suggest the disloyalty of native states, or bringing into disrepute British prestige in the empire'. Any loopholes were then tightened in 1928 by a ban extended to scenes which showed 'British possessions represented as lawless sinks of iniquity' and 'conflict between armed forces of a state and the populace'.

As these rulings indicate, it was the status quo within British-ruled colonies that the BBFC felt duty bound to protect. And even though the Board's examiners sometimes displayed political naïvety, they always applied the preventive medicine with diligence.

To begin with, a whole fleet of films was caught in the BBFC's net of thirties pre-censorship administered by Colonel Hanna and his assistant Miss Shortt. The Colonel's reasons for rejecting scripts almost exclusively concerned themselves with the British military code of conduct. Republic Pictures' *Storm Over India* (1939) was, according to Hanna, 'Another one of these conventional and spectacular stories of frontier fighting in India,' which had been 'written by an American with no knowledge of geography and a complete ignorance of the British army.' The film had in fact been taken almost word for word from Paramount's tub-thumping success of 1934 *The Lives of a Bengal Lancer*. Hanna dismissed the 1939 update of derring-do in native disguise, not because it depicted a mutiny or even miscegenation but because he could not stomach yet one more travesty of British officialdom. 'I think this is an even worse parody of the English officer than any we have had up to now, and I think we are entitled to say definitely we will not allow such caricatures to go out under our certificate.'

Miss Shortt, whose political antennae tended to be more grounded than those of her superior, passed the script of *Storm Over India* as 'suitable for production' with the sole proviso that place names be fictionalised. But Hanna also pointed out in a postscript that 'there is no political significance about the story which is pure fiction and quite harmless.' In one sense Hanna was correct. The plot lines and characters within colonial-set films were interchangeable, especially in Hollywood's imperial epics which the studios sometimes, as with *The Lives of a Bengal Lancer* and *Gunga Din* (1939), remade as westerns.

On the other hand, the assumptions in these 'quite harmless' imperialist epics of the thirties conveyed ideological messages within their gung-ho antics that struck at the heart of native self-sufficiency. After the war, in an essay on the radicalisation of theatre, Bertolt Brecht paused to uncover the poison within just one of these easily swallowed imperial pills, namely RKO's *Gunga Din*.

An Indian tribe – this term itself implies something wild and uncivilized, as against the word 'people' – attacked a body of British troops stationed in India. The Indians were primitive creatures, either comic or wicked: comic when loyal to the British and wicked when hostile. The British soldiers were honest, good-humoured chaps and when they used their fists on the mob and 'knocked some sense' into them the audience laughed. One of the Indians betrayed his compatriots to the British, sacrificed his life so that his fellow-countrymen should be defeated, and earned the audience's heartfelt applause. My heart was touched too: I felt like applauding and laughed in all the right places. Despite the fact that I knew all the time that there was something wrong, that the Indians are not primitive and uncultured people but have a magnificent age-old culture, and that this Gunga Din could also be seen in a very different light, e.g., as a traitor to his people. I was amused and touched because this utterly distorted account was an artistic success and considerable resources in talent and ingenuity had been applied to making it.

Cary Grant with Sam Jaffe as *Gunga Din* (1939). The film's insensitivity towards Hindu customs caused riots so it was belatedly withdrawn from Malaya and India.

If colonial-set films which advocated rebellion were never submitted, let alone made, there was a rich vein which coursed through many an imperial flag-waver that did, literally, carry the seeds of change. Yet inter-racial sex provoked so much concern in the colonial authorities that the censor always avoided the term in favour of the more euphemistic 'liaisons' which were forbidden 'between coloured men and white women' by the BBFC in 1922. This particular exception was then rewritten in 1928 by the Board's President T. P. O'Connor as 'equivocal situations between white girls and men of other races', and if the description seems even more vague the sexual demarcation between the races remained the same.

Unfortunately for the censor, though, miscegenation provided an exotic romantic frisson that paid dividends at the home box office. But as the above rules indicate, there was a clearly delineated gradation between the races, as well as between the sexes within those races. For while certain groups slipped through the BBFC net and were able to make love, others were barely allowed to share the same screen.

European men, for instance, could have sex with whoever they wanted. On the other hand, if they actually married a native woman, they were never allowed to be happy; they could not have children and their spouse was expected to commit suicide as Anna May Wong does when she discovers that her English husband no longer loves her in *Java Head* (1934). The same qualification applied to white women who consorted with Asians; but in this situation, of course the roles were reversed, with the male partners sacrificing their lives for the sake of 'doomed love'. This variation of the respectable western-woman-in-peril theme was more popular with American and British audiences and was therefore constantly repeated in slow-burning melodramas such as *Li-Hang the Cruel* (1920) and *The Wife of General Ling* (1937), as well as in *The Bitter Tea of General Yen*. The Indian spouses of European women were also consigned to the grave but their final moments were usually accorded some dignity, so as to enable the female star to rain down tears upon an expiring body, as Myrna Loy does to great effect upon the browned-up face of Tyrone Power in *The Rains Came* (1939).

One race, however, remains conspicuous by its absence in this roll-call of sexual skin tones. The exclusion of black people of either sex as screen protagonists until the late fifties (with the exception of the all-black 1936 biblical allegory, *Green Pastures* and occasional leading roles from the forceful Marxist actor-singer Paul Robeson) reflected a wider, more general prejudice within the American and British film industries. But even if the producers had been tempted to reverse the starring roles in colonial films and cast leading black actors they would have hit a stumbling block because the BBFC's 1922 rule forbidding 'liaisons between coloured men and white women' was actually the Board's way of distinguishing black men from Asians and other non-Europeans.

For the colonial occupiers and their surrogate censors, the consequences of such a coupling not only diluted the ethnic purity upon which their autonomy depended, it also raised the time-honoured myth of genitally well endowed black males. The thought of sexually frustrated white women being satisfied by such superior equipment would have been anathema for the (male) censor and he must have been grateful that film producers did not depict such sexuality until the empire had all but dissolved.

In theory, or at least by the Board's rules, white men could still dally with black women; but James Robertson, an assiduous researcher of BBFC papers, has found 'no recorded instance of the BBFC's rejection of a film for containing, as the main story line, a mixed marriage between black and white partners'. In fact even unromantic blacks were largely pre-censored by western producers from the screen before 1945. For example, in all of the British films which are set during the Second World War – when 23,000 servicemen from the Caribbean colonies were fighting for the empire – probably the nearest thing to a cinematic representation of blacks was in *The Dam Busters* (1955), and this did not show the British film industry's racial attitudes in a favourable light. At the end of a bombing mission the squadron leader (Richard Todd) climbs out of his plane, crouches down, holds out his arms and then shouts, 'Nigger, Nigger,' as his black labrador runs towards him.

The colonists' fear of black sexuality, however, was not only confined to black skin on the screen. After all, blacks might by tempted by white flesh off,

'Nigger, nigger,' calls out the squadron leader (Richard Todd) after he returns from the famous bombing mission in *The Dam Busters* (1955), demonstrating to modern viewers the blithe disregard prevalent at the time towards the 23,000 black Caribbean soldiers fighting for the Empire alongside their white counterparts in World War II.

as well as on, the screen – especially female. In colonies such as Kenya and Northern Rhodesia, which had large white populations, the local censorship boards insisted upon segregated viewing and they censored films according to the racial audience. A particular cause for concern which the colonists referred to as 'the black peril' could be found in scenes where white women behaved seductively. These were therefore cut from films attended by Africans, presumably for fear of arousing the black male.

These excisions must have been liberally applied because the list for 1948 of scenes prohibited by the Northern Rhodesia board for African audiences included: (a) women in scanty attire, including bathing costumes; (b) undue exhibition of parts of the naked body; (c) women of easy virtue; (d) manhandling of women; (e) prolonged embraces; (f) fights between women.

Needless to say, films were not merely cut for Africans. They were also closed to them. Moreover, the Kenyan censorship board's list of banned films in 1940–1 does not give much hope for other years as it includes such films as *Gone With the Wind* (1939), Michael Curtiz's *Angels With Dirty Faces* (1938) and Alexander Korda's *The Four Feathers* (1939), as well as six other films in which women appeared in 'undignified' roles.

Reinforcing the work of local censorship boards, the Colonial Office provided general outlines of guidance to the local district authorities for the showing of films. Due to the persistently cavalier attitude taken towards the cinema by British banks, however, the Colonial Office was never able to take advan-

tage of the pre-war aphorism, 'trade follows the film'. Lacking the financial means to reinforce an imperial message through the use of actual films, Whitehall, therefore, relegated itself to the less positive, but more easily accomplished, role of censor.

'The success of our government of subject races,' warned a Colonial Office report of 1930, 'depends almost entirely on the degree of respect we can inspire.' Inspiring respect – and fear – naturally meant that the cinematic image of the white man had to be shaped, defined and, if necessary, censored. Once again, though, the quandary facing the authorities lay in the fact that the same film can be interpreted in different ways by different audiences. The bravery of firemen, for instance, in Humphrey Jennings's account of the Blitz in his 1940 documentary *London Can Take It* raised the morale of British cinema-goers at a fateful moment of adversity. For Kenyans, on the other hand, Jennings's scenes of London aflame inspired 'virtual panic' and the widely heard comment, 'the Germans are winning the war.'

Another potentially mixed message which the colonial censor thought could cause disrespect was humour. As long as it did not question their actual validity, poking fun at the authorities was allowed for domestic film audiences. Conversely, the Colonial Office, which was inevitably a prisoner of its own colour bar, would have seen such comedy as a potential attack upon the dignity of the whole white race. Film-makers like Charlie Chaplin, therefore, who based a lot of their humour on bamboozled policemen or undignified

91

clergymen were heavily censored throughout the colonies – especially so in Kenya, where, according to the local censorship board, Chaplin's splayed walk 'provoked much imitation' from the audience.

The work of Britain's colonial censors continued to be undercut, however, by the American film industry which, in the Board of Trade's words, took 'no account of the importance of maintaining the white man's prestige and shows him in the most unfavourable light, exaggerating his weak points and bad qualities.' In fact, the evidence of the time suggests that even though most people in the empire generally preferred Hollywood movies, they could not tell the difference between British and American films. Even so, from the vantage point of the colonial administrators, the American dominance of the world film market constituted a fatal flaw. Not being able to define and disseminate specific messages to the subject peoples at moments of crisis carried obvious dangers. Moreover, Hollywood's occasional embracing of democracy, in such films as Frank Capra's *Mr Smith Goes to Washington* (1939) and John Ford's *The Grapes of Wrath* (1940), raised questions of political representation and civil rights which the British overseers would rather have kept in the dark.

For over 300 years India, the most durable and profitable of Britain's colonial possessions, formed a strategic linchpin in the far-flung empire. Here, however, the British suffered from another, even more crucial disadvantage in their attempt to control film content. One of the avowed aims of the British Raj, again according to the Board of Trade, was to 'substitute Western culture for the Indian' and, at the same time, to create a native class who would be 'Indian in blood and colour but English in tastes, in opinions and in intellect'. In this the British succeeded, but apart from the newly created, anglicised Indian clerical bourgeoisie, the nationalists and the vast illiterate mass still clung to their own religion and culture; and in 1913 that hunger for a cultural echo was satisfied in large part by the advent of the Indian mythological movie.

The first example of this genre, *Raja Harisishchandra*, achieved such instant and widespread popularity that an indigenous film industry was immediately born, first in Bombay and then in Calcutta, Madras and Lahore. Within five years the popularity of Indian as well as American films had achieved such proportions that the British authorities decided to bring the new medium under government control.

A Cinematograph Act of 1918 split Indian censorship amongst four boards, one based in each of the four film-making cities. (Two years later a fifth board was established in Rangoon for the Burmese.) The boards in India usually consisted of the Commissioner of Police – who could override all decisions – a British army officer, an 'upstanding' Hindu or Muslim citizen and 'a European lady representative' or 'a European medical man', as in the case of Lahore, 'who represented the Vigilance Society'. After making allowances for what the

Act called 'a not inconsiderable proportion of illiterate people and those of immature judgement', all five boards adopted T. P. O'Connor's 43 rules of 1916, although, unlike the British censorship system, film distributors in India had thirty days in which to appeal against a decision.

None of the boards encountered much opposition from Indian film-makers until 1929, when the President of the Congress Party, Jawaharlal Nehru, demanded, 'complete freedom from British imperialism'. Under the Emergency Powers Act, which had been brought in a few years before, such calls for independence were automatically removed from all newsreels. The reflection of the country's frustrated mood tended to be less direct and more murky in Indian feature films. Even so, the few attempts to voice resistance, however muted, were cut by the censors. From *Sone Ki Chidia* ('Golden Bird') of 1934, the lines 'May sacrifice for our country become our aim in life. Instead of living without feeling it is better to die like this,' had to be omitted, and three years later the producers of *Iman Farosh* ('He Who Sells His Conscience') were told to remove all cries of '*Inqilab Zindabad*' (Long live the Revolution) uttered by the crowds.

As these cuts imply, the film ban on politics was not specifically directed towards adverse comments upon the British. In fact, it included anything which imparted an incorrect political flavour, and that also applied to British as well as foreign films. In *Knight Without Armour*, a 1937 British anti-Bolshevik saga starring Robert Donat and Marlene Dietrich, this meant, 'In scene of bomb outrage omit all dialogue showing Russian students taking part in revolutionary activities . . . also the preliminary discussion about method of preparing bombs . . . actual explosion can remain.'

The quandary for the colonial censor with anti-Bolshevik melodramas like Alexander Korda's *Knight Without Armour* (1937) was that for the sake of realism poverty had to, at least, be alluded to.

In effect, the exclusion of politics from Indian cinemas became blanket film censorship during the thirties, since any image or piece of dialogue which deviated from the path of mass contentment was removed. The censor had a magpie eye for every possible source of alarm: small-budget, independent American documentaries about the effects of the US depression which were produced outside the studio system were either heavily cut, as in *The Road Back* (1937), or banned, as in the instance of *Black Fury* (1935) for its attempt 'to justify direct action by workers, even to the extent of using explosives to destroy their employers' property'.

At a time of 94 per cent illiteracy, not to mention repeated famines throughout the Indian sub-continent in which over two million people died between 1918 and 1946, all scenes of poverty-stricken peasants teaching each other, holding meetings or making speeches were eliminated by the censor – especially from indigenous films. Indeed, no reference to poverty or the exploitation of the poor by the rich was permitted. Dialogue to be removed, therefore included such speeches as: 'Is humanity in the grip of evil? When men, children of the same maker, live on the blood of their fellow men. The rich feed themselves on the poor. While the poor eat dust and live at the expense of dogs.' (*Bala Joban* ['Youth on Fire'] 1934); or: 'Why should the poor die like rats in their holes? Why should the nobles eat off the fat of the land? Why should we endure this injustice? Food for the poor, food for the poor . . .' from Universal's *The Affairs of Voltaire* in 1934.

Such deletions were a cruel, logical extension of the political censorship in which the effects of the thirties depression could not be seen in British cinemas. But whereas the British working class constituted a presence, albeit usually comic or conciliatory, in popular films of this time, the Indian peasant was only allowed an equivalent dilatory moment on his own screen if he was in a reasonably healthy state. This kind of catch-all censorship threw its net so wide that it can even be traced, in one instance, to the consequences which attached themselves to the request of an image-conscious Hollywood actor for a change in his role.

The plot of the Eddie Cantor vehicle *Kid Millions* (1935) featured a mixture of mistaken identity and a dozen or so songs, and, with the possible exception of its Egyptian background, there was nothing to distinguish it from the usual fare on offer from the highest-paid actor in Hollywood of 1934. Its star noticed from the script, however, that as usual he had not been provided with any romantic interest due to his producer Sam Goldwyn's belief that he had no sex appeal. This time the diminutive, well paid comic demanded that this be remedied.

In the words of his biographer A. Scott Berg, Sam Goldwyn 'counted on his cash crop, Eddie Cantor'. A love interest was therefore supplied forthwith. Unfortunately, though, this translated into a 'comic romance' between Cantor

Opposite Paul Muni in *Black Fury* (1935) a union-financed film set, in the depression which suggested another course for mine workers besides aquiescence – a message that had to be kept out of India during the mass famines.

and a sheik's daughter which, in turn, led to more screen time for the sheik. And the consequence of this was that *Kid Millions* was even more heavily cut in India because the censor said, 'cut all scenes where a person dressed exactly like Mahatma Gandhi is shown.'

Responding to widespread disaffection, towards the end of the thirties the Indian film industry became incensed by the portrayal of their country in American and British films. A campaign was launched in the magazine *Filmindia* in 1939 against Alexander Korda's *The Drum* (1938) and George Stevens's *Gunga Din* (1939) with a protest to the Secretary of State for India against the misrepresentation of India and Indians in such films, and in particular against the caricature of Gandhi as the demented dhoti-clad villain of *Gunga Din*. The opening of both films was accompanied by riots and the censor hastily, but belatedly, withdrew them from Malaya as well as India.

The censor, on the other hand, kept a closer look-out for more favourable representations of India's putative leaders. With the opening of hostilities against Germany in 1939, the Congress Party, while expressing its abhorrence of Nazism, also declared that 'India cannot associate herself in a war said to be for democratic freedom when that very freedom is denied to her.' Casually, in the background, Congress symbols began to be introduced into Indian films: the spinning wheel (Gandhi's motif), a photograph of Nehru or the Muslim leader Mohammed Ali Jinnah or the Congress flag with a Congress song on the sound-track. Often these had no relevance to the plot of the film; nevertheless audiences recognised and cheered them. The censorship boards recognised this enthusiasm and cut them.

In 1942, with Gandhi's terse cry to the British to 'Quit India', the liberation movement gathered momentum, and henceforth no allusion to Gandhi was permitted in films. 'But,' pointed out the *Journal of the Film Industry*, 'excision of photographs of Congress leaders is not going to remove them from the hearts of their followers.' References via photographs in wallets, wall paintings and even playing cards to Congress leaders began to crop up in almost every Indian film which, needless to say, the censor duly chased with his scissors.

As the war progressed, the Indian version of this perpetual universal pursuit of the film-maker by the censor speeded up. Indian directors used officially-sanctioned propaganda against the Japanese to conceal their own urging of the British to 'Go back, go back you foreigners, whether you be Germans or Japanese, India belongs to us.' When audiences cheered such songs, it became clear to the censor that the words equally applied to the British.

Inevitably, any country that fights a war in the name of democracy leaves its own imperialism open to accusations of hypocrisy, and its censorship to the charge of selective standards. Also, because Britain was immediately put on the defensive by Germany and Japan, the colonial authorities had no choice but to try and persuade those within the empire that their lives would not improve under an alternative occupying force. This in turn meant that a political debate about war aims had to be introduced and encouraged. But such a debate destabilises censorship, because once censored topics are resurrected then their value is remembered and therefore retained. It soon becomes clear who is in most danger from the circulation of so-called dangerous ideas – the censor and those he acts for. Thus the colonial system of censorship unravelled during the war, even though many countries under British rule, particularly in Africa, did not gain their independence until the late fifties or early sixties.

Ironically, throughout the fight for India's independence, that country's future leaders never recognised the potency which film could have brought to their cause. In 1938, when a Bombay paper asked Mahatma Gandhi for a message to the Indian film industry on its 25th anniversary, it received this answer from the Mahatma's secretary: 'As a rule Gandhi gives messages only on rare occasions, and these only for causes whose virtue is ever undoubtful. As for the Cinema Industry, he has the least interest in it and one may not expect a word of appreciation from him.'

It is not surprising that an independent India replaced one form of film censorship with another. Before 1947, the British sought to suppress political ideas. After Independence, the Delhi government adopted the more conventional censorship of morality which one Indian film critic has recently pointed out, is almost 'exclusively directed to the bouncing breasts, shapely shanks and luscious legs of our actresses'. Throughout the colonies, this replacement of film censorship was played out according to indigenous custom and priorities. Like India, most of the Commonwealth countries have adopted a film censorship system based upon moral offence. But in the autocracies or dictatorships which are so prevalent in African ex-colonies, censorship is employed as a means of political persuasion and control; although fictional feature films are usually granted more leeway than other media, due to their lack of immediacy and direct political relevance.

The heritage of Britain's film censorship in the empire lasts to this day. The boyhood dream of never-ending heroic conquest of 'virgin' territory – the subject of innumerable pre-war films – continues to hold many in its thrall. Even such an urbane personality as the American writer Gore Vidal has testified to the seductive strength of the empire builders: 'There were ubiquitous newsreels of the new king and queen on coronation day, as well as feature films of gallant little England menaced by Spain's Armada and Napoleon's armies. There were also biographical films of Chatham and Pitt, of Clive and Disraeli, of Wellington and Nelson. It was not until 1939 that we [Americans] got part of our story, *Gone With the Wind*. But by then a whole generation of us filmwatchers had defended the frontiers of the Raj and charged with the Light Brigade at Balaklava. We served neither Lincoln nor Jefferson Davis; we served the Crown.'

Not surprisingly many of the Crown's actual subjects still retain a warm folk memory of a beneficent, virile, romantic mother country which swore itself to justice and fair play. With the aid of Hollywood, this conscience-salving, escapist image dominated and sustained colonial rule in the face of conflict and suppressed hopes amongst many different races. Yet once independence had come, the new film censors were occasionally offered the chance to take revenge upon the memory of their old masters.

The author Salman Rushdie remembers a particularly piquant example of this vengeance from his childhood in Karachi: 'When the Pakistani censors found that the movie *El Cid* ended with a dead Charlton Heston leading the Christians to victory over the live Muslims, they nearly banned it, until they had the idea of simply cutting out the entire climax, so that the film as screened showed El Cid mortally wounded, El Cid dying nobly, and then ended. Muslims 1, Christians 0.' In whatever form he appears the censor always has the last word.

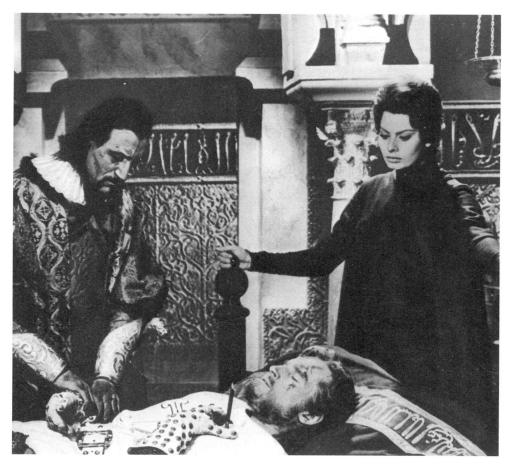

Racial revenge: the dying Cid (Charlton Heston) will be remounted on his white horse to lead the Christians in victory over the Moors. So the Muslim censor in Karachi ended *El Cid* (1961) abruptly with this scene.

It took some time for the news that Britain had declared war on Germany to penetrate the decision-making processes of the BBFC. Ever since 1933 the Board had refused to pass films which might upset the Nazi regime in Berlin, under a rule that banned all films which were 'calculated to wound the susceptibilities of foreign people'. So when a film was set in a foreign country the BBFC would usually seek the advice of the relevant embassy. Thus Alexander Korda's *Lawrence of Arabia*, which was to have starred Robert Donat or Leslie Howard, never got beyond the script stage in 1938 because the Turkish Embassy protested to the BBFC via the Foreign Office that its citizens were being 'represented as tyrants and oppressors of the Arabs'.

This fear of hurt susceptibilities went to ridiculous lengths. One of the reasons given by the script examiner Miss Shortt for her refusal in 1936 to pass the proposed British remake of *The Cabinet of Dr Caligari* was the film's inclusion of a comic waxwork figure of Hitler which, according to the daughter of the BBFC's late President, 'would undoubtedly be resented by Germans and is quite an unnecessary incident'.

Whether it was China, Turkey or Tibet, and however mild the likely hurt, all national feelings had to be taken into account. But the BBFC showed a particular sensitivity towards Germany, and this was apparent even before the Third Reich started on its inglorious reign in 1933.

The Teutonic influence upon Britain's film censors was first exposed in 1928 when the patriotic English director Herbert Wilcox filmed *Dawn*, an account of the trial and execution of the 50-year-old English nurse Edith Cavell at the hands of the German army during the First World War. Hearing of this, the German Foreign Minister, Gustav Stresemann, immediately communicated his displeasure to his British counterpart, Sir Austen Chamberlain, who in turn exerted pressure on the BBFC's President at the time, T. P. O'Connor, to ban the forthcoming film. With alacrity O'Connor obliged the Foreign Secretary's hands-off caution even though he knew that nobody at the BBFC

Dawn (1928) with Sybil Thorndike as Edith Cavell, the First World War nurse who was executed as a spy by the German army. Due to the perseverance of the director, Herbert Wilcox, it was discovered that *Dawn* had been banned on the instructions of the German Foreign Ministry.

or for that matter, at the Foreign Office had even seen Wilcox's film, let alone examined it. Unfortunately for the Board, Wilcox had friends in the House of Commons who provoked the revelation that the government had coerced the BBFC into wielding a rubber stamp on behalf of Britain's recent enemy. *Dawn* remained banned however, and the political strings with which the BBFC had just been seen to be manipulated were immediately reinterred in a welter of government memos and red tape.

Five years later, Hitler's elevation to Chancellor of Germany on 30 January 1933 provoked a series of British anti-Nazi films. But their reception at the BBFC was now guided by the Conservative government's appeasement policy. Gaumont British submitted the scenarios of *A German Tragedy* and *City Without Jews* to the BBFC in June 1933, both of which dealt with Nazi treatment of Jews, but neither of them proceeded any further than the desk of Colonel Hanna, the Board's principal script examiner. He did 'not consider the subject a desirable one at the present juncture', but to their credit, Gaumont British, who normally leapt to the BBFC's command (they were the first production company to submit scenarios to the BBFC), were determined to make a film on the undesirable subject. And they succeeded in doing so because the studio fell back on the time-honoured sidestepping ploy of anaesthetising a controversial issue by placing it in a historical setting.

The only pre-war British film to openly condemn anti-Semitism *Jew Süss* (1934) – with Conrad Veidt – got round the censor because it was set in the historically safe distance of the eighteenth century.

The result was Lothar Mendes's *Jew Süss*, which did not tackle anti-Semitism head-on as a historically based system of oppression; instead the Gaumont British film only showed the effects of Jew-baiting upon the career of one individual, Süss Oppenheimer (Conrad Veidt) in eighteenth-century Würtemberg. In reality, the role of Süss in German history had been so ambiguous the Nazis produced a vicious, Jew-baiting *Jud Süss* of their own in 1942 which Himmler ordered all the SS, including those who served at the concentration camps, to see. Mendes's version, however, did contain one apposite attack on contemporary racism in the line: '1730–1830–1930. They will always persecute us.' This revealing comment somehow managed to elude Colonel Hanna's eye and escape along with the rest of the script into Gaumont's Elstree Studios for production in the early part of 1934.

Anti-racist films safely set in the mists of time, and not so vague anti-

German thrillers such as Hitchcock's *The 39 Steps* (1935) and *The Lady Vanishes* (1938) which didn't actually name their villains' nationality, continued to be passed by the British film censor throughout the thirties. But any film, however anodyne, which put a real name to an evil-doer's guttural accent was automatically – and immediately – referred by the BBFC to the Nazi authorities. For instance, Colonel Hanna conceded that there was 'nothing really objectionable' in *The Dark Invader*, a 1936 Gaumont British spy story based upon the memoirs of an enemy secret agent in the First World War. Nevertheless, because the script contained 'real life characters', Hanna halted the film at pre-production with the words, 'I think the German Embassy should be approached about it.'

As Hitler turned his attention outwards at the end of the decade to the sequestration of Austria and the Sudetenland, followed by the invasion of Czechoslovakia, the BBFC resolutely stuck to its own appeasement policy towards German expansion. Miss Shortt in particular found it difficult to adjust to the deteriorating international situation, as can be judged from her report in 1938 on *The Exiles*, the tale of an Einstein-type figure fleeing from an unnamed European country to the haven of the United States. 'I do not think any exception can be taken to this story,' commented the lady adjudicator, but then she warned the script's overseers at United Artists, 'providing the producers carry out their intention of not making the country identifiable in any way and I suggest the exiles themselves are not made to look [like] unmistakable Jews.'

Miss Shortt need not have worried. The Hollywood studios were just as concerned as she was not to upset the German authorities. It did not matter that the majority of the studio moguls were Jewish, they did not produce any anti-Nazi films because they did not want their films to be excluded from the important German market. This policy only changed when Joe Kaufman, the Jewish representative of Warner Brothers, was chased and clubbed to death by gauleiters in a Berlin back street during the summer of 1938. For the Nazis this particular death had unfortunate consequences, because soon afterwards, with the support and advice of FBI director J. Edgar Hoover, Warner Bros began work on its propaganda movie *Confessions of a Nazi Spy*.

Based on an actual FBI case in which G-man Leon G. Turrou infiltrated and broke up the espionage activities of the New York branch of the German-American Bund, *Confessions of a Nazi Spy* stirred up a hornet's nest in Hollywood. Everyone involved in its production, including its star Edward G. Robinson, received threatening letters from the Bund, but more significantly the film raised issues that the heads of Hollywood's hierarchy would rather have ignored. In other words, the film alarmed the moguls. 'Look Jack, a lot of us are still booking pictures in Germany, and taking money out of there,' Jack Warner later quoted 'one studio owner' as telling him. 'We're not at war with

The set of *Confessions of a Nazi Spy* (1939) is protected by a security guard because of threats to the cast from members of the German-American Bund.

Germany, and you're going to hurt some of our own people.' According to Warner himself his response was forthright: 'Hurt what? Their pocketbooks? Listen, these murdering bastards killed our own man in Germany because he wouldn't "heil Hitler". The Silver Shirts and the Bundists and all the rest of these hoods are marching in Los Angeles right now . . . Is that what you want in exchange for some crummy film royalties out of Germany?'

As more than one critic has noticed, *Confessions of a Nazi Spy* is hardly a landmark in cinema history; its importance lies in the fact that it was the first openly anti-Nazi film produced by Hollywood. On the other hand, that did not augur well with the BBFC. Amongst other rules that the film infringed was its portrayal of contemporary political personalities and a brief mention of British military intelligence; and so, setting a rare example of this kind, the Board's President Lord Tyrell personally examined the film on 1 May 1939. He finally passed it after five weeks' deliberation and Graham Greene subsequently hailed the release in his film review column in the *Spectator* as the BBFC's abandonment of appeasement; but *Confessions* was actually passed by the Board and probably approved by the Foreign Office because the film was set in America.

The anomaly in the censor's attitude to Nazi policy within and outside the

Fatherland only became clear when film scripts that were situated within the borders of Germany were submitted to the BBFC. They were always banned. In fact the curbing of any comment on Nazi domestic politics was being applied less than two months before war broke out. In the latter part of July 1939, the Boulting Brothers submitted the play *Pastor Hall*, a dramatised account of the persecution of Pastor Martin Niemöller, who had been incarcerated in Dachau concentration camp since March 1938 for criticising the Nazis from his pulpit. Miss Shortt did 'not consider this play suitable for production as a film. Even with the nationality disguised,' she insisted, 'it must be evident that the story is anti-Nazi propaganda.'

So one more chance to alert the public to the methods of German National Socialism had been missed. Yet even after the war started, Miss Shortt did not know which side she was supposed to be on. Her comments on a 20th Century Fox scenario, *Reports on a Fugitive* which was submitted on 10 November 1939, betray her concern that this account of the Nazi occupation of Czechoslovakia would name Hitler and Göring. 'I presume the Film Censorship's previous ban on this type of story is now lifted.' Evidently Miss Shortt was correct in thinking that it was now safe for British cinema-goers to know whom they had been fighting for the last two months because the film was indeed made and released in May 1940 under the title *Night Train to Munich*.

Miss Shortt's presumption was right. Though she had not been informed, the BBFC had belatedly changed its rule forbidding the representation on film of living persons. The change only applied to 'enemy aliens' for the duration of the war, but ironically, just when Miss Shortt seemed to be catching up with the events of the day, those very events were about to render any reformation of the BBFC's rules immaterial. This was due to the fact that the government was about to turn on its old ally and shield. It had decided to censor the BBFC.

With its power to pre-censor scripts and then post-censor films through the application of its 43 rules, the BBFC had considerable powers to suppress free expression in the cinema. It was therefore not necessary when the war began for the government to create a vast new machinery to control the content of films. Initially it proposed to adopt the ultimate form of film censorship by stopping the exhibition of films altogether, because cinemas were considered potential death traps in the event of heavy enemy bombing. In fact cinemas were closed for the first two weeks of the war, although the measure was soon reversed when cinephiles protested in large numbers.

The government, however, did feel the need to close certain loopholes in the censorship procedure; so a Ministry of Information was created to issue and vet propaganda of all kinds. First of all the MOI took over the censorship of newsreels, which had been the responsibility of the BBFC during the First World War. Film societies which in the thirties had been allowed to show radical films for the intelligentsia, now had to gain permission from the MOI for the exhibition of non-certificated films. Lastly, the local authorities were squeezed out of the film censorship process through a MOI veto over any council decision to allow the exhibition of a film which had been banned by the BBFC. On the other hand, if a film which the MOI considered to be helpful to the war effort was outlawed by a local authority, the government would not reverse the municipal ban. In a revealing judgement upon the bureaucratic hierarchy within film censorship they acknowledged that the publicity following a council ban would more than compensate for any local irritation.

These were relatively minor regulations, but their real though unspoken effect was to remove the BBFC from political decision-making over films. With the onset of war the government and the MOI had no choice but to instigate a complete about-face in the BBFC's political policies. Far from pursuing Lord Tyrell's rigid adherence in the thirties to 'no controversy' in films, now the British public had to be quickly informed about what they were fighting for. The public had to be woken up, not pacified and the government knew that it possessed the perfect implement for prodding its citizens into political consciousness. 'The screen can be used,' stated the Deputy Director of War Information, 'to give the people a clear, continuous, and total pattern of total war.' Henceforth the wartime purpose of cinema would be the boosting of civilian as well as service morale; because, as the rector in MGM's *Mrs Miniver* (1942) told his congregation, 'This is not only the war of soldiers in uniform, it is a war of the people – of all people – and it must be fought not only on the battlefield, but in the . . . heart of every man, woman and child who loves freedom. This is the people's war. This is our war.'

The imperative then, of the MOI was not to hinder realistic, relevant films but the exact opposite, to encourage their production. And the remarkable figure of only four films banned throughout the war implies that the MOI succeeded in the first stage of its mission to inform. But the second part of its quest was not so easy to perform.

When Brooke Wilkinson, the Secretary of the Board, was told by the Home Office at the beginning of 1939 that once a war began the MOI would consult the film industry on pre-production censorship of planned films, Wilkinson protested that prior consultations made no sense. The film industry would only accept a *fait accompli*. If they were consulted they would interfere. The government spokesman pointed out that as voluntary censorship was intended for the press it was only fair to extend the same freedom to film producers. But the British press, replied Wilkinson, possessed a sense of responsibility lacking in the film industry – which, the BBFC Secretary reminded the government, was in the hands of American producers.

Behind Brooke Wilkinson's vehemence lurked the not unnatural fear of losing influence. The BBFC already faced increasing opposition from production companies before the war. The number of scripts being submitted for examination was dwindling every year and the long-standing Secretary of the Board must have realised that once film censorship was put on a voluntary footing, the BBFC's inflexible pre-war rules would have to be relaxed.

As it turned out, Brooke Wilkinson's fears were justified, but only partly for the reasons he suspected. It was the realities of Britain's survival during the early part of the war as well as the MOI's consultations with the film industry which forced the Board to give up some of its more extreme restrictions. When the Boulting Brothers re-submitted *Pastor Hall* at the end of 1939, the BBFC gave the green light for the script to go into production in spite of the new version's enhancement rather than diminution of Nazi violence. Hall is no longer spared the virtual death sentence of twenty-five lashes each day, as he was in the pre-war screenplay, and although the actual whipping is not seen, the effect is emphasised with a close-up of the clergyman's hands straining within thick leather straps. But then it would have been almost impossible for the BBFC to ban 'a great film' which the Minister of Information Duff Cooper said was 'showing the nature of our present struggle'.

Almost a year after he made this remark, Duff Cooper told his MOI colleague, the writer-politician Harold Nicolson, that if the Nazis wanted to create a civil war within England, they should make sure that every bomb they dropped on London fell east of Tower Bridge. The Minister was pointing in a roundabout way to the dissatisfaction that was emanating at the time from the East End. (The King and Queen had recently been booed when they paid a condolence visit to the East End docks during the Blitz.) Thus it was the present danger of the ruling classes being sustained in comfort at the expense of industrial workers – the example of war-torn Russia in 1917 leapt to Harold

Pastor Hall's screenplay was turned down by the BBFC in 1938 but when the film was finally produced in 1940 the cruelty of this whipping scene was emphasised rather than diminished as it had been in the original script.

Nicolson's mind – that forced the BBFC to abandon its total ban on 'relations between capital and labour' as the principal theme of a film.

So it was that Walter Greenwood's celebrated novel *Love on the Dole*, which had been refused twice by Colonel Hanna before the war, was finally committed to film in 1941. Greenwood's 'sordid story in very sordid surroundings' dealt with the break-up of a Salford family during the thirties depression, and it presented such BBFC transgressions as mob retaliation against truncheon-wielding policemen and a climactic scene that had never been seen in an English film before in which the young, resigned heroine Sally walks away from her down-at-heel family to become a bookie's tart. At last social commentary had come to the British cinema; but, in spite of being praised by contemporary critics for its realism and for its demonstration 'that the one inconceivable war aim would be a return to the status quo ante', this first example of British social realism flopped at the box office. It is now known for the screen debut of the regal twenty-year-old Scottish actress Deborah Kerr in the unlikely role of Sally Hardcastle rather than as the progenitor of the 'kitchen sink' movie.

Due to the necessity of defining war aims this scene from *Love on the Dole* which – for the first time in a film – showed police using their truncheons on protestors was passed by the censor in 1941.

Films that directly criticised the government's social and industrial policies were now passed as automatically as they had previously been banned. In 1939 the two British social dramas *The Proud Valley* and *The Stars Look Down* paid tribute to Welsh miners and their struggles against 'savage' pit managers. Both were ushered into the cinemas without any delay and two years later Hollywood's contribution to the collier genre, *How Green Was My Valley*, received only minor cuts, although the whole film revolved around a pit strike. By this stage in the war, however, the BBFC had been shunted out of its position as unofficial government spokesman on films into the lesser role of cinematic arbiter of the nation's morals.

In a nation that was still being defeated by Germany abroad and constantly subjected to destruction from the skies above, any violence or sexual suggestion that appeared in films must have seemed positively tame when compared with everyday life. Nevertheless the BBFC tried to dampen whatever excesses did occur on screen.

Violence on film in the 1940s initially presented itself in a haphazard pattern: a catfight between Marlene Dietrich and Una Merkel in *Destry Rides Again* (1939), and an unconscious Sam Spade (Humphrey Bogart) being kicked in the head by the vengeful 'gunsel' (Elisha Cook Jnr) in *The Maltese Falcon* two years later, were both allowed, while a torture scene in *The Hunchback of Notre Dame* (1940) in which the gypsy heroine (Maureen O'Hara) is fitted into a steel boot that is slowly tightened, was almost completely cut. At the same time, however, incidents in which women are arbitrarily hit by men started to feature in screenplays for the first time. *This Gun for Hire* (1942) actually opens with Alan Ladd's psychopathic hitman slapping a room maid to the ground, and in *The Next of Kin*, Thorold Dickinson's espionage drama of the same year, Mervyn Johns knocks out Nova Pilbeam with a right hook. Both films were passed in full by the BBFC though Mervyn Johns's fisticuffs were probably considered acceptable because he was playing a German spy.

The Next of Kin also had the distinction of being Britain's first film to show hitherto hidden parts of a woman's body; but the nude made its debut at one remove: in the form of a catalogue picture of a woman stripped to the waist in the magazine *L'Art de Catalon*, which Mervyn Johns gloats over just before his timely death.

Attacks on the status quo, such as Michael Redgrave's call for the nationalisation of mines in *The Stars Look Down* (1939) were passed at a time when national unity demanded that the needs of all classes be expressed.

The Board was particularly careful though about what kind of nudity reached the screen. *This Happy Breed*, a 1944 homage to working-class resolve on the home front, contained a medium-long shot of a girl of eleven sitting in an old-fashioned bathtub which the Board insisted on removing. A few years later, the film's director David Lean described what happened when he sought out a reason for the cut from the Secretary of the Board. '"Because," Brooke Wilkinson explained, "the girl can be seen from the waist up." I said, "But she is only eleven years old, she's flat as a board and you can see this sort of thing any day in any bathing pool." He smiled at me for my naïve approach. "Swimming and bathing take place in the bright light of day. Films are shown in darkened theatres. The sight of this naked girl might very well excite the unnatural passions of certain men in the audience. It is my job to guard against such a happening."'

The almost total lack of physicality on the British screen, however, did not reflect the spirit of a time when the young were afflicted by what was called 'war aphrodisia', the consequence of a more heightened existence in the uneasy expectation of death. According to the documentary film-maker

Humphrey Jennings, this intimation of mortality led to a febrile atmosphere in which people were 'much more prepared to open their arms and fall into somebody else's'.

One screen duo in the early forties did manage to spark off the surrounding sexual charge within the limitation of BBFC-sanctioned violence and restricted sensuality. Margaret Lockwood and James Mason starred in five films together during the war and throughout them they mauled, punched, scratched, slapped and whipped each other in a frenzy of sublimated sex. Within this sado-masochistic format the couple brought sex to the British screen. It was not merely a matter of Mason's sneering charm or Lockwood's famous décolletage in period pictures such as *The Wicked Lady* – which incidentally, caused the American censor at the Hays Office for the first time to cut a British film – their combined screen personae projected a volatile bravado that could never be contained by polite society. And even more importantly from the point of view of future film censorship, it was the sexual gratification sought by Lockwood's characters which ignited the moral mayhem that they both then exploited. Contemporary convention may have demanded that these first screen anti-heroes paid for their hedonism with their lives, but film-goers were quick to forget the moral message as they revelled in the unholy couple's exhilarating ride to damnation.

The BBFC tinkered with or completely left alone such films as the Lockwood/Mason vehicles; and in any case by 1945 when *The Wicked Lady*, the last example of the genre, was released the Board had descended into impotence. The reason for this lay in the ultimate consideration which always determined and still does determine Britain's film censorship: national security.

Back in the early part of 1939, Brooke Wilkinson had complained to the embryonic Ministry of Information that because the British film industry was in the control of Americans, it felt no responsibility to the state. Not for the first time in his career the Secretary of the Board of Film Censors was wrong. From plutocratic producers such as Korda to clapper boys and continuity girls, nearly everyone in the film trade, including the stars with offers from Hollywood, stayed in or fought for Britain throughout the war. What had actually provoked this charge was Wilkinson's fear that the BBFC would be rendered redundant by the creation of British films under the patronage of the Ministry of Information. Such productions would obviously be uncensorable and in that respect, at least, Wilkinson was right.

The wartime compliance of the industry, however, cannot be solely attributed to patriotism. British producers actually had no choice about the matter. First of all, the MOI Films Division allocated film stock through the Board of Trade; the regulations required the submission of scripts, which were passed on to the MOI for examination. The MOI then told the Board of Trade whether or not to allocate film to the production company concerned.

The 1945 release of *The Wicked Lady* – with Margaret Lockwood and James Mason – heralded the BBFC's acceptance of sex outside marriage; by contrast the American censor insisted that Miss Lockwood's décolletage be covered up.

Producers soon discovered that the only way through this bureaucratic maze was to make sure that they employed scriptwriters as well as script consultants who worked for the MOI.

Second, most film technicians and actors had been conscripted into the services, and to gain their release for film work permission had to be sought from the MOI Films Division. Inevitably, the MOI frequently took advantage of the need for such exemptions to dictate to producers who should direct or even who should appear in their films.

109

Lastly, the MOI pre-empted the censorship system because they themselves produced films. In addition to acclaimed documentaries such as *Western Approaches* (1942) and *Desert Victory* (1943), MOI productions mostly consisted of 'information shorts' on such subjects as taking jam straight from the pot and not putting it politely but wastefully in a dish or on your plate. Yet because the MOI could allocate resources and personnel, they were, in effect, financing prestigious fiction films like the David Lean/Noël Coward naval saga *In Which We Serve* (1942) and Michael Powell's relentless anti-Nazi thriller *49th Parallel* (1941). And it was because of this kind of surreptitious feature film sponsorship that producer-directors like Powell, Leslie Howard, Carol Reed, Anthony Asquith and Alexander Korda bypassed the BBFC and dealt directly with the MOI's Film Division when one of their productions was set in contemporary times, involved the services, or touched upon propaganda in any form.

As the repository of so much power, however, the MOI became a target for jealous attacks from other government departments. Fifteen MOI films had to be abandoned during the war because of pressure from other ministries, the most controversial being an official film about the Beveridge Report on national welfare that was part of the MOI's programme to publicise war aims. For progressive ministry officials with socialist tendencies like Harold Nicolson, the encouragement of films, plays and articles which promoted social reform was central to the purpose of the MOI in its propaganda battle against a totalitarian enemy. But the whole programme had to be dropped when the Home Secretary, Sir John Anderson, complained in March 1943 to the Minister of Information, Brendan Bracken, that his department's 'extreme views' on post-war policy 'seem to be catching the public imagination'.

In an effort to reassert its independence, the BBFC also tried to suppress or cut films that the MOI made or supported. In the ongoing battle, for instance, between religion and science the Board had nearly always supported the church, but now technology had the MOI on its side. In 1942 the American drama-documentary *No Greater Sin* was submitted to the BBFC. Its illustration of the dangers of VD contravened the BBFC's pre-war rule rejecting 'Effects of Venereal Disease, inherited or acquired'. *No Greater Sin* specified in detail what precautions should be taken to stop the disease once it was contracted, and because that information would help to lower the high incidence of VD which was beginning to affect the combat ability of front-line troops, the MOI argued that the film should be immediately released. Yet it was for exactly those reasons that the Board wanted the film banned. The BBFC still believed that people should pay for their sins instead of having them painlessly cured by doctors, and indeed the Board's absolutism prevailed against the MOI's amoral pragmatism, with the result that *No Greater Sin* was withheld for nearly a year until the proliferation of sexual diseases amongst the Eighth

Army in Egypt forced the withdrawal of the ban in February 1943.

The Board also reverted to its pre-war habit of counting the precise number of infringements of its code. It insisted that the MOI remove eleven 'bloodies' from its documentary *Western Approaches* and after endless wrangles – the BBFC only allowed the word if it was used in connection with Germans – Brooke Wilkinson conceded that 'Lord Tyrell has granted permission for the word "bloody" to be used on three occasions.' The same problem occurred with the script for *In Which We Serve*. In this case only two 'bloodies' were allowed; permission was also given for two 'bastards', but that was probably because they were applied to German pilots strafing British sailors cast adrift in the ocean.

Most of these bureaucratic battles were won by the MOI because the Ministry was made up of ambitious intellectual propagandists, whereas quasi-government bodies like the BBFC relied on a gerontocracy whose media skills had been honed in the First World War. In other words it was a conflict between amateurs and professionals, with the result that for the first and only time in its history the British film industry had an adroit institution within the government capable of supporting its growth. Indeed, the MOI not so much helped as led the industry into maturity. It encouraged studios to make films that educated while they entertained, and persuaded directors to leave aside the mannered thespians from London's theatres who had stocked British films in the thirties and instead cast unknown actors who did not necessarily have any experience in front of a camera.

Above all, the Ministry favoured film-makers of quality, and under the guidance of officials such as the art historian, Kenneth Clarke, the urbane politician Duff Cooper, the ex-chief of Shell's advertising Jack Beddington, who was in charge of the MOI's Film Division, and, most importantly, Sidney Bernstein, the future TV tycoon who proposed film subjects, documentary and feature film directors were encouraged to mix the best of both mediums. The MOI sustained projects until they reached the screen, and British commercial films improved to the point where they could consistently compete for the first time in the world market.

But what of the MOI's other equally delicate but more prosaic task, that of censor? Would these sophisticated recruits to Whitehall prove capable of applying the same skills to the interdiction of films as they had done to their production?

Before the war Reichsminister Josef Goebbels said that for propaganda to be effective it had to work 'invisibly to penetrate the whole of life without the public having any knowledge at all of the propagandist initiative'. Not surprisingly this same principle underlay the MOI's 'Programme for Film Propaganda' issued at the end of 1939 in which it was stated that the propaganda in feature films directed towards America 'must be kept secret'. It was against such a background of subterfuge that the most notorious and controversial case of MOI film censorship during the war was set.

Michael Powell's partner Emeric Pressburger got the idea for the character of Colonel Blimp from David Low's cartoon of the eponymous archetypal pre-war officer whose motto is, 'Nothing's so good as being a jolly good soldier.' The intention of the film was to disabuse GIs, some of whom would soon be fighting under British command on the Continent, of the notion that the British army was top-heavy with crusty, moustache-twirling nincompoops, who would at best regard their American troops as cannon fodder, or at worst consider the invasion of France an opportunity to reverse the American Revolution. Powell said that the climax of his film would present the conversion of Blimp, and the turning point for the amiable old reactionary comes when his long-standing German friend Theo, who has just escaped from Germany, turns on Blimp and insists that he listens to these words: 'War is no longer a blood sport for gentlemen, but a fight to the finish against the most devilish racism ever invented, if you go on treating it as a gentleman's war you're going to lose it.'

With Laurence Olivier's agreement to play the title role, Powell and Pressburger submitted the script to the MOI. But by this time Winston Churchill had heard about the intended film and was extremely indignant that it would take a German to make a British army officer aware of the enemy's nature. So, as he later recalled, Powell was not altogether surprised when Brendan Bracken told him that without War Office support, which they did not have, the MOI could not release Olivier from the Fleet Air Arm to work on the film.

'Do you forbid us to make the film?' Powell asked.

'Oh, my dear fellow, after all, we are a democracy, aren't we? You know we can't forbid you to do anything, but don't make it, because everyone will be really cross, and the Old Man will be *very* cross, and you'll never get a knighthood.'

Just as predicted, Churchill now fired off a series of his famous memos to Bracken at the MOI: 'Pray propose to me the measures necessary to stop this foolish production before it gets any further. I am not prepared to allow propaganda detrimental to the army . . .' Bracken replied that he had no power to stop the film. Churchill offered to extend the MOI's powers which Bracken politely refused.

Meanwhile Powell had cast the husky-voiced actor Roger Livesey as Blimp and gone ahead with his film. But even for a film-maker with Powell's single-mindedness, it must have been obvious that Churchill was not a man with whom to do battle, so as soon as he had finished in the editing room the director swiftly accepted a documentary assignment in North Africa. Powell's absence meant that it fell to Emeric Pressburger to act as host when the

Prime Minister attended the premiere of *The Life and Death of Colonel Blimp* at the Odeon, Leicester Square in the summer of 1943. 'At the end of the showing,' Pressburger later told Powell, 'the VIPs departed in silence and fast cars.'

However the *Evening Standard* broke the silence with what it assured its readers was the 'inside story'. Churchill did not like the film and moreover had decided to ban it for export because, according to the paper, 'a young army officer wins a victory over Home Guard Colonel Blimp by fighting a "battle" [field exercise] some hours before the appointed zero hour. This, says Whitehall, would advertise abroad that we countenance the ethos of the Japs at Pearl Harbor! Thus are great decisions made.'

Within a month, however, Bracken wrote to Churchill, requesting him to withdraw 'our illegal ban on this wretched film . . . it is now enjoying an extensive run in the suburbs and in all sorts of places, there are notices – "See the Banned Film".' The Prime Minister complied, and three weeks later, on 25 August 1943 the ban on *Colonel Blimp*'s export was lifted.

Powell and Pressburger had scored an astounding victory. They had outflanked the MOI, the most media-astute Ministry in the government. They had defied the War Office and the whole War Cabinet. Indeed, they had scored a victory against the most resolute Prime Minister Britain has ever had.

Such was the censorship record of *Colonel Blimp*. But that record is beginning

Theo (Anton Walbrook) tells his old warhorse friend, the blustering colonel, (Roger Livesey) that 'War is no longer a blood sport for gentlemen.' Churchill took exception to 'a German' explaining the war; but was the officially instigated censorship of *The Life and Death of Colonel Blimp* (1943) an ambitious charade played out for an American audience?

to look curiously inconsistent because of a number of intriguing questions which have since been posed by the film historians Nicholas Pronay and Jeremy Croft. To begin with, Churchill might have had a magnanimous public image, but he was also known to be a dangerous political adversary. Those who crossed him, like Lord Reith the founder of the BBC, paid a heavy price. So did Churchill take revenge on the film-makers for their disobedience, or at least withdraw government patronage from them? It seems not. Powell and Pressburger's next film after *Colonel Blimp* was a documentary called *The Volunteer* (1944) which was commissioned by the MOI. And it starred Laurence Olivier, who this time was somehow able to get a release from the Fleet Air Arm. And that was not the last film that Powell and Pressburger made under the aegis of the MOI. In 1946 they directed *A Matter of Life and Death*, the final film to be secretly sponsored by the MOI, to the following specification: 'Well the war's nearly over, boys, but it's just starting from our point of view. We think you should make a film about Anglo-American relations, because they are deteriorating.'

Then there is the mysterious question of film stock. Due to the success of German submarines in the Atlantic, celluloid had become one of the rarest commodities in Britain. But Powell recalls that as *Colonel Blimp* progressed it 'became more and more an epic, a saga . . .' so he decided not to make it in black and white. Instead he shot it in Technicolor, the rarest material of all; and furthermore, Pronay and Croft point out, Powell 'secured enough [film] to exceed by 60 per cent the limitation on length recently clamped on all productions, even MOI official films and newsreels'. And once Powell had all this film stock in his hands, how did he then manage to obtain all the military vehicles, uniforms and weapons that pack this two and three-quarter hour film, if as it has been claimed, he had been refused help from the War Office and the MOI? Michael Powell's answer is, 'We stole them.' But didn't the army miss all this equipment? Or at least wonder what happened to it?

Lastly, why did the BBFC pass the film when the government supposedly disapproved of it? The Board had certainly never been slow before to carry out government wishes. They had several rules – 'Scenes holding up the King's uniform to contempt and ridicule' being the oldest, and 'British officers in uniform shown in a reprehensible light' being the most recent – to choose from if they had really wanted to stop *Colonel Blimp* from being shown. But the situation need not have even reached that far. Brendan Bracken had been wrong when he wrote to Churchill insisting that he was powerless to ban the film. In fact, under the Defence Regulations, Bracken could ban anything in whatever form it appeared which endangered morale or discipline, and as Minister of Information he would have been well aware of this fact.

So, what was happening? Pronay and Croft suggest that the whole exercise was in fact a charade, a deeply laid piece of MOI double-bluff designed to influence American attitudes towards the British military. For as the two historians point out, the abandonment of *Colonel Blimp*'s export veto 'happily' coincided with the decision taken by Churchill and Roosevelt at Quebec in August 1943 to launch an allied invasion of Italy under overall British command. By this time, say Pronay and Croft, 'American correspondents in London had reported on the "unsuccessful" attempt by Churchill to ban this film from being exported to America. Thereby creating not only far more advance publicity and interest in it than it would have been possible to achieve by any other means, and establishing conclusively the credentials of the film as being anything but official British propaganda, but they also provided a wonderful demonstration for Americans that Britain was indeed a genuine democracy, in which not even an apparently all-powerful Prime Minister such as Churchill had the power to suppress a privately made film.' In short, Powell and Pressburger's new production logo of an arrow thudding into a bull's-eye which introduced *Colonel Blimp* was truly appropriate. What cinema audiences did not know was that the target was themselves.

If in fact the film's eventful passage was a charade played upon the film-goers, then the MOI demonstrated an acute understanding of censorship. They had persuaded the public, and particularly an American public already made wary by British propaganda in the First World War, that the British government had tried and failed to suppress an idea. In reality they actually wanted to disseminate it. And if *Colonel Blimp* was propaganda disguised as a successful commercial feature film, then the MOI had accomplished the trick by making the public forget about the government's real needs and concentrate instead upon the recognition that governments always suppress any information that is inconvenient to their purposes. Or, to put it another way, the MOI had exploited the supposedly fail-safe theory that anything that is censored by the government must contain the truth.

However sophisticated such manoeuvres seem now, in 1945 such sleight of hand was beyond the most surreal imaginings of the examiners at the BBFC. For them the war had been an aberration which should be forgotten as the day-to-day business of applying their expanded pre-war rules – which numbered ninety-eight by 1939 – got under way again. Its ageing team of Lord Tyrell, Colonel Hanna and Brooke Wilkinson – whose eyesight was rapidly failing by this time – were still in harness, and saw no reason to adapt or reform their censorship methods. But the cinema-going public had changed. The possibilities of film had been taken up by a new generation of British film-makers and critics and had even been discovered by establishment figures such as Brendan Bracken. In the decade after the war, the debate widened to include film-goers in general who now demanded that the cinema reflect their lives and not the 'harmless' fantasies foisted on them by unimaginative film directors, paternalistic politicians and compliant censors. Times had changed.

'WHAT'VE YA GOT?' 8 ✂

With the advent of peace in 1945 the BBFC and the local authorities resumed their dominance of British film censorship. That censorship, however, had altered. First, because the debate on the future of British cinema, which had emerged during the war with the encouragement of the Ministry of Information, was leading to an increasingly vocal demand from film-makers and critics for a more independent role in the production and presentation of films; and second, and even more importantly, because the election of a Labour government in 1946 brought with it a commitment to universal social welfare and full employment. In the face of a government whose motto was 'Never again', the BBFC's concern for the political status quo ante was quietly rendered redundant. With one or two relatively minor exceptions political censorship of film within Britain had effectively ended.

Meanwhile, nature was taking its own toll on the BBFC. By the end of the war the Board's President, Lord Tyrell, was in his eighties, and both the chief examiner, Colonel Hanna, and the Board's long-standing Secretary, Joseph Brooke Wilkinson, were not far behind. All were loath to give up their responsibilities. Towards the end of 1946, Hanna's supervision of scenario censorship began to be interrupted by illness and before he finally retired in December his own reports increasingly strayed from recommendations on scripts into maudlin reminiscences about the countryside in which they were set. Six months later, in June 1947, the Board's affable President who had efficiently oversaw the British cinema's 'continued repression of controversy' during the latter half of the thirties died in harness at the age of eighty-three.

The power behind Tyrell's throne, however, clung to his position as Secretary of the Board for another thirteen months and it was not until July 1948 – having been virtually blind for ten years – that 'Brookie' Wilkinson finally gave up his thirty-six-year-reign as administrator of the BBFC.

If there is doubt concerning the blind censor's affection for film there can be no question of Brooke Wilkinson's loyalty to the BBFC. He personally chose T. P. O'Connor as the second President of the Board, took a hand in the selection of Shortt and Tyrell and instituted the BBFC policy of recruiting service officers like Colonel Hanna for a second career as film censors.

Through Brooke Wilkinson the innate ability to search out and uncover

Opposite First attacked and now respectd by the critics, the Boulting Brothers' *Brighton Rock* (1947) featured Richard Attenborough as the snivelling wide-boy Pinkie – whose quick resort to razor blades appalled the censors.

transgression where other souls might find imagination and innovation would also extend to post-war film censorship in Britain. When David Lean visited the Board's offices in Soho during 1947 to discuss the censorship of one of his films, the British director took advantage of his interview with Brooke Wilkinson to ask him why it was forbidden to show 'Platonic scenes between a screen husband and wife in a double bed together'. The seventy-six-year-old Secretary smiled and replied, 'You "pretend" they are husband and wife, but the audience knows very well they are not really married. On further reflection you will realise you are asking me why you are forbidden to show an unmarried actor and actress in bed together.'

Brooke Wilkinson then surprised Lean by asking, 'Do you know one of the most blessed inventions of all time?' the film-maker admitted he didn't. 'It is the invention of the paragraph. My wife,' the Secretary revealed, 'is a great reader and I often see her skip a paragraph, or sometimes a whole page. Do you realise why she does this?' Again the director admitted his ignorance. 'She does it because she has come to an unsavoury passage, and the new paragraph or the new page gives her a guide as to where she can start reading again. . . Now, Mr Lean, you cannot give your audience such guidance. You have no paragraph: they have to sit and watch; and even if they close their eyes they hear the words. I am here to protect thousands of decent men and women like my wife. You're an artistic sort of chap – please don't take me amiss – and perhaps. . . but you see my point, don't you?'

Besides being an admirer of blank spaces, this diminutive, dapper censor directed the course of cinema in Britain to an extent nobody else can claim. Yet even more astounding than the fact that this power lay in the hands of a blind ex-journalist who had never had anything to do with the making of films was the very anonymity of Wilkinson's influence. Undoubtedly this is explained by the mutual dependence on silence between the censor and the censored.

Brooke Wilkinson's own sponsor, the film pioneer Cecil Hepworth declared that, 'There is no name better known through all the industry than that of Brooke Wilkinson. . . He had the most difficult job of all and he held it down with such gentle forceful dignity that he was loved by all and was the friend of every man who might so easily have been his enemy.' And indeed Wilkinson was fêted by the industry; they laid on a lavish luncheon for his golden wedding anniversary in September 1947, paid him a special tribute two months after his death, and in the trade press his obituary notices all mentioned his 'personal charm' and 'unfailing tact'. But for film-makers, if not producers and distributors, a more telling epitaph was provided by the father of the British documentary movement, John Grierson:

Poor dear Wilkinson, with his Blake's poetry and his beloved pre-Raphaelites has, in the jungle of Wardour St., the strength of ten. Great figure he is, for on his charming shoulders, he carries the burden of our servility and our shame. Created by the trade as an image of gratuitous fright, it is not surprising that his slogan of 'No controversy'. . . is abjectly obeyed.

And the ex-Secretary's baleful influence reached beyond the grave. A year before his death Wilkinson arranged for the appointment of Sir Sidney Harris, who had been in charge of the Children's Department of the Home Office, as the new President of the Board. Their acquaintance went all the way back to the origins of Britain's film censorship, when Harris had been part of the Home Office delegation that in 1912 received trade representatives to discuss the setting up of the Board. By 1947, Harris was seventy-one and his outlook upon the cinema reflects a contemporary description of him as 'an English gentleman of the old school'. In the fifties, when one of his censors was discussing with him a French film that had a nude bedroom scene, Sir Sidney said, 'I suppose we shall have to pass it, but men and women don't go to bed together with no clothes on.'

Harris chose his own Secretary of the Board. Arthur Watkins also came to the BBFC from the Home Office's Children's Department and, unlike Brooke Wilkinson, he was interested in film as a vehicle not just for controversy but also for drama. He wrote plays for the theatre, some of which were successful, he visited film sets, talked to producers and directors and tried to impart the sense that films would no longer be arbitrarily eviscerated by an unseen potentate from on high. Undoubtedly the ebullient Welshman did want to liberalise film censorship. To a certain extent he wanted it to reflect post-war changes in Britain – the rise in crime and rediscovery of sexuality – but he soon discovered that this Stendhal-like view of cinema as a mirror of society was opposed by his predecessor's appointments within the BBFC.

In 1946, Brooke Wilkinson had replaced the script supervisor Colonel Hanna with Lieutenant-Colonel Fleetwood-Wilson and earlier in that year another of his appointees, Madge Kitchener, had succeeded Miss Shortt as assistant script examiner. Neither had much sympathy for the new-found tolerance being applied to British films dealing directly with social issues or to a cinema which in the contemporary words of the critic Dilys Powell, 'grows strongly and naturally in its own soil, which . . . springs from the lives and hearts of the people who produce it'.

Miss Kitchener did not believe that scripts should be fertilised or tended. They had to be pruned, and her reports are therefore peppered with the sort of hygienic deletions that Miss Shortt would have wholeheartedly approved. No 'son of a bum', 'bed pans', 'the sign "Gentlemen" over the door' or even 'electric bedwarmers'. Her concern for the dignity of the monarch would also have won her predecessor's approbation: in a Kunderian comment on the 1946 drawing-room comedy *No Nightingales* she reminds the scriptwriter that as 'Queen Mary is living she should not be shown, but I see that the directions are for: – "The Queen's inimitable hat," so if she remains only a hat, all should be well.'

In an era, moreover, when the Labour government was bringing 20 per cent of the economy into public ownership and consequently overturning social privilege, Colonel Fleetwood-Wilson enlarged Kitchener's abhorrence of *lèse-majesté* to include the most blatant example of upper-class decadence. 'Care should be taken,' admonished the chief script examiner, 'that Byron's love affairs' (in Rank's *The Bad Lord Byron* of 1948) 'are not shown in any way immoral or vulgar.' Or to misquote the poet himself, there should be just as much honour left after his name as there is before it.

Like his assistant, Fleetwood-Wilson also indulged in eccentric excisions such as 'the place name "Flannel-under-Neath"', 'slap and tickle', 'where's the 'ot bits' and the removal of a scatological collector's item from a British 1949 army comedy called *Dress Optional*: 'a night pot which has little swastikas running all round its circumference'.

Unlike her superior, Madge Kitchener felt that she was skilled enough in dramaturgy to suggest additions to screenplays as well as deletions. After advising the director of the 1946 gangster film *Smugglers Ahoy* that he should tone down the violence of various robberies, she asks, 'Would it not be possible to delete the crime element altogether and so make the story a child's adventure?' But unlike Shortt, Kitchener did not unearth 'sexual obscenity' where none was intended, and she did at least bring outside interests to her work. She passed over the fact that 'a frieze of half-naked gold Grecian girls' would be presented in the exotic 1946 thriller *Corridor of Mirrors*, while pointing out to the director that 'it is impossible to gild human beings all over without killing them. Leonardo da Vinci tried it for a fête and the child died.' Unfortunately, however, Madge Kitchener's eclectic knowledge of art history was not matched by an equal familiarity with the history of film and the BBFC's role in it.

Fame Is the Spur (1946), which is loosely based on the career of Ramsay MacDonald, charts the ascent of a young working-class socialist (Michael Redgrave) to high office where his political principles are opened to question and compromise. Madge Kitchener had no problem with the basic plot of the Boulting Brothers' script, but she did question the inclusion of a running battle between industrial workers and mounted police. 'These shots,' she said, 'suggest extremes of violence.' That remark might have been accepted by Arthur Watkins and the general public at a time when gang violence was beginning to be publicised by the press; but then she added the cryptic but revealing comment, 'Very reminiscent of the famous montague [*sic*] in the Russian films, "Potemkin" and "Odessa", many shots of which the Board cut.'

An anonymous person at the Board then drew a pencil line through 'montague' and inserted 'montage', which was presumably the expression that Miss Kitchener was looking for. But apart from Eisenstein's crucial innovation in editing technique, the 'Odessa' mentioned was a world-renowned sequence within *Potemkin* and Eisenstein's film had not been cut, it was banned – and it was still banned by the BBFC at the time of Kitchener's comment. And the man who had worked hardest to stop the banning of the film within Britain was the communist film-maker Ivor Montagu.

Miss Kitchener was undoubtedly ignorant of the BBFC's history, but more importantly she was also unaware of its current status. The main difference between Britain's pre- and post-war film censorship was that the 1946 government did not want to be involved in BBFC decisions on films about British industrial relations. So, no doubt with that knowledge in mind, the Boultings ignored Kitchener's advice, shot the riot scene and were not unduly surprised when the film was passed uncut by the Board a year later in August 1947.

This difference though between what the BBFC's script examiners objected to and what its film censors were passing applied not only to films about class conflict, it also included a new British genre, the so-called 'spiv' film. And it was the confusion in the Board's approach to one of these British gangster films that would open up the Board to its most damaging crisis of the late forties.

Before the war a certain amount of violence in American gangster movies was accepted by the Board because of their 'exotic' setting. On the other hand, British crime films had to keep within strict limitations to get past the censor. Any reference to drugs, or prostitution, any scene within a British prison or realistic enactments of crime were all disallowed. Crime therefore had to be represented in anaemic comedies like George Formby's *Spare a Copper* (1941). But as the black market expanded in response to the continuation of rationing after the war, large gangs fought pitched battles to secure control of lucrative territories, and the local spiv, who acted as an intermediary between the gangs and the public, became a common sight on British streets.

The Board acknowledged the presence of these relentless opportunists in kipper ties by granting certificates in 1947 to spiv films such as Robert Hamer's *It Always Rains on Sunday* and David MacDonald's *Good Time Girl*, which was based upon the violent escapades of a Welsh teenager, Betty Jones, and her boyfriend Karl Hulten, an American deserter. (In turn it would become the basis for the Emily Lloyd–Kiefer Sutherland vehicle *Chicago Joe and the Showgirl* in 1989.) Then, three days after issuing a certificate to MacDonald's film, the Board ignored the advice of its own script department and passed the most famous example of the cycle, *Brighton Rock*.

Graham Greene's original novel had been inspired by the 'Battle of Lewes' in 1937 between the Darby Sabini Mob and Alf White's King's Cross Gang which first brought British organised crime to public attention. According to Madge Kitchener, Graham Greene's screen adaptation for the Boulting Brothers relied too heavily upon gangland realities. 'This is,' she reported, 'a sordid and in some parts a brutal story of a gangster's revenge upon a rival crook,' and amongst the various scenes and details to which she took 'exception' were: 'Pinkie's habit of carrying a bottle of vitriol', 'fixing of razor blades to his fingers', the seventeen-year-old gang leader's minimal comment on sex, 'I used to watch it . . . didn't bother', and the 'brutal details' of his death. Lastly Kitchener brought up an old BBFC hobby-horse: defamation of the place where a film is set. 'Brighton Town Council,' she pointed out, 'may not appreciate having this unpleasant and sinister tale located in their holiday resort.'

The Boulting Brothers had been through all this the year before with *Fame Is the Spur*, so they went ahead anyway and shot the film in Brighton – where, apparently, they did not have to look hard to find unsavoury-looking characters for gangland scenes. They reinstated all Kitchener's deletions, including a shot of Pinkie (played by the young Richard Attenborough) slicing open the cheek of an informer and again one of their films which had been heavily censored at script stage was passed uncut by the actual Board.

The film's reception by the press in the latter part of 1947 should have put the Board on its guard. Somewhat surprisingly dismissed as 'the sadistic norm of British gangster films' and 'false, cheap, nasty sensationalism', *Brighton Rock* was a success with the public at a time when spiv films dominated the British box office. But the critics disapproved of the home-grown genre. Dilys Powell of the *Sunday Times* complained of the 'taste of blood which I am beginning to find all pervasive in the contemporary cinema' and one 'spiv' director was accused of 'hauling muck to the surface and smearing it, for our minute inspection under glass'.

Into this febrile atmosphere, there now stepped a British gangster movie with grand ambitions. Taken from the James Hadley Chase thriller, *No Orchids for Miss Blandish* was going to be the first big budget, high production value, all-American starring spiv film. In fact it turned out to be a modestly budgeted, easily forgettable thriller, the sole exception to its all-English cast being an American 'B' movie star, Jack La Rue. Nevertheless, this shoddy imitation of an American *film noir* would turn the clock back on British film censorship by ten years.

Rejected by Colonel Hanna in 1944 as 'unsuitable', the script of *No Orchids* was resubmitted to the Board three months later. But in spite of drastic revisions the Colonel remained unimpressed. 'It still seems to be a story of pretty sordid crime and violence, with a highly improbable love story in the background.'

There matters rested for three years when yet another version of the screenplay was passed by the new team of scenario scrutineers in March 1947 with only a few minor cuts. This was not altogether surprising, since the only elements of Chase's original story that now remained were the characters' names and his title. In the book, Miss Blandish is abducted, roughed up, raped and reduced to a state of drugged catatonia for three months by the highly sexed psychopath Slim Grissom. In the film, Slim courts Miss Blandish from a callow distance, saves her from the attentions of his inept gang, changes his mind about extracting her ransom and dies in a shoot-out leaving Miss Blandish to commit suicide rather than submit herself once again to a life of upper-class monotony.

For reasons which have remained mysterious to future generations the critics fell on this mélange, when it opened the next year, like a pack of wolves. The film possessed 'all the morals of an alleycat and all the sweetness of the sewer'. It was 'a piece of nauseating muck', 'a wicked disgrace to the British film industry', and according to the *Monthly Film Bulletin* 'the most sickening display of brutality, perversion, sex and sadism ever to be shown on the screen'. This normally sedate magazine then turned on the censor. 'It is an extraordinary oversight on the part of the British Board of Film Censors that

In spite of being toned down between book and screen the release of James Hadley Chase's *No Orchids for Miss Blandish* in 1947 unleashed so much critical opprobrium, the head censor had to apologise for passing it.

this monstrosity has been passed for public showing . . . ' Finally in an open letter to the BBFC published in the *Sunday Times* Dilys Powell twisted the knife. Apparently, *No Orchids for Miss Blandish* deserved no less than a new classification. It should be branded with 'a "D" certificate for disgusting'.

Within days politicians responding to ever-present concerns about violent crime asserted that the film would 'pervert the minds of the British people'. Even the flamboyant Labour MP Tom Driberg called for the appointment of a Royal Commission to investigate BBFC methods. Two days later, on 23 April, in a rare show of defiance, the LCC overruled the BBFC, instructing St John Clowes, the director of *No Orchids*, that he had until the following Monday to cut the film according to their specifications or face an LCC ban. (That same evening the director complied under the eyes of a censorious council official.) Other councils then demanded their own cuts and while some accepted the BBFC decision or even reinstated the Board's cuts many of the councils' watch committees banned the film.

Not since the twenties had the BBFC and the local authorities been so divided, and the Board tried their best to repair the damage, 'We don't know what the excitement is about,' they claimed. '*No Orchids* underwent drastic revision at the Board's behest . . . As far as we are concerned it is a normal gangster film, no more brutal than many made in Hollywood.' But within a week of the film's London release on 15 April 1948, the BBFC had already conceded defeat with an apology from its President, Sir Sidney Harris, to the Home Office for having 'failed to protect the public'.

Harris and his new Secretary Arthur Watkins had been almost drowned by their baptism at the font of censorship. Watkins, in particular, wanted to update the censorship system so that 'unquestionably adult films' could be passed 'instead of having to refuse a certificate'. But any hopes of changing the 'A' category, which was still open to those under sixteen if accompanied by an adult, had now been dashed by the *No Orchids* débâcle. Over the next two or three years the new sexually 'adult' films arriving from the Continent would pay the price for this one oversight by the Board.

The Miracle, a contemporary parable on the virgin birth of Christ, directed by Roberto Rossellini, with a script by his young assistant Federico Fellini, was refused a certificate in 1949 because of overall blasphemy and in particular Anna Magnani's intense depiction of 'labour pains' when she delivers the 'Messiah'. Claude Autant-Lara's *Occupe-toi d'Amélie* received the same treatment from the Board that year because of its general sexual exuberance, with particular exception being taken to one of Amélie's suitors waiting for her trouserless 'to save time'. Also Henri-Georges Clouzot's *Manon* (1948), a modernisation of the Abbé Prévost's didactic eighteenth-century novel reset in wartime Paris, eluded British film-goers owing to the hero's passionate fondling of the eponymous heroine's corpse at the end of the film.

On the other hand, in a period when nearly half the films being submitted to the BBFC were cut, it is perhaps questionable whether it was worth the sacrifice to receive an 'A' certificate. In effect, any film that did not make an allowance for the presence of children within the audience was altered by the censor. The young hero in Buñuel's *Los Olivados* (1950) lost his motivation for revenge with a pivotal scene in which one of the street kids is bludgeoned to death with a rock; Autant-Lara's tragic love story, *Le Diable au Corps*, whose international success revived the French film industry in 1946, had over ten minutes removed from its British version; even more footage was cut from *Bitter Rice* (1948), including the scene from the famous poster featuring Silvana Mangano in a rice field with skirts tucked up exposing her thighs above black stockings, which, according to one frustrated critic, 'looked infinitely worth the parting', and the reason for Ray Milland's dipsomania disappeared amongst two major sequences from Billy Wilder's *Lost Weekend*. Four years later, in 1950, the same director had a crucial line revealing Norma Desmond's (Gloria Swanson) past affair with her butler (Erich von Stroheim) deleted from his bittersweet homage to Hollywood, *Sunset Boulevard*.

Italian neo-realist films such as the rural *Bitter Rice* (1948) proved too realistic for the censor.

By 1950 Watkins himself admitted that the situation had got out of hand. 'I went to the premiere of the French film *Passionelle* (1949),' he was reported as saying, 'and I found that some of the cuts made by my own Board so absurd that I had them restored next morning.'

Ironically, the Board's opponents in local government brought about the solution to Watkins's problem. Responding to pressure from the local councils, the government set up a committee in December 1949 to investigate the censorship system, and the following year the Wheare Committee recommended: 'A single category of films, which should include the present "H" [Horror] category from which children should be excluded . . . The category might be called "X".'

Once the Board had adopted the 'X' certificate in January 1951, it was assumed by critics that films which came within the new category would no longer be cut. Those commentators would soon be disabused. Fewer pictures were banned and under the new category British audiences were introduced to a golden age of world cinema through the films of Fellini, Bergman, Kurosawa, Mizoguchi, Rossellini, Renoir and many others. But in order to squeeze every film into the new classification system cuts became longer, more extensive, and even more outlandish than at any other time in the BBFC's history. For instance, Henri-Georges Clouzot's nail-biting thriller *The Wages of Fear* (1953) in which Yves Montand's character delivers a truckload of nitro-glycerine across 600 miles of pot-holed terrain lost a lot of its tension along with seventeen minutes of cuts. By contrast, only a few frames disclosing the actress, Eva Dahlbeck's left nipple had to be removed from Bergman's *Smiles of a Summer Night* (1955). Faced with this demand the Swedish film director told *The Times* that he had not even been aware that the nipple could be seen; he had to run the film backwards and forwards on a viewer to find the offending shot. It took him some time, he said, but eventually he tracked it down. The nipple was visible for less than one second, but the Board spotted it.

It was not uncommon for a film at this time to lose a third of its length; occasionally, though, the removal of so much footage only made matters worse. In Alexander Mackendrick's *The Sweet Smell of Success* (1957), Tony Curtis asks his girlfriend to sleep with a man who can help him in his career. Originally the woman protested before agreeing, but the Board ordered her arguments to be cut. Consequently she appears to be amoral as well as a fool. Cinema-goers could also get the wrong message from the BBFC's inclination to censor film titles as well as films. After chopping Visconti's genteel period melodrama *Senso* (1954), to ribbons, the Board refused to allow the title, or Visconti's alternative suggestion, *Sensuality*. Instead they insisted on *The Wanton Duchess*.

Celluloid continued to build up on the BBFC's floor throughout the fifties. As the decade progressed, however, the criteria by which films were being censored underwent a change. The realignment largely came about due to the increasing public interest in film which had been fostered by the creation of the National Film Theatre in 1951 and by the influence of film critics such as Dilys Powell and Derek Hill of *Tribune*. A 1956 report on the 'X' in the British Film Institute's house magazine *Sight and Sound* summed up their argument for reform: 'The effect on an audience of an episode of violence in, say, Los Olivados is very different from that of the savage beating-ups in the conventionally brutal American thrillers.' As it happened this tied in with Arthur Watkins's own beliefs. According to the Secretary of the Board, 'a good censor' had 'to judge each film on its merits and give full weight to that cardinal factor in the censorship of films, the "intention" of the director.'

Thus the Board moved from its pre-war political rationale to an artistic

basis for adult film censorship, and this aesthetic provision is still a mainstay
from which the BBFC oversees '18' certificated films today. Back in the fifties
Watkins's prescient belief in the auteur theory created a loophole for such
sequences as the rape scenes in Kurosawa's *Rashomon* (1951) to squeeze
unscathed through his office; as did the poignant circular sexual couplings of
Max Ophuls's *La Ronde* (1950) which the Secretary called 'witty and charming'. (In America, by contrast, where *La Ronde* was tried for obscenity, the
prosecution asked 'Do you realise that this picture will be seen by a large
group of people in a darkened theatre?')

The 'intention' of a director, is of course, a difficult thing to gauge and while
Japanese films could be welcomed in Britain as a glimpse into the inscrutable,
or French sex comedies waved on as the predilection of an over-sexed nation,
the depiction of violence as directed against the authorities carried unwelcome
associations for both critic and censor. For most British film commentators
violence against authority had yet to become part of a character's motivation,
and it was therefore inartistic and still unnecessary; for the censor, moreover,
it was a direct threat to his validity: the more volatile sections of society, those
without the education to know or want to know about their place in the class

Passed with no cuts
La Ronde (1950) –
with Simone
Signoret, Gerard
Philipe and Anton
Walbrook – was the
exception to the rule
of heavy-handed
cutting during the
fifties.

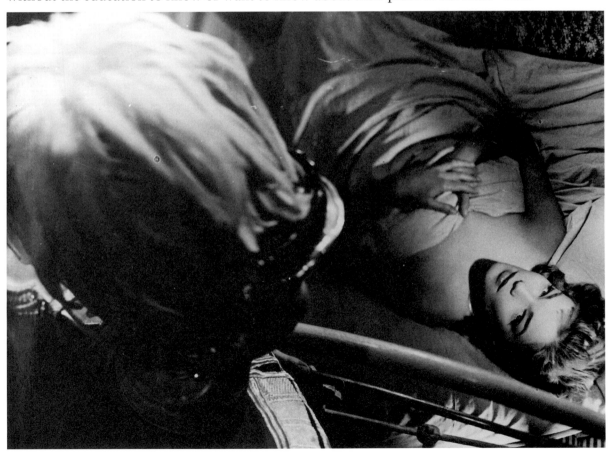

structure might identify with the source of violence and then undermine or even physically attack the traditional institutions which censorship was supposed to protect.

The Board thought that the cause which would set off just such an effect had been presented with the arrival in Britain at the beginning of 1954 of *The Wild One*. Laslo Benedek's film portrays the descent on a small Californian town of two motorcycle gangs, one led by Johnny (Marlon Brando) the other by Chino (Lee Marvin). First they intimidate the townsfolk – 'What're you rebelling against, Johnny?' asks a friendly local. 'What've ya got?' he replies – then they run amok on their motorbikes while the sheriff wrings his hands within the safety of his own gaol. Meanwhile Johnny falls in love with a local girl (Mary Murphy) who persuades him to call a halt to the gang's mayhem. But by this time the townspeople have taken the law into their own hands and when the gangs are forced to leave a local bystander is killed by a skidding bike.

All seven of the Board's examiners, including Madge Kitchener and the future Secretary John Trevelyan, agreed that Benedek's motorcycle-western should be banned. 'Having regard,' they told the producers at Columbia, 'to the present widespread concern about the increase in juvenile crime, the Board is not prepared to pass any film dealing with this subject unless the compensating moral values are so firmly presented as to justify its exhibition to audiences likely to contain (even with an "X" certificate) a large number of young and immature persons.'

Columbia refused to accept the decision. They proposed a new ending (which unfortunately has been lost from the BBFC's records). They even asked the BBFC to suggest its own ending, but after the film was viewed at the beginning of December the Board reaffirmed its rejection. Columbia then took the battle out into the provinces where they made applications to all the leading councils, but once again they were rebuffed. Moreover the Board was antagonised by this campaign and Harris made his sentiments known by personally thanking Dilys Powell for her support of the BBFC's ban.

The battle in the provinces, however, was not over. At the prompting of Leslie Halliwell, the author of the film catalogue, the Cambridge magistrates examined *The Wild One* in the spring of 1955 and granted it an 'X' certificate. Five local authorities then passed the film (including Lanarkshire, which awarded it a 'U'), which in turn meant that the source of so much controversy could be coolly evaluated in the national press. Not all the reviews of *The Wild One* were favourable, but enough of them were to put renewed pressure on the Board. However, constant publicity about teddy-boy violence ensured that the Board rejected the film twice in July and October of 1955. 'Our objection,' insisted an increasingly irate Watkins, 'is to the unrestricted hooliganism. Without the hooliganism there can be no film and with it there can be no certificate.'

Opposite Marlon Brando's leather-clad leader of the pack in *The Wild One* (1953) became a static photographic icon for generations of British youth because the actual film was banned in Britain for fifteen years.

The following December, Columbia recut, adding a preface and a new scene to the end of the film, and the Board agreed to view the new version as long as there was no publicity in the meantime about the resubmission. Again it was rejected and one of the longest-running campaigns in Britain to unban a film then subsided until April 1959, when the persistent studio tried once more.

By this time John Trevelyan had become Secretary of the Board, but he was still feeling his way into the job. He did not want to repeat Watkins's mistake of passing a controversial film while the BBFC was vulnerable during a changeover; so he upheld the ban but his tone was more conciliatory. 'There has been a lot of publicity,' he told Columbia, 'about adolescent gangs in London and elsewhere recently and, while in some ways the present gangs are more vicious than those depicted in the film, the behaviour of Brando and the two gangs to authority and adults generally is of the kind that provides a dangerous example to those wretched young people who take every opportunity of throwing their weight about . . . Once again we have made this decision with reluctance because we think it is a splendid picture. I only hope that the time will come, and come soon, when we do not have to worry about this kind of thing, but I am afraid that we do have to worry about it now.'

The time did not come and the film was rejected twice again, the second time following a riot at Clacton between 2,000 mods and rockers at the end of March 1964. For the next two years Columbia received an annual rejection slip, although Trevelyan raised no objection at the time to a TV showing since 'the young people for whom it might be harmful are generally not frequent television viewers.'

The BBFC had boxed itself into a corner. While juvenile delinquency continued to be reported in the press they could not unban this contentious film and it therefore took someone at the Board who had not seen it and who had not been pressurised by Columbia to break the vicious circle. David Harlech, the Welsh aristocrat who had assumed the Presidency of the Board in 1965, watched *The Wild One* for the first time towards the end of 1967 and he judged that 'it would no longer be likely to have its original impact.' *The Wild One* was finally granted a certificate on 6 November 1967.

The following February, when the fifteen-year-old film received its belated premiere at the Columbia Cinema in Shaftesbury Avenue, John Trevelyan justifiably described the film as 'almost a period piece', but then he disingenuously pointed out that 'our own brand of rockers are now just a prehistoric race. The film's dangerous appeal was aimed mainly at them.'

For the Board, *The Wild One*'s dangerous appeal had actually been aimed 'mainly' at the spivs, then the teddy boys and then the rockers, and presumably if a window of opportunity had not presented itself with the appearance of peace-loving hippies in the mid to late sixties the film would have been shackled to each successive teenage fashion and remained banned in perpetuity. A reported explanation from the BBFC for the repeated rejections was that 'the police were shown as weak characters and the teenagers did not get the punishment that they deserved.' Thus the film was banned for fifteen years not because Watkins or Trevelyan considered it immoral or too violent, but because its morality was too subtle and too generous. It did not categorically condemn those who defied authority and without that condemnation, the censor feared the possibility of local emulation. Usually this kind of conjectural explanation for a film's banning cannot be tested by any practical means. Unfortunately for the censor, in the case of *The Wild One* it could be.

In fact *The Wild One* did not cause juvenile violence of any kind in the districts where it was allowed to be shown in the mid-fifties. As with most political bodies, however, when the empirical evidence did not fulfil the argument, the BBFC ignored the evidence, retained their fears and then repeatedly restated the argument.

The power of the BBFC's prophecy was also found wanting in the next film of the fifties to deal with teenage gangs. This time the Board forecast calm seas ahead and almost in consequence a hurricane ensued. Unhappily for cinema-owners though, the signal for juvenile mayhem was not contained in the actual film.

Submitted to the Board on 15 March 1955, *The Blackboard Jungle* starred Glenn Ford as an altruistic teacher trying to 'get through' to his New York City students. He is opposed from the back of the classroom by Artie West (Vic Morrow) and his flick-knife-wielding gang who, inevitably, are more interested in the pursuit of 'kicks' than of knowledge. This was the first Hollywood movie to bring teenage 'heptalk' to the screen and the BBFC was appalled. They demanded that MGM cut 'Tell me about your stinking sister' and 'No, it's cheaper to steal one. That's arithmetic, Teach'; and they were absolutely insistent that the studio remove the film's climax in which Artie stands up in the classroom and flicks open his switchblade to taunt Glenn Ford: 'Come on, step right up and taste a little o' this, Daddy-oh . . . Where do you want it? You want it in the belly? Or how about the face, huh?'

'A most unpleasant film,' was the opinion of the Board, but after a series of heated conversations both sides climbed down from obdurate positions and *The Blackboard Jungle* was released, with six minutes of cuts, in mid-September 1955. Press reviews mostly criticised the film's limp liberal ending in which order and respect for authority is unrealistically restored. The Board was right, though, to be worried about the reception of the film's 'unbridled revolting hooliganism'. British teddy boys flocked to see *The Blackboard Jungle* and they did not identify with Glenn Ford's soppy student supporters. Instead they cheered when Ford's collection of old jazz records is stomped on by Artie and his crew. They released their own flick-knives when Artie threatens

Dadier (Glenn Ford), the teacher-hero of *The Blackboard Jungle* (1955), is consoled by his wife (Anne Francis). It was the rock-and-roll soundtrack though, rather than the film itself, that signalled the destruction of many a British cinema in the summer of 1956.

to slice open his teacher's cheek. By this time, however, the 'teds' in the audience would have already been on their feet hollering. What had brought them to fever pitch was the insistent rumbling sound which opened the film: 'One, two, three o'clock, four o'clock. Rock.' Bill Haley's 'Rock Around the Clock' played over the credits of *The Blackboard Jungle* and throughout Britain in 1955–6 the song was usually accompanied by the sound of teds slashing cinema seats.

Incredibly, the Board received no public complaints at their decision to unleash the film on cinema owners. But the avoidance of a critical backlash upon the censors probably had less to do with the lack of BBFC foresight and more to do with *The Blackboard Jungle*'s reception from the press, who were equally blind to the film's future effect.

To the surprise of most members of the Board, Britain's film reviewers gave a warm reception in 1956 to the next teen-movie which would come to exemplify the problems of post-war youth and the growing generation gap between parents and their children. At its first showing before the Board on 14 October 1955 those examiners were impervious both to *Rebel Without a Cause*, and the impact of its star James Dean who, within days of the film's release, became a prototype for angst-ridden, adolescent alienation.

'Although we did not like the film on censorship grounds,' commented the examiner Audrey Field, 'and although it would be no loss from an artistic

point of view, it was not thought practicable to reject it, in view of the action which we had taken on *The Blackboard Jungle* – a better, but also a more violent, film.' With not even the offer of a certificate to *Rebel*'s distributors, a resolute Field concluded that the Board would be prepared to look at the film again, but only if nineteen cuts were made in the meantime.

Once again a series of cuts was motivated by the Board's determination that compensating moral values be sufficiently presented 'to outweigh any harmful influence which the film might otherwise have on young and impressionable members of a cinema audience'. But in common with other tightly constructed films *Rebel Without a Cause* did not lend itself easily to a sudden change in narrative emphasis. For, as the French director, Erich Rohmer observed at the time, Nicholas Ray's direction and James Dean's performance might have been purposely nonconformist but the story itself fell neatly into the five acts of classical tragedy. Also, in an acknowledgement of Aristotle's rules, the film's action is all but contained within twenty-four hours.

The censors immediately recognised the problem of cutting into a film in which successive scenes were successfully interdependent on each other. From the first of 'the five acts' – the exposition of Jim's (James Dean) conflict with his parents – the chief censor, Arthur Watkins complained that, 'What we cannot get out of the picture is the spectacle of ridiculous and ineffectual parents which is the main case for the "X" certificate.' But then the Secretary seems to

Warner Brothers regarded this knife-fight scene with James Dean from *Rebel Without a Cause* (1956) as integral to their film. But the British censor asked for – and won – its removal.

133

have had second thoughts about the adult certificate. 'At the same time, I still have a feeling that our "X" may appear too heavy handed a category for the rubbish that this picture undoubtedly is.' In an appended, handwritten note, a junior colleague had to bring his superior back to the point. 'I agree that it is rubbish for adults but poisonous stuff for the teddy inclined adolescent.'

A battle between the BBFC and the distributors at Warner Bros over cuts and categories then ensued. Out went 'Jim punching and kicking a probation officer', 'shots of Jim trying to throttle his father' (Jim Backus), 'shots of Judy's (Natalie Wood) hysterical excitement over the [chicken run] contest on the cliff top', and the 'removal of the *entire* knife duel between Jim and Buzz (Corey Allen) outside the planetarium'. But these concessions only reduced a banning to an 'X'. If Warners wanted an 'A' instead of an 'X' various other scenes and lines including 'Jim's drunken mimicking of the sound of a police car' would have to be sacrificed.

After watching the rushes of the knife-fight scene during *Rebel*'s production, Jack L. Warner had notified Ray that this was now a 'very important picture'; none the less his London office pleaded that, 'Not only have we taken out a terrifying and distasteful knife fight . . . but in doing so we have left in a line of dialogue in which the "hero" refuses to fight with knives.' They 'hoped' that the Board could 'reconsider your classification and allow it to be seen by young people, accompanied by their parents, rather than force us to cater to the morbid element of the population by branding it with an X.'

Unfortunately of course, the Board was more concerned with the effect of Warner's film on young people rather than on the morbid element. It had to remind the distributor of 'the serious view' with which the Board looked at any film that dealt with juvenile delinquency, 'especially in these times when there is such widespread public anxiety about the problem'. A cut-down *Rebel* was therefore released under an 'X' certificate at the beginning of 1956. Soon after, Watkins noted that 'rather to our surprise, and also to our relief, the film received universal praise from the critics in this country, and is enjoying a great success.'

The released film had undoubtedly been damaged. As Bernard Eisenschitz points out in his biography of Nicholas Ray, 'Group scenes provide the film's best moments,' and those had either been deeply cut or removed altogether. Whether an intact *Rebel*, on the other hand, would have caused riots like *The Blackboard Jungle* is doubtful because, unlike the latter film, *Rebel* never threatened to turn cinemas into rock-and-roll clubs. It was after all a film about internalised rather than externalised rebellion and James Dean, who, as Ray said, was bound up 'in the conflict between giving himself and fear of giving in to his own feelings' personified for a teenage audience that indecision between impulse and defiance. But for a clue to the potential effect of *Rebel Without a Cause* the censors could have done worse than look to its title.

What in fact had happened in the British censorship of these three 'teen dream' films is that the censor had completely misread their ideology. Contrary to popular belief, Marlon Brando's Johnny never wanted to be a 'wild one'. As the film's director, Laslo Benedek said at the time, 'The subject of the movie isn't juvenile delinquency: it's youth without ideals, without goals, which doesn't know what to do with the enormous energy it possesses.' In short, Johnny wants to be making love to the local girl, Kathie, not running around with his gang. Similarly, if he can possibly avoid it, James Dean's Jim would prefer not to rebel. Instead, as the film writer Peter Biskind notes in his book on Hollywood in the fifties, *Seeing is Believing*, 'Jim craves authority.' 'Please lock me up,' he begs the police, 'I'm gonna hit someone, do something . . . ' After the knife fight he wants to go to the police but his irresponsible parents won't let him. 'We're all involved,' he pleads in vain. Jim in fact wants to start a family with Judy and for that reason there is no room for his surrogate son Plato (Sal Mineo) who therefore has to be sacrificed because he has become a liability and a rival to Judy for Jim's affections. It is for the same reason that Vic Morrow's Artie West is sacrificed on the altar of institutional authority at the end of *The Blackboard Jungle*. For the sake of social control his fellow students have not only to reject Artie's pre-hippie protest against authority, they have to offer him up to that authority – the headmaster – and by doing so they remind the audience that delinquency is the exception, not the rule and that rebellion can only go so far before it is stopped short in the name of the majority.

Towards the end of 1956, the BBFC's Secretary, Arthur Watkins, defined the censor's task. The Board 'believes,' he said, 'that it is performing a service both to the public and to the film industry if it removes offensive and distasteful material which cannot be regarded as entertainment and which if not excluded would in the long run do harm to the kinema's claim to that universal patronage on which its economy rests.' He then beseeched the industry never to reveal the Board's cuts, arguing, 'If the public think that something has been cut from a picture there is less incentive for them to see it.'

But from 1951 onwards the film industry had to confront a new competitor which was pulling audiences out of cinemas and entertaining them in the living-room. In 1951 the number of television licences issued in Britain had barely reached three-quarters of a million; by the end of the decade that had risen to ten-and-a-half million and was still increasing. In the face of this immediate threat from the small screen the industry realised that the only way to staunch the haemorrhage was to put subjects on to the screen that were not allowed on TV: social realism, horror, and explicit sex. Needless to say, these were the very kinds of films which were most subject to censorship: for the first time, therefore, in the intertwined history of cinema and censor the Board would not be able to rely upon the vital silent support of the British film industry. On the contrary, the industry was about to do battle with the BBFC.

In the face of the imminent threat posed by the film industry the BBFC was fortunate to have a changing of the guard towards the end of 1956. In November, the Board's Secretary Arthur Watkins retired and in his place Sir Sidney Harris appointed John Nichols from the Cultural Section of the Foreign Office. Nichols was later described by the censor and future Secretary, John Trevelyan, as 'a delightful man with special qualifications and experience in the fine arts', and indeed Nichols pursued Watkins's policy of applying artistic criteria to film censorship.

The new Secretary had a special fondness for mid-fifties Japanese cinema and Ingmar Bergman films, all of which he refused to cut. He also showed some sympathy for early examples of the British 'social problem' film by granting 'A' certificates in 1958 to *The Young and the Guilty*, a hyperbolical tale about the frustrations of adolescent celibacy and the more aggressively naturalistic *Violent Playground* which starred the young New Zealand actor David McCallum as Johnny, a 'mixed-up kid' who is transformed by rock and roll into a savage. (He symbolically keeps his gun in a guitar case.) On the other hand, Nichols's decisions were also arbitrary and often biased in favour of American film-makers. Hollywood gangster movies which featured pistol-whippings or close-ups of pulped faces such as *The Joker Is Wild* (1958) and *Baby Face Nelson* (1958) were both granted 'A' certificates; in the latter case because Nichols described it as 'an historical subject'. But very little help was offered to commercial British film directors who, in the meantime, were carrying on an increasingly desperate fight against television.

With no aid in sight from the censor, the industry broke ranks and turned on their traditional ally. The opening salvo was fired off by J. Lee Thompson, the director of *Ice Cold in Alex* (1958), in the June 1958 issue of *Films and Filming*. After informing his readers that the censor had demanded 'over ninety cuts' from the script of *Ice Cold in Alex*, Thompson accused the Board of 'alarming inconsistencies among films of similar types, which suggest that the whole business of censorship is becoming more a matter of luck than judgement.' The remedy, according to the Bristol-born director, lay in an Appeal Panel composed of film critics which would arbitrate disputes between the Board and film producers.

The Board could afford to ignore the opinions of a single disgruntled film-maker, even a successful one like Lee Thompson, but the frustrated director then followed up his criticisms in an interview given to the trade journal *Kine Weekly*. There he called upon the British Film Producers Association to organise an all-industry meeting with the BBFC to discuss the possibilities of a 'more enlightened and adult approach to censorship' through the incorporation of an appeals panel. Three years before, in 1955, the BFPA had planned the setting up of a committee to consider members' grievances against the censors, but they had shelved the proposal. Now they demanded a meeting with the Board.

Previous pages
J. Lee Thompson, the director of *Ice Cold in Alex* (1958), issued a broadside from an increasingly frustrated film industry to the censor during 1958. The strength of his opposition might be explained by the BBFC's treatment of his film.

Under the auspices of the Kinematograph Renters Society the confrontation took place on 17 May 1958. The three main charges lodged against the BBFC were: arbitrary categorisation of films; taking no account of what was permissible on television; and, lastly, that the Board was operating 'artistic censorship' in taking quality into account. From the Board's point of view none of these criticisms mattered. They could simply promise to do better in the future. But they had to avoid the imposition of an appeals panel. Once that was installed their decisions would have to be explained and defended. Even worse, they would no longer be able to carry out censorship under the carapace of anonymity; therefore the mystery from which their power as censors came would be lost. A concession was needed, but one that would not compromise the identity of the examiners.

The Board's solution appeared in the form of a sacrificial offering laid at the feet of J. Lee Thompson. Under his article in *Films and Filming* a postscript had been added: 'Since inviting Mr Lee Thompson to contribute this article, the British Board of Film Censors has announced that its secretary, Mr John Nichols, has resigned 'due to his decision to return to work connected with the fine arts'.

Since then, film commentators have alluded to 'circumstances that have never been explained' or stated that, 'It is not possible now to judge how far these criticisms were fair.' But in *Films and Filming*, Lee Thompson had specifically stated that 'I want it to be clear that I am not attacking any individual at the British Board of Film Censors.' In fact, like any government or bureaucratic institution which is faced by a potentially fatal crisis, the BBFC decided that for the rest of the body to live on it had to cut off its own head.

Not surprisingly the President of the Board, Sir Sidney Harris, felt wary of choosing another administrative head of the BBFC himself. Instead the new Secretary, John Trevelyan, was appointed by a committee representing the industry which in 1960 would formalise the administrator's role as that of 'executive responsibility', while the President was relegated to the position of 'consultant'. Also, by 1958 Harris had reached eighty and he felt less and less inclined to take part in the Board's decisions. Trevelyan, therefore, had far more autonomy within the BBFC than his predecessors. Indeed, the future of Britain's film censorship would now be in his hands.

Before he joined the BBFC as a part-time censor in 1951, John Trevelyan had been a teacher and then an administrator in local government education – which may explain why he wanted *The Blackboard Jungle* to be banned and *The Wild One* to remain banned. In the late 1960s this tall, stooping figure with a cigarette permanently cupped in his hand would become a ubiquitous, avuncular presence on television, empathising with the creative problems of auteurs, conceding the injustice of adult censorship while at the same time declaring his reluctance to 'modify' the work of great artists. In the late fifties,

The graphic climax of this love scene between Jeanne Moreau and Jean-Marc Boreau in *Les Amants* (1958) was cut short by a pair of scissors.

though, he was a wily conservative censor, waiting to see which way the wind blew, aware that he was at his most vulnerable during his first six months as Secretary.

To begin with he hugged the same shadowy path as his predecessors. 'The Board's examiners,' he said, 'would be encouraged if it were realised that the majority of their decisions are not criticised at all . . . ' He let through cuts that left immense meaningless holes in films which he would later refer to as works of art. For instance, Louis Malle's *Les Amants* (1958), one of the key films of the French 'New Wave', led up to the gratification of a sensual woman (Jeanne Moreau) by the skilled mouth of a stranger. After the ending had been lopped off by the Board, however, it led nowhere but to what the critic Derek Hill called 'one of the Board's interruptions'.

Like Watkins and Nichols, Trevelyan also passed films which would be hard put to gain the same certificate today. One such example, *The Stranglers of Bombay* (1959) even appalled its own director, Terence Fisher, when he came to see it assembled. Publicised as being in 'Strangloscope' this 'factually based' drama about India's Kali-worshipping thuggees caused a minor sensation on the Continent where cinephiles reportedly crossed frontiers in the hope of see-

Released in
'Strangloscope',
Terence Fisher's
relentless homage to
sadism (as well as to
sado-masochism) in
*The Stranglers of
Bombay* mysteriously
eluded the grasp of
the BBFC.

ing it. What they came to see, according to the rapt French critic, M. Caine, was 'a very beautiful catalogue of tortures . . . a young Hindu girl (Marie Devereux) whose stunningly exposed bosom is of quite demential sumptuousness, contemplates the atrocities with a pleasure so intense (and so evidently erotic) that she glistens with sweat. I am astonished by the presence of this proud figurehead of female sadoscophilia who can have escaped from the scissors of Auntie Censorship only by some miracle.'

Yet films which kept more closely to historical fact did not necessarily receive the same blessing from Trevelyan. While domestic politics within British films had flown the BBFC's coop since 1939 foreign issues in foreign films could still be snared if they strayed within the borders of Britain. Two East German documentaries, *Holiday on Sylt* and *Operation Teutonic Sword*, which argued that Nazi war criminals occupied prominent political positions in post-war West Germany, were banned in 1958 because they were, as an internal BBFC memo noted, 'critical of a government with which this country has friendly diplomatic relations'.

Coupled with the lengthy cuts applied at this time to other films from communist countries, such decisions reminded long-standing opponents of the

141

'Oh Joe, wasn't it super?' Heather Sears asks Laurence Harvey during this love scene in *Room At the Top* (1958) and with those sighing words sex came to the British cinema.

BBFC, like Ivor Montagu, of unregretted days when controversy and politics were not allowed to mix in a film. 'For all the ritual denials of political censorship,' the old Marxist film-maker asserted, 'the ultimate political powers remain crouched in reserve; first as the film life of Nurse Cavell could be banned by the "independent" B. B. of F. C. at a moment when Neville Chamberlain was making up to Hitler, so the Board at the present day could invent reasons for forbidding film revelations of the Nazi past of West German functionaries when Macmillan was making up to Bonn.'

The reason for rejecting these two films was, of course, kept secret, but after the Board's action was criticised in the House of Commons, Trevelyan publicly defended the decision. 'We refused [the films], but not on political grounds. We did not think that cinema entertainment was the right place for putting over defamatory material about living persons.' Some years later, when he belatedly sought legal advice about the apparent defamation, Trevelyan discovered that the new reason was not justified – and never would be justified – because 'it was most unlikely that the Board would be involved in any libel proceedings since it was not an accessory in the publication of a libel.' 'On receiving this opinion,' the Secretary commented, 'we immediately abandoned our former policy.'

But he did not. In fact he adapted it in an attempt to steer British cinema away from social realism. 'Social comment and entertainment don't necessarily mix. Most people,' he said, 'pay one-and-nine to be entertained rather than receive social comment.' Trevelyan had fallen back on the BBFC's long-serving as well as self-serving, proposition that films would wither on the commercial vine unless censorship made them palatable for the discerning film-goer. Events, however, would prove him wrong.

As the number of television licences steadily rose and cinema attendances dramatically fell in the fifties, directors looked for material which would differentiate their films from TV. 'Daring' 'X' films like the Diana Dors vehicle *Yield to the Night* (1956), which pleaded for the abolition of capital punishment, or *The Flesh is Weak* (1957), which 'gave the lowdown on white slavery', could perform that function, but the major exhibitors disapproved of the category. Rank's chairman, John Davis, liked to remind producers that 'fundamentally a film production is intended to satisfy the demand for family entertainment.' In consequence, Rank cinemas only showed six 'X' films between 1951 and 1957.

From a film-maker's point of view, an informal alliance had been drawn up between the industry and the Board against the 'X' film. But this unwritten agreement also created a loophole for the new independent production companies that were coming into existence by the late fifties. These smaller companies did not release their films through the major exhibitors but through individually designated cinemas (such as the Academy in Oxford Street); so they had less to lose by producing 'X'-rated movies. Thus the Hammer horror cycle was born, along with so-called 'social problem' films covering such issues as juvenile delinquency, like *The Young and the Guilty* (1958), or racial prejudice in *Sapphire* (1959).

The subsequent success of most of these films at the British box office revealed that a crucial distinction was now opening up between the favoured choice of the exhibitors and the censor and what a young cinema audience actually wanted to see on the screen. Nowhere would this difference be more clearly epitomised than in the newly emerging strain of gritty social realism now commonly known as 'kitchen sink'. And once again, because of their position outside the mainstream, the independent film companies were better placed to exploit the new film genre. Thus it was an independent film company called Remus Films Ltd, which produced the first of the kitchen-sink dramas in 1958.

Taken from John Braine's novel, *Room At the Top* recounts the ruthless rise of Joe Lampton (Laurence Harvey) up the social ladder of a northern industrial town. Joe's goal is achieved when he seduces Susan Brown (Heather Sears), the daughter of the town's top businessman; but in order to marry her he has to give up Alice Aisgill (Simone Signoret), the woman he loves, and any chance of personal happiness.

Rather than its action, though, it was *Room At the Top*'s dialogue that struck home with audiences in the late fifties, particularly in a scene when Joe seduces Susan, the industrialist's daughter, by a river bank. 'Oh Joe,' she sighs, 'wasn't it super?' But Joe looks coolly off into the distance stranded in post-coital ennui and disappointment as Susan happily chatters on about their future together. The British screen had finally made a direct reference to sex, and more daringly still it had acknowledged that women can take pleasure from the experience.

Yet *Room At the Top* did not cause undue excitement when it was delivered to the Board's offices in September 1958. Apart from the substitution of the word 'witch' for 'bitch', and the deletion of a line in which Joe overhears the news of Alice Aisgill's suicide in a car crash – 'she was scalped' – the BBFC left the film alone. Fourteen years later, in his memoir *What the Censor Saw*, Trevelyan explains the Board's unusual reticence and provided an insight into a changing era:

> In retrospect one can see that Jack Clayton's film was a milestone in the history of British films and in a way a milestone in the history of British film censorship. Up to this time the cinema with rare exceptions had presented a fantasy world; this film dealt with real people and real problems. At the time its sex scenes were regarded as sensational, and some of the critics who praised the film congratulated the Board on having had the courage to pass it. Ten years later these scenes seemed very mild and unsensational . . . There was no nudity or simulated cop-ulation, but there was rather more frankness about sexual relations in the dialogue than people had been used to.

Yet what shocked contemporary film-goers even more than the racy dia-logue was Joe's determined use of his sexuality to leap the class barrier. 'The new dimension of the film,' said the book's original author, John Braine, 'was in presenting a boy from the working class not as a downtrodden victim, but as he "really" was. It wasn't important that Joe Lampton was honest about sex, what was important was that Joe was honest about class. Most ambitious working-class boys want to get the hell out of the working class. That was the simple truth that had never been stated before.'

The critics recognised that truth and welcomed the advent of social realism. 'Here was a British film,' said the *Daily Express*, 'which at long last got its teeth into those subjects which have always been part and parcel of our lives, but have hitherto been taboo subjects on the prissy British screen.' Genuflecting to the film's northern roots, the *Daily Sketch* trumpeted, 'Now Britain joins the bedroom brigade – and adds a slice of Yorkshire pudding,' and after conceding that 'This is in no sense a U story,' the *Sunday Express* stated, 'But it is real and straightforward, and rings true. In this case at least, and at last, the X certificate looks like a badge of honour.'

When *Room At the Top* was released in Britain at the beginning of 1959 audiences also agreed that the film reflected their own lives. At the time two-thirds of the population was working class, and young working men, in particular, identified with Joe's rebellion against post-war austerity and the class system. Like Joe they had heard their relatives claim, 'I'm working class and proud of it.' But the rebels in the audience felt no such pride. On the contrary, they were fed up with being stuck in a cultural and economic cul de sac with no opportunity to advance themselves. It was a time of protests and demonstrations. The young seized their rebellious role models from pop music, theatre and films, and it was these real-life 'angry young men' that drove *Room At the Top* to box-office success.

Faced with incontrovertible evidence of support for an 'X' film, the Board acted after the event. Albeit late in the day, they were forced to accept that the British working class was no longer satisfied with its lot and was prepared, like Joe Lampton, to vent its frustration on the middle classes. No doubt the BBFC's attitude to such an irate social message was being tempered by the critics' overwhelming praise for *Room At the Top*, but what actually changed BBFC policy was the fact that this 'X'-rated picture became the third most successful film of 1959 – for the Board was always impressed by a film's takings.

The BBFC, and especially Trevelyan, therefore conceded that from then on the working class would have to be represented more realistically in British films. Yet the Board had had a minimal influence on this sea change. Just as in 1939 when the Ministry of Information had overruled the Board, forcing them to accept political controversy within films, now two decades later in 1959 a whole new swathe of dramatic content was being foisted upon the censor. In this case, though, the agent for reform was not a government organisation but a single film. *Room At the Top* proved that post-war film censorship in Britain had been designed for maintenance of the status quo and not, as had been repeatedly stated, for the protection of the censored.

The 'X' film had proved its viability at the box office and it now moved into the mainstream of British cinema. (Even Rank jumped on the bandwagon with *The Wild and the Willing* in 1962, now that the territory was commercially approved.) Moreover, because Hollywood films were still restrained by a censorship code that had been drawn up in the late twenties, British directors were well placed to exploit the need for adult-themed movies amongst the vast American audience. This they proceeded to do. In the following five years new British film-makers with fresh ideas would bring to the screen a sense of immediacy and social awareness that would revive a moribund industry and turn the censor round. Sex and class were no longer excluded; and with the breaking of those two crucial taboos the stranglehold over film content that had been exerted by the BBFC ever since its creation in 1912 would finally be broken.

NC 62
20 MARS
CE FILM HORAIRE SPECIAL
à 21h même le SAMEDI
EVA-MARIE SAINT
m Dramatique
DUS
EN COULEURS
BON
ANSEUR
EN
5
LEÇONS
33 rue de
VAUGIRARD
GEORGE
LIT. 20-76
LE ZO
VAU. 29.47
du 7 au LUNDI
RECORD
DANN
DOU
DU G
EN SCO
du MERCRE
LES P
ARTIST
AM
CEL
EN SCOPE
VARI
17, Bd CROIX-NIVE
PAUL
ARNA
EN CINE

THE BOARD BREAKS OUT 10 ✂

As in no other decade, the practice of film censorship in Britain would be transformed during the sixties. The BBFC, permanently on the defensive, would try to shore up newly adopted positions only to see them almost immediately undercut and overrun by innovative film directors and scriptwriters. On the other hand, during this traumatic period the Board possessed in John Trevelyan a Secretary who had found his feet, who fought best on the run, and who, in his willingness to contradict himself, provided the personification of a 'moving target'.

For the opponents of censorship the seeds of change had been sown in 1958 by J. Lee Thompson. Because the director had attacked the Board's 'inconsistencies' in public with no apparent harm to his career, the chimera of an all-powerful, autonomous BBFC was exposed to rational argument. Of course, personal conviction also played a part in the unveiling of a previously inviolate censorship. In a coruscating article published in the July 1960 issue of *Encounter*, the film critic Derek Hill adopted a Zola-like stance enumerating various instances of the Board's 'amendments' to 300 of the 550 features submitted each year. He concluded by accusing the Board of being responsible, at least in part, for the British cinema's avoidance of 'worthwhile themes' and called for it to be replaced by the Obscene Publications Act.

Hill's list of censorial quirks was underlined in the next issue of *Encounter* when the playwright John Osborne and the film director Tony Richardson added their own comments about the Board. With barbed irony, Osborne amplified Hill's criticism of the BBFC to reveal that: 'The Board's history of dedicated prejudice and devotion to mediocrity has been very helpfully and consistently sustained by most British film producers, since these are the qualities they both have in common.' Even more tellingly, Richardson explained exactly why Trevelyan was trying to stop the new school of social realism from reaching the screen – not so much because of the BBFC's avowed belief that people went to the pictures 'to get away from it all' as from their fear of the incalculable consequences that an innovative film can set in motion: 'I believe that the basis of the censor's attitude is that films must not be serious – that they must work within the limits of a formula. Over both the films that I made [*Look Back in Anger* (1959) and *The Entertainer* (1960)], Mr Trevelyan has

Opposite Anna Karina at work in Jean-Luc Godard's day-in-the-life-of-a-prostitute *Vivre Sa Vie* (1962). Amongst others, the films of Bergman, Antonioni, Hitchcock, Pasolini, Billy Wilder and other films by Godard were cut during the sixties.

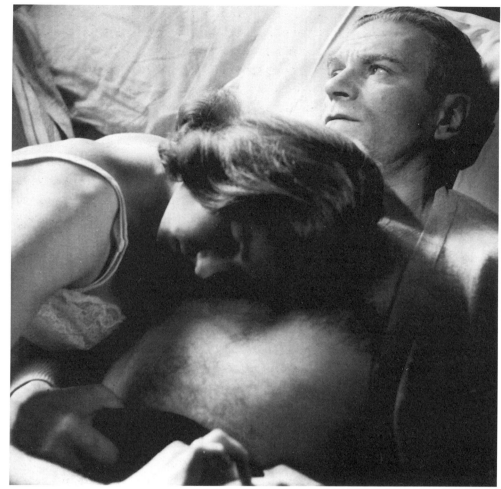

The BBFC insisted that this bedroom scene with Laurence Olivier and Shirley Anne Field in *The Entertainer* (1960) carried with it an 'A' rather than a 'U' certificate, because Olivier's Archie Rice 'had obviously been making love mechanically, and without any pleasure.'

insisted that these created problems for him – not because they themselves could possibly have corrupted anyone . . . but because they were too "real". Audiences it was implied, must not recognize their own world and must not relate what they see on the screens back to their social experience. It would be too disturbing.'

Richardson obviously felt – and would have good reason in the next few years to continue to feel – constrained by the BBFC. But what must have particularly irritated authors like Osborne was the censoring of both film scripts and finished films. Yet this was unavoidable, even for prestigious writers. Following the lead of his predecessor, Arthur Watkins, Trevelyan had rapidly built up a network of contacts amongst producers and distributors in the film industry. Through them he nurtured pre-censorship of films to such an extent that by 1960 over 80 per cent of British scripts were being submitted to the BBFC before production began on the studio floor. Trevelyan protested that this was 'the film-maker's choice. They needn't send any script to us. Nobody needs to.' None the less, it is very unlikely that the 'ever-friendly' Secretary would have failed to bring to the notice of reluctant producers the considerable cost advantage to be gained from not having to re-shoot censored scenes.

Use of the BBFC's 'script censorship service' was not encouraged for the vetting of mainstream commercial films or cheap B-movies. (As Tony Richardson pointed out, for the censor those kinds of films fell within a predictable formula.) Trevelyan, in fact, was attempting to snare scripts which, due to controversy, could rebound on the censor if they were allowed to develop without impediment between the page and production. Yet, in this quest, producers not only acceded to the censor's wishes, they sometimes made finance for a film dependent upon BBFC approval of a script. Under the terms on which Warner-Seven Arts produced *Lolita* in 1961 for instance, the director Stanley Kubrick had to consult Trevelyan and the American censor at the Motion Picture Association of America, and adjust Vladmir Nabokov's screenplay accordingly.

Initially, in this case at least, such a condition seemed to presage disaster. Trevelyan overreacted to a letter from Kubrick informing him that he intended to shoot Lolita as a comedy and not, as Trevelyan advised, as a tragedy. But in his next letter Trevelyan admitted that he had misunderstood the American director's intentions. 'I must apologise for my use of the phrase "it seems to us fantastic to play it for cheap laughs." Your record and the standing of your artists, make this a completely unfair comment.'

What had become apparent to Trevelyan in the interval between the two letters was that Kubrick and Nabokov had anticipated and then pre-empted censorship concerns. First of all, the author had raised the age of his nubile heroine from twelve in his book to fourteen in the film; then, presumably with the knowledge that the MPAA held a 'moral compensation' clause that required a character's misdemeanours to be punished (which also applied unofficially in Britain), Nabokov opened his screenplay with a scene of retribution. Here the paedophiliac protagonist, Humbert Humbert, takes revenge on his successor to Lolita's favours by shooting his rival down under a cascade of surrealistic gunfire. Thus the censor's qualms were almost but not quite settled on both sides of the Atlantic by a prescient author. But in spite of all these precautions by Nabokov the chief censor held out for one more important change.

This involved the Humbert Humbert 'nymphet theory' which Nabokov enunciated as follows: 'Between the age limits of nine and fourteen there occur maidens who, to certain bewitched travellers, twice or many times older than they, reveal their true nature which is not human, but nymphic (that is demoniac); and those chosen creatures I designate as "nymphets".' Nabokov transposed this passage from the novel to the off-screen voice of James Mason as Humbert in the film with various illustrations in the background of the

149

James Mason's Humbert Humbert tries to tempt his teen lover away from Coca Cola in *Lolita* (1962). Script-censorship demanded that Nabokov raise the age of his 'nymphet' from twelve to fourteen.

nymphet type such as cheerleaders, schoolgirls in bobby socks, and so on.

Trevelyan's objection to this scene lay in the generalised depiction of Humbert Humbert's predicament. If paedophilia was particularised in one eccentric and rare individual the condition would appear concomitant with Humbert himself. However, the censor argued, this sequence acted as an illustrated guide which would entice and stimulate would-be practitioners without demarcating the hero's demoralising fall from conventional grace. Nabokov, who waved aside the slightest alteration to his manuscript by literary editors, unfortunately never recorded his response to Trevelyan's presumption. Yet for once the autonomy of the great writer's work would be punctured because Humbert Humbert's theory never was divulged to the audience.

As can be inferred from Trevelyan's correspondence with Kubrick, the Secretary of the Board considered himself to be a cultivated man of the world who empathised with the creative side of film-making. Under his administration script supervision therefore became a matter of negotiation or horse trading, where it had previously been imposed by unilateral dictat. Nevertheless, for writers who were new to film this could still be a disillusioning process.

Alan Sillitoe, who adapted his own novel *Saturday Night and Sunday Morning* for the screen in the latter half of 1959, insisted six months later that the main reason why Karel Reisz's film was unfaithful to the book was due to BBFC hindrance. 'It seems to me,' he said, 'that censorship in the British film industry is in its own way as hidebound as that of Soviet Russia.' In fact, like

all other film productions of the sixties, pre-censorship of the *Saturday Night and Sunday Morning* screenplay was dictated by compromise.

Admittedly the opening comment from the Board's examiner left room for accusations of bias: 'I see from the accompanying compliments slip that this is the company in which John Osborne is involved; we might almost have known it from the language of the script.' But then, like many others before and after him, the BBFC reader was seduced by Sillitoe's work-shy, womanising, anti-hero Arthur Seaton and his ill-fated struggle to avoid the work-bench as well as retribution following an affair with the wife of a fellow factory worker. 'The hero is an immoral fellow who would doubtless end up in jail in real life, but I enjoyed him a lot more than the people in *Look Back in Anger* and *A Taste of Honey* (other products of the new school of Young Writers Speaking for the People), because I could believe in him, and even got to like him towards the end.'

In an acknowledgement of the influence upon the BBFC of *Room At the Top* the examiner allowed the inclusion of numerous 'bloodies', 'bleddys', 'bleedings' and 'bastards'. But he baulked at 'bogger', 'Christ' and 'sod'. Trevelyan himself informed *Saturday Night and Sunday Morning*'s producer, Harry Saltzman, 'We have not yet accepted the use of the word "bugger" in films and the substitution of the letter "o" for the letter "u" makes no significant difference: on the soundtrack the word will certainly sound like "bugger".' (The word eventually made its first screen appearance in Mike Nichols's

151

Who's Afraid of Virginia Woolf? in 1966.) Unfortunately, this was not merely a question of semantics. A lot of Sillitoe's Nottinghamshire dialect which lent so much conviction to the novel had been bound up in the pronunciation of swear-words, and much of this provincial flavour was therefore lost in the film.

A pivotal reference to an off-screen abortion scene in which the married woman successfully terminates an unwanted pregnancy resulting from her affair with Arthur was also lost; in the final film the pregnancy mysteriously subsides 'without' as the censor had insisted 'any outside interference'. But because Saltzman gave way on this and the 'excessive brutality' in the fight scenes, the Board conceded that the main differences now had to do with tone rather than actual cuts.

A sense of the minutiae in which the Board and the producers then immersed themselves can be gained from the fate of Arthur's phrase, 'I'd been knocking on wi' a married woman.' The BBFC reader observed, 'They want love making of a *Room At the Top* directness, and should be allowed to have it.' But he was in a quandary. 'I don't know how obscene this phrase is.' Trevelyan then suggested the alternative, 'mucking about wi' . . .' This was discarded though, and the more direct 'I'd been knocking about wi' a married woman' became the film's final word.

'They have not done all we asked,' the Board's examiner concluded, 'but they have done what we wanted most.' What neither Sillitoe nor the censor knew, however, was that the sheer presence of Albert Finney as Arthur Seaton would not only reinstate but enhance the shock value of the original script. 'With his wary eye, cocky banter, short neck and jutting chin,' noted the critic Alexander Walker, 'Finney possessed the naturalistic vitality of a working-class environment where survival bred swift responses and not too much care for other people's feelings. The Beatles were soon going to turn such an attitude into stock-in-trade. But its novelty was brand new in *Saturday Night and Sunday Morning*.' It is therefore not surprising that Arthur Seaton's uncensored maxim, 'Don't let the bastards grind you down,' would become an emblem of working-class solace and fraternity in the sixties.

The same hesitant motion of two steps forward and one step back governed the pre-censorship of other box-office successes of the British realism movement. 'We certainly had a tussle with the censor,' recalled the director John Schlesinger, 'at the script stage over *A Kind of Loving* [1962], particularly with the scene where the young man [Alan Bates] was shown trying to buy contraceptives from a female chemist's assistant, only to emerge with a bottle of Lucozade. There were other, less comic references to contraceptives in the script,' added the director, 'and the censor's advance view was that, if the mention of contraceptives was allowed here in an admittedly legitimate context, it weakened the position of opposing it in some other context where it might be exploited.' In the end, however, Schlesinger won the argument because he believed, 'we introduced the subject honestly and without sensation.'

More stringent treatment, however, was accorded to the writer-director of the other social-realist success of 1962, *The L-Shaped Room*. Among thirty-one changes imposed upon Bryan Forbes, every reference in his screenplay to 'breast rubbing or thigh rubbing' was struck out; nor would the censor allow 'copulatory dancing'. Also among many other lines the Board thought that it was 'most unlikely to pass "That's the sort of thing that makes me want to fornicate right in the middle of Westminster Abbey during a Royal Wedding."' Forbes was even forced to inform his leading actress, Leslie Caron, that he had been instructed to cover her nipples with Elastoplast during a nude scene.

John Schlesinger's assertion that, 'a greater leniency seems to exist if sex is treated lightly' had some basis in reality at this time. Trevelyan later regretted that the first Bond films, *Dr No* (1962) and in the next year *From Russia With Love* both glided past the BBFC with their facile but suggestive misogyny still intact. In contrast, the physical reality of love-making in *This Sporting Life* (1963) – its own sexism incidentally, is cleverly contextualised in the world of Rugby League – was treated by the Board as if it were a symptom of physical sickness. 'We would not want to see,' Trevelyan told the director, Lindsay Anderson, 'Frank [Richard Harris] moving his hands over Mrs Hammond [Rachel Roberts], bearing down on her and lying on top of her, and we would certainly not want what I imagine would be visually described by the phrase, "Their bodies are suddenly in spasm".'

To the sound of the Liverpool Beat and the appearance of the miniskirt, cultural commentators date the rise of the 'permissive tide' which swept over sixties Britain; yet at the BBFC John Trevelyan seemed to take on the persona of King Canute. For instance, the famous eating sequence in *Tom Jones* (1963), in which the food consumed by Albert Finney's Tom and Joyce Redman's Mrs Walters symbolises their increasing hunger for each other, was subjected to intense scrutiny by the Secretary. The director, Tony Richardson, held out for an 'A' certificate so that the film could be shown to an under-sixteen-year-old audience; but Trevelyan made that conditional upon the removal of the shot of Mrs Walters cradling an oyster in her tongue before it slides down her upturned throat. This kind of threat by the censor normally worked because, in spite of the success of other 'X' films, it was difficult to book the category into the major cinema circuits: ABC and Rank, as well as the censor, still disapproved of non-family films. The film proved to be an overwhelming success as an 'X', but Richardson had taken a gamble when he refused to make the cut.

One of the many apocryphal stories that the scriptwriter Herman Mankiewicz used to tell about Hollywood in the thirties was that the MGM mogul Louis B. Mayer employed an assistant solely for the task of sticking his

Alan Bates settles
down to married life
with his bride (June
Ritchie) and his
mother-in-law
(Thora Hurd) in John
Schlesinger's *A Kind
of Loving* (1962).

For this scene with
Tom Bell in *The L-
Shaped Room* (1962)
Leslie Caron had –
on the instructions
of the censor – to
have Elastoplast
covering her nipples.

Like many social-
realist films of the
sixties, *This Sporting
Life* (1963) – with
Richard Harris and
Rachel Roberts –
had to endure cuts
which reduced its
naturalism.

The famous gastro-duel between Albert Finney and Joyce Redman in *Tom Jones* (1963) was nearly impaired by censorship.

head out of a studio window to see which way the wind was blowing. In his thirteen years as Secretary of the Board, John Trevelyan never relinquished his place by a window. He never stopped 'gauging public opinion', but like everybody else he also never found out the exact spot where the so-called boundaries of decency lie. All he seemed to be sure of, during the many pre-lapsarian moments of film censorship in the sixties was that there were moral limits outside which the majority of the British people felt decidedly uncomfortable.

Thus in 1958, in a reference to the artistic milieu in which he socialised he declared, 'In our circles we can talk about homosexuality, but the general public is embarrassed by the subject, so until it becomes a subject that can be mentioned without offence it will be banned.' Admittedly the Secretary had to tread warily on this particular ground because up until then homosexuality in any form had been virtually invisible, not just in British cinemas, but on screens around the world.

Two weeks later, however, in a decision which probably marks the high point of moral courage in Britain's film censorship, the Secretary announced that he had changed his mind. From now on films with homosexual themes would not be banned provided the subject was treated 'responsibly'. 'Responsibly' was a codeword for 'consultation', which in turn meant that the producers of such films would be advised to submit their scripts to the BBFC. Within two years three British screenplays – *Serious Charge* (1959), *Oscar Wilde* (1960) and *The Trials of Oscar Wilde* (1960) – had been submitted; but none of them posed a censorship problem for the Board, either because sex between men was only referred to within the clinical confines of a courtroom or, in the case of *Serious Charge*, because homosexuality was merely employed as a device to further a plot concerning a vicar (Anthony Quayle) falsely accused of abusing a teenage boy.

In May 1960, though, the producer Michael Relph informed the Board that

155

a script entitled *Victim* was almost complete. Could the BBFC advise his production company, Allied Film Makers, whether or not they should proceed with the film?

The intention of *Victim*'s script was to validate the recommendations of the 1958 Wolfenden Report, which advocated the partial decriminalisation of male homosexuality. Janet Green's screenplay highlighted Wolfenden's statistic that 90 per cent of all blackmail cases in England at the time involved homosexuals; the need, therefore, for gay men to hide their sexuality, to remain silent and pass as 'normal' provided the engine for the story.

To a contemporary eye, Green's plot initially appears to be hopelessly contrived and compromised. Melville Farr (Dirk Bogarde), a handsome, upper-middle-class barrister married to a loving, patient woman is gay but he has always restrained his physical urges. Several years previously he had a relationship with a working-class youth called Boy Barret (Peter McEnery), but it was sexless as well as brief. When their platonic affair is threatened by exposure through blackmail, Barret selflessly commits suicide in an attempt to save Farr's marriage and career. Sacrificing that career and possibly his marriage, Farr then sets out to challenge the existing law against homosexuals and avenge Boy's death by bringing the blackmailers to justice.

Melville Farr, the crusading lawyer-hero of *Victim* (1961) on the receiving end of an early example of 'outing'.

The American film critic Vito Russo commented, in his lively survey of homosexuality in cinema, *The Celluloid Closet*, that *Victim* 'creates a gay hero with credentials enough to get into heaven, let alone society.' Yet Russo also attributes the role of gay militant to Farr. The middle-class barrister becomes 'a hero in the gay perspective because he is willing to lend a little dignity to his homosexual relationship by fighting to legitimize its existence.' In the middle of 1960, however, when the recommendations of the Wolfenden Report still had to wait another three years to be acted upon by Parliament, such advocacy struck the censor as precocious.

'I can't help feeling,' noted one of the BBFC's senior censors, Newton Branch, in an internal report, 'that the acceptance of homosexuality is too ready in this script. Examples of special pleading are . . . P.108 Melville tells Harris [a police inspector]: "We are behind the times. The law is the culprit. The blackmailer's charter offers unrivalled opportunities to any extortionist. That's what I've learnt." I feel,' affirmed Branch, 'that the majority of people in this country are not in agreement that the law is the culprit. I for one don't care a fig about what homosexuals do in private. But in ninety per cent of such men there is a curious recklessness in the choice of their companions and often in their public behaviour.'

More to the point, Branch's fellow censor Audrey Field, who had been elevated to this post from her previous position as a secretary at the Board during the war, expressed concern about Melville Farr's trawl through London's gay demi-monde to ensnare the blackmailer. 'It is very oppressive,' she warned, 'to be confronted with a world peopled with practically no one but "queers"; and there are precious few other characters in this synopsis. Great tact and discretion will be needed if this project is to come off, and the "queerness" must not be laid on with a trowel. The more we can see of the various characters going about their daily life in association with other people who are not queers and the less we need have of "covens" of queers lurking about in bars and clubs the better.'

Trevelyan then summarised these internal reports; but the Chief Censor tended to be less conservative as well as more flexible than his examiners. (This was probably the reason why Sir Sidney Harris had appointed him as Secretary in 1958 over the heads of two senior censors, both of whom had joined the BBFC before Trevelyan.) So he softened his examiners' criticisms and blunted their evident fear of 'otherness' when he wrote to Janet Green at the end of June 1960. Nevertheless, he was not afraid to dictate the content of her story.

'On the subject of homosexuality there is a division of public opinion,' the Secretary informed her, 'and, if this week's debate in the House of Commons is anything to go by, it appears that there is still a majority opposed to any compassionate treatment of it. In these circumstances a film-maker dealing with this subject is treading on dangerous ground and will have to proceed with caution . . .' The film, Trevelyan suggested, should somehow reflect this division, but then he inadvertently offered Green the opportunity to explore Farr's ambivalence from a homosexual perspective when he highlighted the emotional conflict at the heart of the movie: 'It would I think help to show that he [Melville Farr] has had a normal relationship with his wife but that his homosexual impulses, although always controlled, remain with him. In fact I would like this film to be essentially a story of this tragedy.'

Whereas Trevelyan demonstrated a politician's judgement concerning the adjustable level of tolerance to be accorded to every controversial issue in film, including 'homosexual practices', the film industry treated this subject with obvious distaste. Dirk Bogarde revealed in his autobiography *Snakes and Ladders* that when Allied Film Makers began casting for *Victim*, 'very few of the actors approached to play in it accepted; most flatly refused and every actress asked to play the wife turned it down without even reading the script, except for Sylvia Sims.' The cast and crew were sometimes treated 'as if we were attacking the Bible' and the lawyer who was responsible for drawing up pre-production contracts, told Bogarde that he wanted 'to wash his hands after reading the script'.

Once the film had been produced the censors returned to their ordained task in the cutting-room. Along with the senior examiners Trevelyan requested the removal of a number of scenes in which the film's statement that 'adolescent boys' knew whether or not they were homosexual was 'too sweeping' or where the case for gay sex was 'too plausibly put and not sufficiently countered – there was more from Mel about self-control in the last script we read.'

What the examiners, and to a lesser extent Trevelyan, were trying to do was to excise any dialogue which challenged gay stereotypes; in other words, all the scenes which showed that homosexuals are not confined to the upper class; that they are not solely defined by their sexual urges; and that those sexual desires are not simply chosen behaviour which can be altered at will – in short, any scenes that said homosexuality is an orientation, not an act. The Board did, however, win these battles. The producer, Michael Relph, fought hard to retain any dialogue which punctured gay myths but in order to gain an 'X' certificate he had to give up nearly all of those lines. However, there was one vital exception.

After the script had been written new dialogue was inserted into the film. In the original screenplay, *Victim* ends with Melville Farr admitting to his wife that homosexuality is wrong. Only religion can help a man of his persuasion and henceforth he will deny himself in the interests of society. In the new version the barrister confronts his wife, and then, two full decades before it became a convention in gay movies, the film shows a homosexual coming out of the closet. 'You were attracted to that boy "as a man would be to a girl"?' his wife screams. 'Because I wanted him,' he cries. 'Do you understand? Because I "wanted" him.' Of course, the BBFC demanded the immediate removal of these words. But while Relph was prepared to sacrifice other scenes he refused to back down in this instance – in spite of Trevelyan's threats to withdraw the agreed certificate. So a film finally came to the screen in which a homosexual was allowed to express his love.

Several years later the sudden inclusion of this revelatory scene was accounted for in an interview that Dirk Bogarde gave to Barry Norman in *The Times*. 'I wrote that scene in. I said, "there's no point in half measures. We either make a film about queers or we don't." I believe that picture made a lot of difference to people's lives.' The critic Vito Russo shared that belief: 'For gays in the closet . . . it was one of the first indications on film of the knowledge of shared oppression.'

For Trevelyan, however, there remained one last hitch before he could release *Victim*. 'I must submit this project at the appropriate time,' he

Melville Farr (Dirk Bogarde) in *Victim* (1961) is poised to tell his wife (Sylvia Sims) 'I wanted him' – thus becoming the first gay character to 'come out' in a film.

informed Relph, 'to Lord Morrison our new President. If there should be criticism it would reflect on him and, since he must take personal responsibility, it is only right that he should do it with full knowledge of the project.' Herein lay a problem. As the critic Alexander Walker later noted, the new President 'made no secret of the fact that he disapproved forcefully of homosexuality, of loose living among teenage youth, and of whores and tarts, and his disapproval was vented on films which featured these things.'

The successor to Sir Sidney Harris as President of the BBFC had risen through the ranks of the Labour Party by virtue of his organisational and tactical skills to become Home Secretary in Churchill's wartime coalition cabinet, and then Leader of the Commons in Attlee's post-war Labour government. A short, stocky figure with a quiff of ginger hair combed back from his forehead, Herbert Morrison, according to Trevelyan, took great pride in his humble background. The seventh son of a Brixton-based police constable who had a weakness for the bottle, the BBFC's President always bought his clothes and furniture from the Co-Op, and among his favourite phrases was, 'I'm working class and proud of it.'

A Secretary of the Board who talked about the differences between the effect of films on 'our circle' as distinct from the 'general public' was not very likely to form a tight bond with a man who had left school at fourteen to

159

become an errand boy, shop assistant and switchboard operator. The class conflict, again according to Trevelyan, was also exacerbated by Morrison's 'prejudice against anyone who had been to university'. The Secretary, who happened to possess various degrees, soon learned that Morrison held this belief because 'he had not been to a university himself and would have liked to have been.' In this sort of climate, maybe it was fortunate for the Secretary that Morrison rarely made public statements about films; one of the few that he did make, during his five years at the head of the Board, carries the general flavour of the new President's attitude towards contemporary cinema. It related to *The World of Suzie Wong* (1960): 'Now there was a very beautiful film. There was some prostitution in it, but it didn't protrude itself.'

As for *Victim*, the Secretary devised a simple means to bypass Morrison's homophobia. There is no evidence in the BBFC records that the President of the Board actually viewed the film; so it can be safely assumed that Trevelyan did not 'submit this project' to the head of the BBFC 'at the appropriate time', or, for that matter, at any other time. If, indeed, Morrison did insist that he view the film he would have seen very little of it, anyway. For the Labour politician had only possessed the use of one eye since his teens and the sight in that was now failing him.

In spite of the assertion by the Rank Organisation's Chairman John Davis in 1962 that he would not like to see 'his' company make a film on homosexuality, British film-makers did act on the example provided by *Victim* and produce gay-themed movies during the early part of the sixties. Tony Richardson's *A Taste of Honey* (1961), and Sidney J. Furie's *The Leather Boys* (1963) both met with the censor's requirement of responsibility and were duly passed by the Board.

The homosexual scenes in Joseph Losey's *The Servant* (1963), as played by Dirk Bogarde, the manipulative manservant, and James Fox as his ineffectual master, presented Trevelyan with a different kind of moral dilemma. Harold Pinter's tale of calculated corruption drags its idle, upper-class victim down into sexual as well as economic impotence and such calculated debauchery poses an unavoidable question for the censor. Does he take the amoral story at face value or extract a social message from the plot in which an upper-class parasite is overthrown? In this instance, Trevelyan was persuaded by Losey that the film was an uncomfortable but serious study of natural justice at work. (Losey also had fortune on his side when *The Servant* was passed uncut in France because the two members of the state censorship's Commission de Contrôle present at its screening both slept throughout the film.)

Trevelyan's opinion was largely formed because he had held pre-censorship discussions with Losey during the script stage of the film. And, to this arm of pre-censorship, the Secretary now added his immediate predecessor's use of aesthetics as a factor in post-censorship. In 1961 he told the press that 'when

Passed as uncut by the Board, Joseph Losey's sexually ambivalent *The Servant* (1963) – with James Fox and Dirk Bogarde – probably received such hands-off treatment because of the friendship between Losey and BBFC Secretary John Trevelyan.

you're dealing with people of quality and integrity and artists there is practically nothing they can't do because they do it for valid reasons . . .' Such aesthetic criteria made it possible for the Board to pass the current films of Bergman – *The Silence* (1963), Antonioni – *L'Eclisse* (1962), and Roman Polanski's first production – *Knife in the Water* (1961), as well as the work of many other prestigious directors during the sixties, with only minor cuts.

The disadvantage of a demarcation line that is circumscribed by a particular censor's sense of aesthetics inevitably lies in its dependency on that person's taste. When they fell outside this arbitrary bracket, productions from other respected directors did not prompt Trevelyan's reaction to Bergman's *The Silence* – 'this is a work of art.' After excising four minutes from Jean-Luc

161

Anna Karina with client in *Vivre Sa Vie* (1962). Body shots were cut for fear that Jean-Luc Godard's detached look at prostitution 'might provoke critical comment' outside London.

Godard's *Vivre Sa Vie* (1962), Trevelyan conceded: 'it was a very fine film, a cold clinical analysis of prostitution which was perfectly fair. But from our angle we have to be cautious about the admission of something [voyeurism] which will probably . . . be brought into other pictures of lesser quality.'

The censorship of mainstream movies which did not fit into an artistic pigeonhole, such as Sam Fuller's crime melodrama *Underworld USA* (1960) or Robert Aldrich's biblical epic *Sodom and Gomorrah* (1963), could exact an even greater toll from their footage. Structural scenes were lifted out of these two films, as they were from J. Lee Thompson's original version of *Cape Fear* in 1962 which received 161 'trims', as Trevelyan called them.

The Board also added insult to injury over this period when BBFC cuts reduced explicitness to innuendo, as they did in *The Chapman Report* (1962) where the trims made the film 'look much dirtier' according to one of its stars, Claire Bloom. Sometimes they muddied a scene's meaning. Although John

Julie Christie surveys a night-club sex act in *Darling* (1965) but the male half of the act had been removed by the censor.

Schlesinger submitted the script of *Darling* (1965) for pre-censorship in 1964, the completed film suffered from an odd interruption. The original version contained a sequence in which the characters played by Laurence Harvey and Julie Christie visit a Paris brothel and watch a couple making love, but the film is cut as the woman waits on a bed for the arrival of her male partner; thereby giving the impression that the spectators are about to witness an adroit, inventive solo performance.

Trevelyan's dependency on pre-censorship also courted mishaps; for this pre-production policy was determined by the availability of scripts for BBFC supervision. Because the British market was relatively unimportant, many American and European directors did not submit screenplays to the BBFC during the sixties; with the result that if the Board banned a film it was usually a foreign production. In addition to this hurdle, mainstream foreign films could also fall foul of the Secretary's increasing inclination to gauge public opinion, one of its effects being that he preferred to reject a picture outright rather than be attacked in the press for cutting it too severely.

Such a consideration undoubtedly applied to Paramount's *Lady in a Cage* (1965). Trevelyan would have known that the banning of this plodding horror movie, in which a crippled Olivia de Havilland is discovered trapped in a lift by three psychopaths and then tormented to the point of dementia, was unlikely to be attacked in the press. But because the film does possess such a

163

threadbare plot, and also because its violence is on-going rather than accumulative, multiple cuts would have presented technical difficulties for the censor. The fear of British juveniles attacking defenceless people, though, rather than shortcomings in the censor's skill, was the official explanation given for the rejection of *Lady in a Cage* in the summer of 1965.

The other two foreign films which were refused at this time were banned for reasons that were more unconventional, but equally irrational. Both came from the rumbustious American director Sam Fuller, the first being set in a location that had always been regarded as a no-go area by the BBFC – the mental hospital. The various reasons cited by the Board for its refusal to grant a certificate to *Shock Corridor* in 1963 are confusing as well as contradictory. First of all the Board said that its depiction of conditions in an American mental asylum bore no comparison with those in hospitals within Britain. But this could equally apply to gangster films, Westerns or, for that matter, musicals. Secondly, the film could frighten cinema-goers who had relatives in mental institutions. This had been the rationale behind the BBFC's rather extensive cutting of the German Expressionist film *The Cabinet of Dr Caligari* back in 1928, and even then it appeared to be a catch-all excuse.

The last three reasons given by the Board did at least concern themselves with the film's plot: it was irresponsible to suggest that a sane person could gain admission to a mental hospital by pretending to be insane (maybe the Board thought that this would be imitated); or to suggest that residence in a mental hospital could cause insanity; finally, it was considered that the film might have 'bad, possibly dangerous, effects' on film-goers who were susceptible to mental disturbance. But the charge of an irresponsible story device is merely an attack on Fuller's ingeniousness and the last two clauses cancel each other out because, presumably, if a film can cause insanity then a mental hospital must have the same capability.

The following year, Fuller made *The Naked Kiss* which opens with the now-famous scene of a bald prostitute (Constance Towers) knocking out her pimp. The Board refused the film with the single comment, 'The employment of the girl [Towers] in a home for spastic children was not an adequate compensation for the rest of the material in this film.'

A revealing look at small-town American morals, *The Naked Kiss* rivets the viewer from the first frame of Towers stalking towards the camera, but Trevelyan ignored Fuller's command of his 'material', or the necessity of sensationalism to his style; instead he seized upon the American censor's compensation clause, in which wrongs have to be righted, and he even attacked the MPPA, in his memoir *What the Censor Saw*, for ignoring their own clause when they granted Fuller's film a Code Seal in 1964.

In the case of *The Naked Kiss*, Trevelyan did not want to be caught out on a limb as the sole censor in Britain to ban a film – a precarious position that the

Secretary would try to avoid in the future through various manoeuvres. The overriding reason though for the banning of *Shock Corridor* the year before can be found once again in pre-censorship.

Trevelyan's usual procedure with a film that involved insanity was to call in the services of a psychiatrist to scour the script for any possible cause of psychiatric trauma. For example, in the screenplay of Roman Polanski's *Repulsion* (1965) the BBFC's consultant Dr Stephen Black expressed 'concern about the fantasy rape scenes', in which Carol (Catherine Deneuve) has nightmares after hearing her sister make love in the next room. (Incidentally, this was the first orgasm to be heard in a British film.) In turn, Polanski was worried that his plot would be irredeemably diluted by medical advice, so he leaked the information to the *Sunday Telegraph* that Trevelyan was consulting a psychiatrist about *Repulsion*. That prompted the admonition: 'I would prefer all our negotiations to be kept confidential . . . As I have already made clear to

Constance Towers discovers that the private investigator-hero (Brock Peters) of *Shock Corridor* is going mad. Sam Fuller's film was banned in 1963 for suggesting that residency in a mental hospital could induce insanity.

you, my comments are entirely personal comments.' Later on, though, when Trevelyan was called upon to explain why he had not cut *Repulsion*, the unequivocal response was 'We kept our eyes on it during production. I like Roman.'

Yet as well as being unable to claim an acquaintanceship with Trevelyan through the aid of pre-censorship discussions, Sam Fuller and his film fell through a fault line which distinguishes censorship in whatever form it appears: namely that it is stuck in time, that it cannot tell today's cheap exploitation movie from tomorrow's classic. *Shock Corridor* and *The Naked Kiss* were both dismissed at the time by the critics as 'the overripe leftovers of a brutal imagination'; but they are now acknowledged as 'distinguished examples of the baroque B-picture' from 'one of the most harsh artistic presences in cinema'. For a censor like Trevelyan, who laid great store by critical opinion, Fuller therefore became an easy target for exclusion. For Fuller, the critical and censorial reception of *Shock Corridor* and *The Naked Kiss* nearly ended his career. Except for *Shark Kill* in 1970, which he disowns, Sam Fuller did not direct again until he made *The Big Red One* in 1980.

Carol (Catherine Deneuve) listens to her sister making love in *Repulsion* (1965) and then hears the first orgasm in British cinema.

Neither of these mid-sixties films was consigned to darkness, however, as both immediately gained an 'X' certificate from the GLC. Now it seemed that what one censor could take away, another one in the form of a local authority could give back; but Britain's local authorities had not expressed an interest in film censorship for nearly forty years. What had woken the councils from their long slumber? And even more to the point, who was responsible for prodding this 470-headed demon awake? The answer to both questions is John Trevelyan.

What had happened was that the Board was beginning to pay a price for its Secretary's gauging of public opinion. And this ironic situation had come about in turn because of Trevelyan's adoption of a devious strategy to unban certain controversial films, such as Joseph Strick's *The Balcony* in 1963, which in this case the Secretary personally admired, but which he felt the Board had to refuse because of potential public reaction. For, paradoxically, Trevelyan had to avoid praise almost as much as censure. 'As soon as we are praised anywhere in the press for our intelligence in letting through something uncut,' he pointed out, 'some local authority somewhere thinks "Aha, so they're passing dirty films now, so we'll have to look at that, and then the harm is done."' The trick that Trevelyan had to accomplish was to make the local authorities think that the Board was reluctant to pass a particular film which, in reality, it wanted to pass.

The Secretary achieved this seemingly contradictory aim, first of all by suggesting to the distributors of these films that they apply to the Greater London Council for a licence enabling them to show a particular film in London. Once the licence had been issued, Trevelyan would wait for the critics' opinion and if they were generally favourable he would then grant the film a BBFC certificate. With the knowledge that public opinion now supported him and that he had kept his part of the bargain, he would then tell the distributor that his film – usually 'X' rated – could now be shown outside London.

But the down side of this Machiavellian manoeuvre was its delegation of censorship to local authorities; and they seized the bit between their teeth. For the last twenty-five years there had been no central authority in the form of the Home Office twisting their arms through government memos to enforce censorship uniformity. Now they had been given a lead by Britain's chief film censor. They had been sanctioned to censor and they therefore had a duty to demonstrate their liberality, or their sense of propriety, to their cinema-going constituents. As he was soon to discover, Trevelyan had unknowingly revived the Board's most capable opponent.

For the remainder of the decade the local authorities proceeded to carry out their moral imperative; they banned films which the Board passed, and unbanned films which the Board refused. Inconsistency became the only reliable guide to censorship; and amidst all the differences in gradation and new opportunities for the curious cinema-goer the terrain where the struggle between Britain's film censors would be at its most intense was shaped in the celluloid image of man's most taboo-ridden subject, himself.

LETTING IT ALL HANG OUT:
the sexual breakthrough

11 ✂

It was the appearance of nudity on the screen that had first aroused the local authorities from their somnolence. Sponsored by the American Sunbathing Association, *The Garden of Eden* had appeared before the Board's examiners in January 1955. The film featured the rejuvenation of a cranky middle-aged man through the recuperative powers of naturism, and needless to say the cinematic debut of white women's naked breasts (in the fifties the BBFC permitted black women to be seen nude in documentaries) proved too much for the Board. They rejected it 'entirely' in spite of one examiner's protest that 'I can hardly believe that the nude males in back view would arouse any female.' Significantly, amongst the examiners proposing that *The Garden of Eden* could be sexually stimulating for 'the man in the street' was the BBFC's new part-time censor, John Trevelyan.

Within two years, however, *The Garden of Eden* was showing in a London cinema because the LCC had granted the film a certificate. The Board's current Secretary, Arthur Watkins, plaintively asked, 'Where are we to draw the line?' Two years later, in 1958, when he succeeded to Watkins's job, Trevelyan supplied the answer: henceforth breasts and buttocks, but not genitalia, would be accepted by the Board 'provided that the setting was recognisable as a nudist camp or nature reserve'.

The BBFC's founding rule of 'no nudity' had finally been abandoned. But then the new Secretary could hardly have done otherwise; while the Board had been making its mind up over *The Garden of Eden*, 300 of the local authorities had followed the LCC's lead, many of them granting the first nudist picture a 'U' certificate.

The BBFC and Trevelyan's new-found toleration of the nude was also aided by the passing of the 1959 Obscene Publications Act in which a defence could be mounted on the grounds of published material being 'in the interests of science, literature, art or learning, or of other objects of general concern'. Presumably Trevelyan took notice of the Act because he affixed 'A' certificates to such forthcoming 'nudies' as Michael Winner's *Some Like It Cool* (1960), *Around the World with Nothing On* (1959) and the first British example of the genre, *Nudist Paradise*, which was shot in the summer of 1959 at the Duke of Bedford's stately home, Woburn Abbey.

Opposite Then as now, unconventional screen sex was rejected by the BBFC during the sixties, unless the film-maker had an international reputation. Predictably, the BBFC did not know of the French intellectual writer Alain Robbe-Grillet in 1967 so his film of that year *Trans-Europe Express* was duly banned.

169

Making a splash. *Garden of Eden* (1954), the first nudist picture to arrive on British shores, was greeted with averted eyes by the BBFC.

In his history of British sex films, *Doing Rude Things*, David McGillivray recounts that Nat Miller, the reticent producer of *Nudist Paradise* insisted to him that 'There were no full . . . er . . . frontals or anything like that at all' in his picture. In spite of this, the actresses in this 'trailblazer' had to observe the contemporary niceties imposed on nudist pictures by shaving their pubic hair.

But if, according to Trevelyan, 'British film-makers followed my advice, and gave us no problems', this was not the case with imported sex films which caused repeated headaches for the Board. The released print of the German exposé, *Girl of Shame* (1959), whose loose-living heroine originally appeared naked in every reel, was thirteen minutes shorter than the version which was originally submitted to the BBFC, and *La Plume de Ma Tante* (1960), a comedy revue by Robert Dhéry, was offered a certificate only if all its non-marmoreal, mobile stage nudity was cut, an adjustment which would have reduced it to about twenty minutes.

At the same time, sex films in America were starting to escape from the confines of the naturist camp into nude comedy. Although these so-called 'farcical' nudies only displayed rare, brief glimpses of actual flesh, they also attracted the ire of the BBFC. Thus *Promises, Promises* (1963) starring Jayne Mansfield – 'I have fine, healthy, normal girlish impulses and I always make sure to obey them' – and a year later the Mamie Van Doren vehicle *Three Nuts in Search of a Bolt* both came up against the Board's 'firm line'.

Their prototype, the first skinflick, *The Immoral Mr Teas* had been shot in

Starting at the
bottom. The film-
maker Michael
Winner began his
career directing the
'nudie' *Some Like It
Cool* in 1960.

four days during 1959 at a cost of $24,000 by the 'King of the Nudies', Russ
Meyer. Film critic Roger Ebert's fanciful plot of a Hollywood messenger boy
who has hallucinations of nudity every time his job brings him into contact
with a beautiful woman would become a staple of sex films. Meyer himself
estimated that there were about 150 imitations of his $2 million grossing
'epoch-making' movie in circulation by 1963. The original, however, did not
get beyond the BBFC and to the disappointment of nudie aficionados Russ
Meyer's debut has never had a British release.

One of the imitations was *Career Girl* (1959), a British sex melodrama
which in spite of being duly banned by the BBFC gained a certificate from
numerous councils. Once again, the Board had been outflanked, as it would be
the following year by the most famous British nudie of them all, *Naked As
Nature Intended*. This film production started out as a mere glimmer in the
imagination of a pin-up photographer called Harrison Marks. The name has
since become synonymous with Soho smut, but Marks claims he learned his
(film) trade at the knee of one of the creators of British cinema, Cecil
Hepworth – who ironically, was largely responsible in 1912 for setting up the
BBFC – when the elderly pioneer 'used to bugger about on a Moviola' at
Elstree Studios.

In any event, according to David McGillivray, before shooting began on
Nature, Marks went to see John Trevelyan at the Board's offices in Soho
Square: 'I told Trevelyan what I wanted to do. He said, "No, no, no, no, no."

171

I said, "It's going to be a genuine film about British naturism. I'm going to be waving the banner for nudists."'

'You were lying?' asked McGillivray.

'Well, of course I was. I didn't have a script. I only had an idea. All I knew was that I wanted to put nudes on the screen.'

Trevelyan must have accepted this bare synopsis because Marks went ahead with the film, which was shot at the Spielplatz Sun Club, to meet the BBFC's ruling on nudie location. Starring Pamela Green, Marks's favourite model, *Naked As Nature Intended* shows bikini-clad girls exploring a succession of tourist traps including Stonehenge and the Minack open-air theatre in Porthcurno; the film's notoriety now seems incongruous, since only in the last twenty seconds does Pamela take the plunge and reveal all.

In his memoirs, Trevelyan does not recall his meeting with Marks; instead he remembers that: 'A well known commercial photographer of nudes, Harrison Marks, made a film called *Naked As Nature Intended* which consisted of a series of comedy sketches with "pin-up" nudity. We decided not to pass this film . . .' Once again the 'doffing' had strayed outside the nudie remit because Pamela and the girls had not 'put up the pretence of advocating naturism'. But once again a sex film was passed by the LCC, making the Board look ignorant of what the public would now accept.

The British nudie struggled on for another two or three years until it gave way to the 'shocking but true' social documentary genre in such exposés as *West End Jungle* (1961), which was banned in spite of the Reverend Donald Soper's support – 'It should be generally released' – or *London in the Raw* (1964), which featured a hair transplant operation as well as a more crowd-pleasing striptease act. But, as their own directors conceded, the censor-appeasing morality within these films reduced audiences to near-catatonia. 'We had these dreadful advisory psychiatrists,' recalls the exploitation-film director Stanley Long, 'explaining the social behaviour patterns and all that crap, which no one was interested in in the slightest. I remember taking a psychiatrist up to see John Trevelyan and trying to convince him that the purpose of making *The Wife Swappers* (1969) was not to make money, but to try and improve society. It was a charade.'

Neither was Trevelyan impressed. He continued to snip away at sex films, refusing to accept the premise that the cinema should cater to the 'frustrated sexuality of urbanised men'. The sex films that the Board refused to certificate were usually accepted by one or more of the local authorities. The newly established Greater London Council, in particular, passed BBFC-banned nudies as well as other controversial films due to a crucial decision in October 1966 to change its licensing conditions for cinemas. The council set aside the arbitrary criterion of 'offensive to public feeling' in favour of a revised rule which forbade the exhibition of any film which, 'if taken as a whole' would 'tend to deprave and corrupt persons who are likely to see it'.

By restricting censorship in this way to material already forbidden by common law, the GLC had in effect provided film exhibitors and distributors with an appeals panel with which to challenge BBFC decisions. The historian of film law Dr Neville Hunnings wrote at the time: 'On the surface the general working of the censorship is not altered . . . But in practice the Board is likely to amend its approach gradually under pain of seeing itself overruled by the Council if it does not restrict itself fairly carefully to the Council's new criteria.'

The canny, ever-cautious Secretary of the Board took note of the GLC's tolerant attitude towards sexuality on film and followed suit with the granting of certificates to various skinflicks; but by then it was too late for Britain's nudie producers. Better-financed mainstream film companies such as Hammer had stepped into the exploitation market in the meantime, and stolen the patronage of the 'frustrated urban male' with barely disguised sexploitation like *The Vampire Lovers* (1970) and its even more prurient sequel, *Lust for a Vampire* (1970).

Paradoxically, the censorship of celluloid sex would be loosened by other, more respectable visitors to Trevelyan than Harrison Marks or Stanley Long. These were the reputable directors of artistic films. But by this time the structure of the BBFC itself had changed to suit the more liberal and intellectually questioning climate.

Fortunately for the BBFC, it was not possible for Herbert Morrison, the deeply conservative, aggressively working-class President of the Board, to have a catastrophic influence upon British film censorship for the first half of the 1960s. A vigorously anti-intellectual stance, together with the lack of sight in one eye, had resulted in the adjustment of his BBFC role at the beginning of the decade to that of 'consultant' as opposed to the Secretary's overall 'executive' responsibility for censorship. Nevertheless, during the last five years of his presidency the Labour peer did his best to resist his enforced relegation.

Clement Attlee had complained in 1947 that 'Herbert cannot distinguish between big things and little things,' and indeed, this lack of balance coloured Morrison's BBFC presidency. The ex-politician squandered his argumentative skills on irrelevant details, such as his futile attempt to ban *West Side Story* (1961) on account of its gang-fight scenes – which had been shot as a modern ballet with choreography by Jerome Robbins. Alternatively, he disingenuously pretended not to understand the crucial importance of pre-censoring scripts so that films could be quietly passed without public rows in the press detailing the Board's 'savagery'.

Morrison's death in 1965 must therefore have provoked mixed feelings in John Trevelyan. Film censorship during this period was in flux; and its loyalty to the status quo was questioned almost every time a film can revealed its contents to the Board's examiners. The BBFC, in consequence, needed a President whose morality had been formed more recently than the Edwardian era. What was required was an articulate public figure who agreed with the Secretary's constant realignment of BBFC decisions, and the film industry's choice for this demanding post was David Harlech.

Lord Harlech, formerly David Orsmby-Gore, had followed his father's footsteps into politics, Parliament and on to the government front bench. He left the Commons in 1961 to become British ambassador in Washington where he rose to prominence as a confidant of President Kennedy in the White House 'Camelot' court. His politics were generally centralist, those of the Tory 'one nation' school, and, according to the politician Roy Jenkins, in the psyche of this egalitarian aristocrat a large part 'was played by pleasure, tempered by high public spirit, good judgement and unselfish instincts'.

Though clearly part of the establishment, Harlech also held many of the anti-authoritarian views that had become common currency during the 1960s. At his weekend home in North Wales he would examine films with his teenage children and wait for their opinions before he committed his own to paper. At the BBFC, where at forty-seven he was the youngest figure on the Board, the new President's patrician charm elicited 'the highest regard'; although his radical views on film content would prove to be an irritant to the older, more recalcitrant examiners.

By the time Harlech had assumed the Presidency, however, Trevelyan had updated his public image and was no longer making references to 'offending and disgusting' films. On the contrary, in 1964, the Secretary stated that, 'The British Board of Film Censors cannot assume responsibility for the guardianship of morality. It cannot refuse for exhibition to adults, films that show behaviour which contravenes the accepted moral code, and it does not demand that "the wicked" should always be punished. It cannot legitimately refuse to pass films which criticize "the Establishment" and films which express minority opinions.'

In effect, if not in word, the Secretary and the new President now formed a progressive front against the rest of the Board in their quest for the relaxation of film censorship; and if it can be said about such an institution as film censorship, the BBFC enjoyed a golden age under this duopoly.

Yet the liberal advance in censorship, particularly with regard to sexual material, can also be attributed to the contemporary influence on the Board of film critics: if Trevelyan banned an exploitation film it might be passed by a more easy-going local authority, but if he, a supposed friend of the cinema, 'the seventh art', so much as cut a frame from a distinguished director's oeuvre he would be lambasted where it was most painful – in the press. BBFC reports continually show that Trevelyan, along with his fellow examiners, had become surprisingly thin-skinned where news coverage of their activities was con-

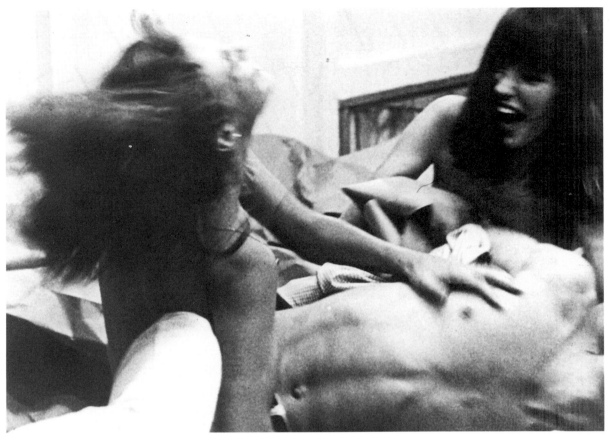

cerned. They seemed to have been wracked by a recurring nightmare in which all fingers point in their direction and a collective cry rises up of: 'Philistine!'

Whether that fear was justified or not, an aesthetic slide rule would now be applied by the Board in its treatment of the notorious ground-breaking sexual scenes from late sixties cinema. The first famed example, from a BBFC report dated 13 January 1967, and signed N. K. B. (Newton Branch) A. O. F. (Audrey Field), examined Michelangelo Antonioni's distant, elegiac fable of swinging London, *Blow-Up*.

'We were disappointed by this extremely uneven film. A. O. F. feels, because of the general nature of this particular piece, we would be justified in passing it uncut. There is the consideration of a certain hullabaloo if we do make cuts also.' Then with grinding inevitability the examiners note that their President, who had viewed the film alongside them, 'was a little dubious about the scene in reel 5, in which David Hemmings frolics with two girls who end up nude. He thought this might be shortened by cutting to a point before the 2nd girl is de-leotarded. I am inclined to agree. There is nothing *very* erotic about the incident. But we have not previously had a man behaving this [way] with either one or two naked women. The fact that he has made love to them both

Group sex is still frowned upon by the BBFC, and in 1967 the Board wanted to remove this scene from *Blow-Up* (1966) in which David Hemmings is the laughing torso in the throes of frolicking with Jane Birkin and Gillian Hills.

175

Luis Buñuel's classic account of the sexual degradation of a bored housewife (Catherine Deneuve) in *Belle de Jour* (1967) was sufficiently artistic to win the approval of the BBFC.

is brought out later, when we see him looking exhausted "afterwards" and by his remark that he cannot take photos of them because "he is too whacked".'

Thus were the minutiae of sexual precedent delved into; but Trevelyan had already been forewarned in a frank letter from John Davis, the new Chairman of the Cinematograph Exhibitors Association and current Chairman of the Rank Organisation, to be on his guard with this particular film. 'As you probably know,' Davis wrote, 'the films of Antonioni are always of interest to highbrow critics, and any cut that we ask for in such films is liable to produce criticism of the Board from these sources.' The film potentate then explained exactly why the critics must not be offended: 'At the present time the anti-censorship pressures have increased, and we have to be particularly careful not to lay ourselves open to attacks on points of censorship that we cannot fully defend.'

In short, choose your battleground. But by 1967, this was a lesson that Trevelyan could recite in his sleep. That year he had banned two foreign films: Alain Robbe-Grillet's *Trans-Europe Express*, because of its sexual sadism, and Roger Corman's *The Wild Angels* for its gang violence. Neither director could claim to be well known in Britain at the time and the exclusion of their pictures therefore did not cause too much of a 'hullabaloo'. On the other hand, the reputations of the Spanish film-maker Luis Buñuel and the American director Arthur Penn gave the censor pause for thought; and the inconvenient fact that their respective films of 1967, *Belle de Jour* and *Bonnie and Clyde*, also contained sexual sadism and gang violence did not hinder their journey through customs at the BBFC.

Trevelyan's ubiquitous use of selective judgement also influenced his attitude towards the next sexual precedent to be set by the cinema: pubic hair. A back view of the female body having been provided by *Blow-Up*, the censor, in the meantime, nervously awaited the cinematic arrival of the notorious 'full-frontal'. It was duly presented in a Swedish picture called *Hugs and Kisses* (1968), in which the film's heroine undresses in front of a mirror, wanders around the room and looks at her reflection. This is then repeatedly intercut to shots of her oblivious husband chatting with a friend in the next room. The critic Philip French says that the sequence visually reflects the woman's boredom and lack of interest in her disintegrating marriage: nevertheless, Trevelyan insisted upon its removal, citing the scene's use of what he called 'flash frames'. But the film's distributor called a press conference to protest against the Board's cut. Here, Trevelyan explained that he had demanded the removal of the scene because the Obscenity Law was so vague; if it remained, he said, charges might be preferred against the film's distributors, exhibitors and even the Board itself.

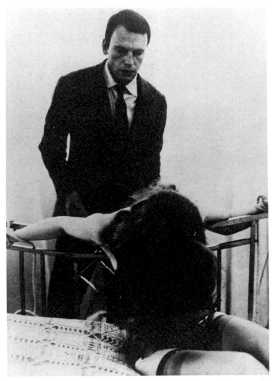

A more naturalistic and less stylised approach to female sexual degradation in Alain Robbe-Grillet's *Trans-Europe Express* (1967) (with Jean-Louis Trintignant and Marie-France Pisier) received a rejection.

Meanwhile, Lindsay Anderson's passionate attack in *If* (1968) upon the British establishment and their breeding grounds, the public schools, was winding its way through BBFC reports, letters and replies. And there amongst the scenes singled out for exception was, ' . . . the front-view shot of Mrs Kemp [the housemaster's wife] walking naked down the corridor'; but 'the subsequent back view shots of her in the dormitory would probably pass.' Lindsay Anderson, though, was wise in the ways of censorship. 'Mrs Kemp,' he wrote to Trevelyan, 'in the dormitory corridor, I am hoping will be so obviously aesthetic as to avoid any suggestion of offence. It reveals no more, after all, than any member of the public can see at the National Gallery free of charge.'

As Trevelyan himself said four years earlier about putting the knife to the films of the great Swedish master Ingmar Bergman: 'It's the equivalent of taking a first-rate painting, and saying "cut out three square inches on the right hand side, four and a half inches down." I don't think one should do that.' So Mrs Kemp was allowed to walk down the dormitory corridor into film censorship history. The lady in *Hugs and Kisses* had to wait awhile for her

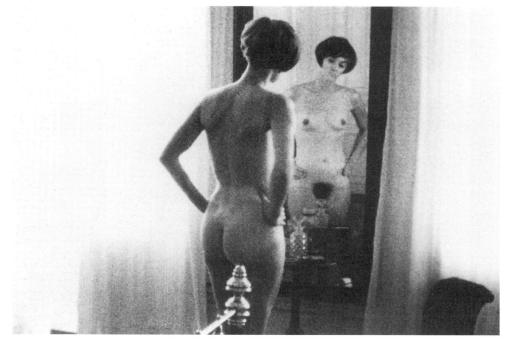

1968 – the first female full frontal. Originally cut from Jonas Cornell's *Hugs and Kisses*, but then reinstated due to popular demand, this view of Agneta Ekmanner's genitals started a pubic war.

restoration; not for long, however, because in the meantime Trevelyan had been called upon to explain the Board's anomalous attitude towards her full frontal.

Putting aside for one moment any expectation of being charged under the Obscene Publications Act, the Secretary of the BBFC declared, 'When my Board asked for cuts in the nude scene in the Swedish film *Hugs and Kisses* we were really testing public opinion. There was no massive outcry one way or another, and some local authorities even passed the film with the pubic hair left in. So we decided to leave the film *If* intact in this respect.' Public opinion having been assuaged, the Swedish heroine's pubic hair was untrimmed.

Now, of course, it was the turn of men to present their own full frontal. For film censors, however, male genitalia are the most taboo-ridden area of human anatomy. Probably this is because of the masculine monopoly of the BBFC – not to mention the establishment at large – and the notorious heterosexual male aversion to the exposure and resultant demystification of the male crotch. Even today, in sex education video tapes such as 'Erection' which is part of the Dutch series, *Sex: A Lifelong Pleasure* (1992), the male performer's penis always appears only to be slightly tumescent due to the current BBFC rule forbidding total and incontrovertible erection.

In 1969, the slightest inclination on the part of a naked actor to turn towards the camera initiated a BBFC blackout. Two years before, Trevelyan had told Lindsay Anderson he would pass *If*, 'provided that you trim the scene in the shower baths in such a way as to avoid clear shots of the boy's genitals.

The housemaster's
wife walks along a
school corridor in
Lindsay Anderson's
If (1968). By claiming
an aesthetic
motivation, the
director snatched
this shot back from
the censor.

If you will send me a letter assuring me that this has been done I will issue an
'X' certificate for this film.' Having won the more easily attainable retention of
Mrs Kemp in frontal nudity, Anderson, in this instance, agreed to the cut.

Like Lindsay Anderson, the American producer Larry Kramer was also
adept at nudging the censor past a sexual milestone. In his negotiations with
Trevelyan over the censorship of Ken Russell's *Women in Love* (1969),
Kramer demonstrated the emollient skills of a diplomat. First, he established
the literary credentials of his subject: 'I am sure you will appreciate,' he wrote
to Trevelyan, 'what an ambitious film this is, and what an extraordinary novel
we are tackling. [Dr F. R.] Leavis at Cambridge considers it [D. H.] Lawrence's
major work and one of the greatest novels of the twentieth century. We have
been extraordinarily faithful in our adaptation, and nothing appears in the
script which does not come from the novel.' Then, after having given a brief
résumé of the suitability of Ken Russell as the film's director, he ended his
appropriately unctuous letter with a direct appeal to Trevelyan as a fellow
artist. 'We feel that we are embarking on an extraordinary creative experience,
which we would like to have you share with us.'

Trevelyan subsequently expressed to Kramer his admiration for 'a brilliant
film', yet at the time the Secretary was being asked to pass a sequence in which
Alan Bates and Oliver Reed strip naked and wrestle with each other in the firelight. (Russell persuaded the two actors to perform the scene with the help of a
bottle and a half of vodka.) The incident was faithful to the novel but, from
Trevelyan's vantage point, such an unabashed sequence demanded the utmost

vigilance. The year before he had passed the fleeting appearance of Terence Stamp's penis in Pasolini's *Theorem* (1968) but few people noticed it, so he suggested to Russell that, 'While we are prepared to accept the wrestling scene, we would like you to remove if possible full-length shots in which genitals are clearly visible . . .The main trouble lies in shots where the two boys are standing still.'

Even after these shots had been removed Trevelyan was still not satisfied. The print of the film that he had seen showed the sequence as if illuminated by the sun, not the dim flames of the fire. He, along with the other examiners, was aghast at what he saw. The scene was then darkened to replicate firelight, which the Secretary found 'helpful'. He was still worried, however, by a full-length shot of Gerald (Oliver Reed) showing his genitals. Russell promised to darken this shot as well and when Trevelyan disapproved yet again the director claimed that he could do no more 'owing to the fact that the material available in the cutting rooms was not as "helpful as he thought it would be".'

Such is the public phobia surrounding any penile representation that Trevelyan probably felt that the Board could only pass a film that implied but did not actually show what makes reproduction possible for the human species. The BBFC file on *Women in Love* suggests that he was prepared to continue the fight over Gerald's genital chiaroscuro but was persuaded by David Harlech to accept what the Board had already won in deletions from other sexual scenes. Before he put the file to bed he noted in his last memo that the President 'appreciated the technical problems, and felt that there was nothing more that we could do. After careful consideration he had decided that the quality and integrity of the film justified these rather extreme scenes, and that it would be of help to us if we were criticised as Ken Russell had a big reputation in this country as a director of artistic films, especially for television. In the circumstances,' Harlech had 'decided that we should accept the modifications they had made and not ask for more.'

To the victor, then, of this landmark in film censorship the last word. At the time of *Women in Love*'s release Ken Russell summed up his attitude to nudity in the apposite remark: 'the full nude has a dignity that half a body does not have.'

The film historian James Robertson has argued that in the late sixties Harlech and Trevelyan 'pressed too far and too fast ahead of influential public opinion.' But influential public opinion also demanded that the BBFC did press ahead. As John Davis pointed out to Trevelyan at the time of *Blow-Up*'s censorship in 1967, a social consensus in favour of censorship no longer existed. Indeed, institutional and state authority was under attack from writers, musicians and artists as well as from playwrights – whose own liability to censorship had been abolished in 1968. The administrator of Britain's film censorship therefore had to enforce a means of cultural control in the midst of a social revolution, one of whose main rallying cries was freedom of speech.

The effect of this cultural explosion can be seen not only in the more radical films of the period but also in the way those films circumvented censorship. For instance, in 1967 the Board banned Dusan Makavejev's *The Switchboard Operator* because it included a glimpse of pubic hair. (The distributor did not help his own cause by appending a note to the BBFC which stated, 'I am sending you a film with a few tits in it. I don't think much of it but I can sell it to the sex theatres.') At the time the Board dismissed Makavejev's Reichian call for sexual freedom as a confusing film by an unknown Yugoslav director who possessed no critical pedigree; so it could be safely assumed that no one would notice the film's disappearance.

But Derek Hill, the film critic and nemesis of the BBFC in the sixties, chose this moment to intervene, reminding the Board that they had just passed a similar scene in Antonioni's censor-proof *Blow-Up*. Disgusted by the Board's subsequent lack of response, Hill established the 'Forbidden Film Festival' which for the next seven years exhibited banned and uncut films first at the ICA and then at the New Cinema Club in London's Notting Hill. This in turn inspired companies like Gala and Compton to set up their own film clubs to show uncertificated films; although the more esoteric examples of the banned genre were soon supplanted in these clubs by skinflicks or reissued under more alluring titles, as in the case of *The Switchboard Operator* which became *Love Dossier*.

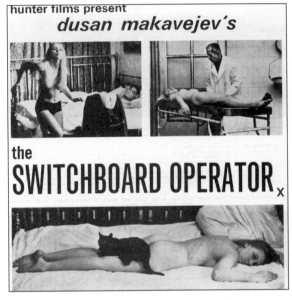

By emphasising sex and not the critical reputation of the director, the British distributor of Dusan Makavejev's *The Switchboard Operator* (1966) ruined the film's chances for release.

In an attack upon the use of the Board by producers and distributors to nudge renegade film-makers into conformity, Derek Hill described the BBFC of the sixties as 'a sort of protection racket run by the film industry for the film industry'. By establishing the Forbidden Film Festival, Hill helped to expose this form of trouble-shooting. Because of him, film-goers could see for the first time exactly what the Board and the film industry had agreed to censor. The all-important mystery of censorship, the arcane priesthood in which the censor envelops himself, where it is implied but never stated that only he is able to withstand what would shrivel the eyes of others, would be put to its ultimate test – the judgement of the public.

The BBFC's own judgement was also being increasingly questioned in the sixties by another force in film just as potent as the newspaper critics. Film-makers no longer backed away from the BBFC nodding their heads in silent

181

approval as they tucked their traumatised celluloid under a protective arm; the censor's schoolmasterly salve of 'this hurts me more than you' no longer recompensed directors excluded from the cinema. When, in 1967, the BBFC refused to give a certificate to Joseph Strick's screen version of James Joyce's novel *Ulysses* unless substantial cuts were made, the American director not only refused to alter his film: he publicly called Trevelyan 'your friendly neighbourhood film mortician'.

Cynics might suggest, not without justification, that Strick would not have made this remark if his portentous film could have been stopped dead in its tracks by the BBFC. But of course Strick now had another means of appeal besides Derek Hill's cinema in Notting Hill.

Twenty-six local authorities granted the complete version of *Ulysses* an 'X' certificate in the summer of 1967. (This included the celebrated Molly Bloom soliloquy in which the word 'fuck' was heard for the first time on the British screen.) Joseph Strick undoubtedly discovered, though, that Britain's local councils tended to take a varied approach towards the task of film censorship. Fifty-six councils rejected his film, four of them without having seen it. One such authority revealed that the BBFC had sent extracts to which it objected from Strick's script to all 600 local councils. One of the recipients, Southampton, duly ignored the script as well as the actual film; instead they examined the Board's extracts and when the film was subsequently banned by Alderman Michael Petit, the Chairman of that city's Public Safety Committee explained that he had read the book about thirty years before: 'I believe that without its obscenities and blasphemies a film version of *Ulysses* would not be worth seeing anyway.' He then advised local people not to 'waste their money on this kind of rubbish'.

On the other hand, Hawick Council passed Strick's film, also without seeing it. Their Provost James Henderson asked, 'Who are we to set ourselves up as an unofficial Board of Censors?' and his Senior Baillie, Sidney Irvine, answered him, 'I would like to think that we are sufficiently broadminded to let the individual decide for himself. We have no right to dictate to 16,000 people.'

While such a discrepancy was partly accounted for by regional variations and identity, the waywardness of local council decisions also had its roots in the different kinds of committees that administer local film censorship. In Brighton, for instance, the job was allocated to the Fire Brigade Committee, in Tynemouth to the Civil Defence and Traffic Committee, and in Bradford films were judged by the Standards and Cemeteries Executive Group. In Beaconsfield, local censorship during the sixties was rendered somewhat easier because the one local cinema was owned by Beaconsfield Urban Council. In effect the council's entertainment manager acted as his own censor, but that did not stop him from being strict with himself. In 1967, for example, he banned the Beatles' *Yellow Submarine*, 'Not,' he explained, 'because there was anything naughty in it, oh, there was nothing naughty about it. It was just pure unadulterated rubbish.'

Other, more liberal local authorities, however, were taking a different kind of initiative. While Trevelyan had been encouraging councils to pass one or two esoteric non-certificated films, such as *The Balcony* in 1963 or Jean-Luc Godard's *One Plus One* in 1968, those same councils had also been passing films which they had not been asked to pardon such as Russ Meyer's *Fanny Hill* in 1965 and the Danish sexploitation success of the same year *Seventeen*. But because various local authorities were reasserting their legal right to ignore as well as rubber-stamp BBFC decisions, Britain's censorship system now began to resemble not so much a moral shield as large colander; if a film was rejected by one council, a bus ride would often provide would-be viewers with the chance to see it in a neighbouring district. And it was this multiplicity of choice within municipal censorship that prompted the last notorious sexual breakthrough of sixties cinema in Britain.

Throughout this decade the BBFC had displayed a relatively tolerant attitude towards female homosexuality on the screen. Unlike their male counterparts, a certain amount of suggestive but discreet physical contact between attractive-looking women was considered acceptable by the preponderantly male Board. Thus they eventually passed a delicate lesbian kiss in *The Balcony*, Stéphane Audran's elegant canoodling with Jacqueline Sassard in Claude Chabrol's *Les Biches* in 1967 and a moody, prettily lit coupling of Anne Heywood and Sandy Dennis in *The Fox* (1968). But the following year the Board flatly refused to pass Robert Aldrich's raw, tragi-comic account of a 'pathetic old dyke' in *The Killing of Sister George*.

Taken from the play by Frank Marcus, Aldrich's film charts the fall of June Buckridge (Beryl Reid) a BBC soap-opera actress who plays the cheerful, kindly country nurse, Sister George, on a weekly TV series. In real life George is a loud-mouthed, insecure, butch lesbian whose alcoholic binges bring about her downfall. First she loses her job, then her child-like lover (Susannah York) is seduced away from her by a reptilian BBC executive (Coral Browne).

The two-minute seduction scene between Coral Browne and Susannah York did not appear in Frank Marcus's play and Aldrich's decision to make his treatment sexually explicit caused an outcry. Critics accused the American director of gratuitous sensationalism, and certainly lesbian kissing, breast fondling and nipple sucking were without precedent in a film scene. But the censor had already anticipated the furore and taken steps to restrain Aldrich's sense of sexual adventure on the screen.

'We are not prepared as yet to accept lesbian sex to this point,' said Trevelyan in a letter to the film's distributor. 'You can arrange to try another re-editing of the scene, but I can hold out little hope that it will be acceptable if submitted here.'

183

'I really think,' he went on, 'that we have not been unfair in our decision on this film. We have accepted a number of other things in the film which we might well have asked you to cut, and I do not think that you have any justified grievance about our decision to remove the entire lesbian sex scene. The cut seemed to me to work very well, and I really see no point in replacing a small part of the scene. However, as I have said, you may try again if you wish to.'

Aldrich felt that at least part of the scene was essential to the audience's understanding of the film. 'After all,' he said, 'unlike the stage version, the picture had to play out the betrayal, and the story itself is so genteel, it's possible you could be sitting in Sheboygan and the film could be so "well done" that nobody would know what the hell you were talking about.' Rather than accept the Board's cuts, therefore, and a national release under a BBFC certificate, the production company opted for a more limited distribution. They approached half a dozen councils who were selected for their likelihood to pass a very slightly reduced version of the troublesome scene.

But Trevelyan immediately fired off a warning letter to all 600 local authorities, in which the film's plot could be read off like a charge sheet: 'The woman who acts the part of "Sister George" in the serial is an active lesbian who lives with a young girl who is emotionally and mentally retarded, and they both drink to excess. Arising out of this incident, "Sister George" is disciplined by the BBC, and this is undertaken by a woman executive, who is also a strong lesbian.' Trevelyan ended with an appeal to the comradely spirit of fellow censors. 'The Board has no wish to encourage film material of this kind at a time when it is becoming increasingly frequent and I hope that your council will take the same view.'

Unfortunately for the Secretary, twelve councils including the GLC, took a divergent view and passed *The Killing of Sister George* with their own 'X' certificate at the end of 1969. Conversely, many of the councils who decided to reject the film did so because of the seduction scene. 'I was embarrassed by the scene,' revealed Reg Munn, the Chairman of Sheffield's Licensing Sub-Committee, 'and wanted to look away. Perhaps it was some deep Freudian reflex in me that made me react in this way. But these things are not pretty to watch any more than it is pretty to see someone sitting on a bed pan. I'm all for watching girls dancing round in the nude. But when it comes to watching people make love – no. It's a private matter and I don't think it is necessary to put it on the screen.' However, Mr Munn then conceded, 'I'm no expert on the cinema – and most of my time on the Licensing Sub-Committee is taken up with dealing with licence applications from taxi drivers, people who want to install one-armed bandits and so on. But I don't think it is necessary to be an expert for this sort of job. You don't have to have any special qualifications. Almost anybody would do really. It's just people.'

Opposite The censor wanted to leapfrog over the lesbian sex scene in *The Killing of Sister George* (1969) to this shot when George (Beryl Reid) discovers her BBC boss (Coral Browne) with her baby-doll lover Childie (Susannah York). They partially succeeded.

One person, namely John Trevelyan, had once again been outflanked by a distributor. Aldrich's film was about to go on release in twelve separate municipalities, including London. Trevelyan therefore had no choice, if he wanted to avoid the stigma of impotence, but to reopen negotiations with *The Killing of Sister George*'s distributor. But, of course, this did not stop him from haggling.

'We are still not prepared,' the obdurate Secretary wrote, 'to pass the full scene, or even the scene as reduced, which was passed by the Greater London Council and other authorities, but we are prepared to pass the scene up to the point at which the young girl starts to writhe and gasp orgasmically. We would not accept the two women kissing passionately, but we would accept a few shots which lead satisfactorily up to the entry of Sister George.'

After some horse-trading the inevitable compromise was reached. The kissing was reduced, but the breast manipulation (in which a body double had been substituted for Susannah York) remained. The BBFC 'X' certificated film made absolutely clear 'what the hell' Aldrich was talking about. In America, the doyenne of film critics Pauline Kael had previously remarked, in respect of another film, that 'lesbians needed sympathy – because there isn't much that they *can* do.' When she saw in *The Killing of Sister George* exactly what lesbians could do her review of the film appeared under the title 'Frightening the Horses'.

Aldrich's film also became the subject of homophobic abuse in British newspapers with much of the tabloid onslaught being directed at the 'weak-kneed, lezzie-loving' Board. But in fact *The Killing of Sister George* had been coupled by tabloid journalists with a far more troubling issue which was beginning to stymie the British film industry at the end of the decade – the resurgence of the 'sexploitation' movie.

In the first of its post-war crises the British film industry faced bankruptcy in 1969 because American finance had been withdrawn from British producers. The film trade took what it thought would be the one road leading to salvation – sexploitation. Trevelyan knew that sex films were 'a licence to print money' but in interviews with the press he resorted to wishful thinking. 'The British people do not like dirty films,' he commented, 'and they will never prosper.' Of course they did, and the proof was supplied in 1970 by the managing director of the ABC circuit, which so recently had rejected films in the 'X' category, when he said: 'If we put on sex films the takings go up 10 to 15 per cent.'

This set in train a sexual cycle in which producers had to create more and more explicit films to attract audiences; by this time, though, another even more alarming ingredient than sex, namely violence, had been added to the censor's brew by film-makers from a country which had provided surprisingly few problems for the Board over the last two decades.

By 1969, the Hollywood Production Code had virtually disintegrated. Their strict rules of do's and don'ts had initially been flouted by British and continental films of the late fifties and early sixties; but then that casual defiance had been transformed into a frontal assault by independent producers such as Warren Beatty and by directors who worked outside the studio system like Sam Peckinpah and Roger Corman. Their respective films of the late sixties, *Bonnie and Clyde* (1967), *The Wild Bunch* (1969) and *Bloody Mama* (1969) introduced the British cinema-goer and censor to the slow-motion bloodbath in which the impact of each individual bullet on the human anatomy could be discerned with the same detail that had previously been afforded only to sexual discovery.

The Motion Picture Association of America responded with the adoption in 1969 of a similar rating system to Britain's; nevertheless the subsequent insertion of letters after American film titles did not help the BBFC to deflect the inevitable charge from conservative critics that the exhibition of these films contributed to the steady escalation of violent crime.

While sex in films tends to embarrass older film-goers, screen violence can shock all age groups. But John Trevelyan reacted to the American tweaking of this sensitive nerve in the same way that he reacted to all pressures on the Board which possessed inherent economic or political leverage. He gave way and allowed the films. This may have been an appropriate response in an era of progressive social liberalisation, but a new player was about to enter the censorship roundelay and this new participant did not approve of excess in any form whether in sex or in violence.

In the meantime the Secretary had become 'increasingly tired'. He was now approaching his seventies and he had been looking for a successor since 1968. But he could not retire yet. For the enemies of permissive films were gathering under a new leader and somebody from within the Board had to lead the forces of moderation against this unknown housewife from Manchester called Mary Whitehouse.

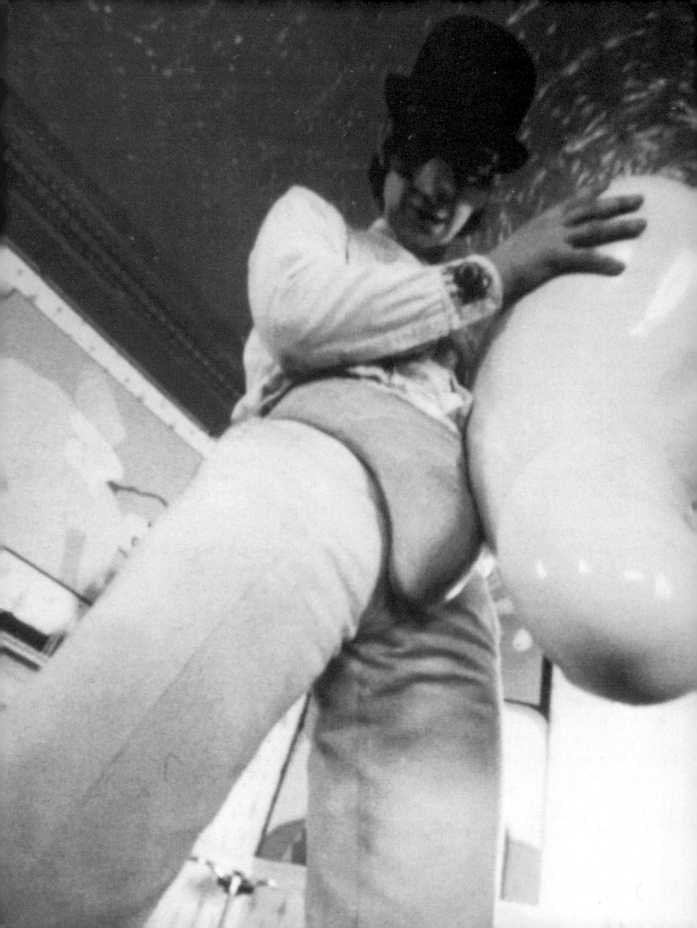

UNDER SIEGE: 1970–75   12 ✂

As John Trevelyan embarked upon what would be the most explosive period in the Board's history he put into practice a reform that he had devised for the censorship system eight years before in 1962. It would, in effect, act as an insurance policy against three films, *The Devils* (1970), *A Clockwork Orange* (1971) and *Last Tango in Paris* (1972), which together almost provoked the downfall of British film censorship. The raising of the age limit for the 'X' category in 1970 from sixteen to eighteen did not protect the BBFC from attack, particularly from the backlash that the battalions for moral reform were about to unleash upon the 'backsliding Board', but this seemingly minor example of retrenchment did indicate a willingness to censor film-goers, if not actual films, and possibly even saved the institution of censorship from being absorbed into the state.

That the new 'X' category did not take even longer to implement is a tribute to the political skill of the 'tirelessly articulate' Secretary. Not only did the film industry oppose the new age limit, because teenagers now made up the largest part of their audience, the Greater London Council, the most easy-going of the licensing authorities, also objected to it as yet another curtailment of the 'freedom to view'. For some months the country's most influential council threatened to stick to the old system, but, as the film critic Alexander Walker pointed out in his book *The Celluloid Sacrifice*, Trevelyan 'might have been created by C. P. Snow for one of his "Corridors of Power" novels about the dying art of secret negotiation and the cagey confrontations of the devious and the devout.'

The chosen method with which the devious, if not devout, censor persuaded the reluctant council to come round to his point of view has since become part of the censor's canon and, indeed, it was employed by a later Secretary, James Ferman, when he first met Britain's municipal censors in February 1977. Trevelyan had a special reel made up consisting solely of the most extreme cuts from various films, which, needless to say, was shown to the grey-faced councillors as an awful warning of the fetid flood on the other side of the dyke which only the Secretary's nicotine-stained, discriminating forefinger was keeping out.

Maybe Trevelyan justified this kind of factitious manipulation with the excuse that the local authorities should not, as he later said, 'make judgements

Opposite *A Clockwork Orange* (1971) would unleash just one of the many storms that buffeted the BBFC during the most turbulent period of its history.

as censors since they have no experience or expertise in this job'. Nevertheless, the upgrading of the 'X' classification in 1970 did enable Trevelyan to pass with only minor cuts a slate of films which would have previously been refused or altered beyond recognition. That year *M*A*S*H*, *Woodstock*, *Zabriskie Point*, *The Boys in the Band*, and *Fellini Satyricon* broke down various sexual and verbal barriers; and the passing of a detailed rape scene, with dismemberment and decapitation of American Indians, in Ralph Nelson's relentlessly brutal *Soldier Blue* deposited a tide mark in cinematic violence which would be approached with trepidation by film directors today.

If the new age bracket prevented fatalities, it did not stop the annual roll-call of the walking wounded, the most notable victim of 1970 being Donald Cammell and Nicolas Roeg's *Performance*. This particular film could ill afford to be severely cut by the BBFC as it had already been heavily pre-censored by its own production company, Warner-Seven Arts.

The studio found it difficult to say exactly what they objected to when a group of their executives viewed *Performance*'s rushes three weeks into the shooting of the film in the autumn of 1968. They were apparently expecting a sequel to *Easy Rider* (1969), but what the executives actually saw was a psychedelic mobster movie in which Chas (James Fox), an East End gangster on the run after killing a man he was supposed to be protecting, seeks refuge in the townhouse of a reclusive pop star (Mick Jagger). Once within the sanctuary of the basement he is offered 'magic mushrooms', then seduced by his host's two girlfriends (Anita Pallenberg and Michèle Breton) who in turn are replaced by his host the following morning. The plot was secondary, however, to the film's theme of merging identities amidst drug-induced paranoia.

It would be fair to say that the Hollywood executives in that viewing-room felt hesitant about bringing this production out under the Warner Bros logo. More immediately, they wondered why the film did not get to Mick Jagger until half an hour had gone by. And did the scenes between Jagger and the two women in the bath and Jagger in bed with James Fox mean that all these characters were 'bi'? 'Bi what?' asked Cammell and Roeg, unfamiliar with the American expression for bisexual. 'I knew we were in trouble then,' recalled the producer Sandy Lieberson. And the feeling must have been confirmed when one of the Americans was heard to say as he left the meeting, 'Even the bath water is dirty.'

Warners removed twenty minutes of footage, mostly from the beginning of the film, which lent a jarring note to what was already a confusing plot for those uninitiated in drug lore. But the studio perpetrated an even more blatant form of censorship in February 1969 when it decided to shelve the film for nearly two years. After this the official censorship began, and in its British guise this consisted of sixteen further cuts. Trevelyan was particularly insistent that a shot of Chas being flogged, which is intercut with his back being clawed

by a girlfriend during a love scene, should be extensively re-edited. Yet it was the clawing, not the sight of Fox's torso being shredded by a whip that Trevelyan wanted removed. He said he could not endorse an explicit statement of Chas's sado-masochism and when Donald Cammell pointed out that the deletion of this piece of character development would render the scene gratuitously violent Trevelyan replied, 'so be it.' The argument was then rendered redundant, anyway, because Warners pre-empted the Board and took out the intercutting.

The new classification did at least allow Trevelyan to retrieve one film that he had banned with some misgivings at about the same time that *Performance* went into production in 1968. Loosely based on *Midnight Cowboy*, which was simultaneously being filmed in Manhattan, Andy Warhol's *Flesh* revolved around a day in the life of a male prostitute (Joe Dallessandro) who is persuaded by his wife to get out of bed and go to work in order to hustle the money for a friend's abortion. Shot in four days at a cost of $4,000, the film reflected the cinematic style of Warhol's earlier films, of which he said: 'The lighting is bad, the camera work is bad, the sound is bad, but the people are beautiful.'

In spite of a scene in which a teenage girl (Geraldine Smith) ties a bow around Joe Dallessandro's penis – thereby engendering the first erection to be shown on the British screen – Trevelyan personally liked *Flesh*; but being wary once again of public reaction he suggested to the film's distributor, Jimmie

Vaughan that he forgo a certificate and instead approach the Open Space Theatre in London's Tottenham Court Road for club-controlled screenings.

In his thirteen years of office as Secretary of the Board, Trevelyan's finest hour was now at hand. On 3 February 1970, 'acting on information received' (a member of the public had complained that *Flesh* was obscene), thirty-two policemen led by a Chief Superintendent descended upon the Open Space Theatre. They halted the screening, took the names and addresses of everyone present and seized the film along with the projector, the screen and the theatre records. Vaughan immediately phoned Trevelyan who arrived on the scene within minutes. The Secretary energetically defended the film and the theatre's right to show it, calling the police action 'unjustified and preposterous'. Trevelyan's contacts in the press immediately whipped up the case into a public row, insisting that the Home Secretary, James Callaghan, explain the 'peremptory' police behaviour. Callaghan could only splutter, 'It is the general desire of the average person in this country that it [obscenity] should stop.'

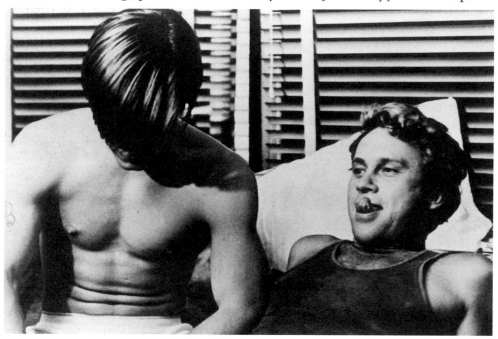

Thirty-two policemen seized Andy Warhol's day in the life of a street hustler, *Flesh* (1968) but one censor set it free.

Just as suddenly as the affair had erupted the police backed down and dropped the obscenity charge on the grounds that films were not subject to the Obscene Publications Act; but the theatre was fined £200 for admitting non-members to see a film, a sum which the distributor Jimmie Vaughan, did not have and which it took some persuasion from his friend-in-need, John Trevelyan, to extract from the notoriously penny-pinching superstar director Andy Warhol. After this imbroglio Trevelyan had little choice but to grant a certificate to *Flesh*, and although one of the more elderly examiners wanted the 'shot showing Joe with an erection' to be deleted, the film was in fact passed in full on 27 October 1970.

In spite of a snide suggestion in *Time Out* that the Open Space Theatre was raided because it was probably mistaken for a sex cinema, this was a notable victory for Trevelyan. He had drawn a demarcation line around films, reminding the authorities that whether a film wore a BBFC certificate or not it still had protection under the law, and by doing so provided the British film industry with a bulwark upon which they could – and would – fall back more than once in the next few years.

It was also an unprecedented compliment to Trevelyan, as Alexander Walker pointed out at the time, for a distributor to call upon the help of a censor when one of his films was under threat. In his autobiography, Trevelyan said, 'I have loved films all my life,' and whilst this is stretching the point – many of the less intellectually fashionable film-makers of his time would have jeered at that remark – it is true that Trevelyan was one of those rare public figures who instead of becoming more conservative become more liberal with age. With his urbane manners and his easy willingness to bring film censorship out into the open, where it could become part of the debate on freedom of information, Trevelyan almost succeeded in squaring the circle and resolving the inherent contradictions within censorship. 'To an extent,' said the critic David Robinson, 'the brilliance of Trevelyan's own work at the BBFC has been a beautiful conjuring trick, dazzling enough to distract us, most of the time at least, from the essential anomaly of the Board, its peculiar division of function between censorship and classification, its uncertainty between protection of minors and moral guardianship of adults.'

BBFC Secretary John Trevelyan discusses the finer points of film editing with Andy Warhol.

But there was also another less well known side to Britain's best known censor. According to the critic Philip French, the 'clubbable' Secretary curried favour with selected directors, such as Joseph Losey, whose films rarely received cuts, and Vittorio de Sica, from whom a realistic rape scene featuring Sophia Loren in *Two Women* was accepted as early as 1961. But while conceding that he was 'dirty-minded' and used 'extraordinarily bad language' for a man in his position, French's predecessor as film critic at the *Observer*, George Melly, also points out that Trevelyan was 'a censor who tried to censor the least he could'. Perhaps a true picture of this liberal hypocrite is caught by his daily greeting, usually delivered to his colleagues after a lengthy Italian lunch in Soho: 'Well, who's been fucking who today?'

At the end of 1970, Trevelyan said that he thought that fewer and fewer good films were being made, a surprising comment considering that this period is now regarded by most critics as the heyday of world cinema. More relevantly perhaps, Trevelyan felt out of touch with British cinema-goers, three-quarters of whom were between the ages of sixteen and thirty-five in 1970, and he thought that the time had arrived for a Secretary of the Board to be put in place who reflected the attitudes of that age group. He himself had lost faith in the necessity of film censorship for adults. 'I would like to think,' he said, 'that the role of the censor is beginning to disappear'; and two years after his retirement he joined the Campaign for the Abolition of Film Censorship for Adults, an offshoot of the National Council of Civil Liberties. Ironically, though, before he retired in June 1971 the Secretary passed a film which not only became a poisoned chalice for his successor, but also ensured that adult film censorship would continue up to the present day.

For the BBFC, Ken Russell's *The Devils* possessed the repercussive effects of a firestorm. It seemed to thrive on the oxygen expended in attacks on its 'integrity', 'prurience', and overall 'validity' as a film. Before the production had even finished shooting at Pinewood towards the end of 1970 the tabloids opened hostilities with a report from the set that five actresses who had been required to walk naked through a crowd had been assaulted by nude male extras. The following month another paper reported that a fourteen-year-old child actor had appeared in a bedroom scene with a naked actress playing a nun. Inevitably both allegations proved to be false, but of course by then *The Devils* had already gained a reputation for sensationalism.

Admittedly, the plot of the film did seem designed to inflame public reaction. *The Devils*, as its director has recently said, is about the destruction of a six-teenth-century citadel 'from within'. While its walls still stood the provincial city of Loudon posed a threat to the political ambitions of Louis XV's chief minister Cardinal Richelieu. His Grace therefore sends agents to the town where they discover that Sister Jeanne (Vanessa Redgrave), the hunch-back Mother Superior of an enclosed Ursuline convent, has fallen in love with Grandier, a wanton priest and leader of the community played by Oliver Reed. When Grandier spurns Sister Jeanne she claims to be possessed by the Devil in the form of her erstwhile seducer, and thus the scene is set for the arrival of the Inquisitor, Father Barre (Michael Gothard), who induces hysteria in the nuns, tortures and burns to death the hapless Grandier, and finally oversees the destruction of the city's walls.

Russell wrote to Trevelyan that 'the events in the film are true as anyone who has read [Aldous] Huxley's documentary masterpiece "The Devils of Loudon" will testify.' However, when his version was submitted to the BBFC at the beginning of February 1971, its claimed veracity did not stop the BBFC's examiners from reacting as though they were attempting to separate meat from offal. 'I consider this to be a nauseating piece of film making,' began the report of the long-standing adjudicator Ken Penry. 'We would all be glad,' added his colleague Audrey Field, 'if the picture could be left to the local authorities.'

The third examiner, Newton Branch, however, had been put on his mettle by a scene in Russell's previous film, *The Music Lovers*, in which 'the demented woman [Glenda Jackson], shaved and filthy, squatted on a grating and allowed the madmen beneath to fondle her etc.' Yet the apoplectic censor wrote, 'This was a mere foretaste of Ken Russell's *nostalgie de la boue* which, in *The Devils*, plumbs really filthy depths. This relish for the putrid starts here with maggots falling out of the eye sockets of a skull and ends with the nun [Vanessa Redgrave] using the freshly charred tibia of her "lover" as a dildo – this, a relic of Christ in her deranged mind . . . No doubt the other examiners will have suggested specific cuts. My object here is to demolish any argument by Ken Russell that his film is a serious work of art. The theme is extremely important. His treatment of theme – done in 15 weeks apparently – is sex sensationalist [*sic*] and utterly muddled. We should say to him: "Oh come off it, Ken!" Any cuts that we make in his grossness and excesses, to the bare bone, will improve the film. It is thoroughly sick and kinky.'

The examiners duly went in search of bare bone, since any possible banning of the film had been precluded by Trevelyan and the Board's President, Lord Harlech, who both believed in the essential honesty of Russell's approach. The examiners accordingly drew up a two-page list of recommended cuts which Russell largely agreed to. The director resubmitted the film at the beginning of April, by which time the examiners had their scissors freshly sharpened in preparation. But Russell balked at any more concessions.

In an attempt to stave off the imminent second dissection of *The Devils* the controversial director wrote to Trevelyan defending himself against the charge of sensationalism. 'What I set out to do was to make a deeply felt religious statement – and I believe that despite the fact that I have butchered the film at your bidding far and away beyond anything I dreamed of – especially in view of the new rating system – what remains still just about retains my intentions – albeit in a watered down version. After all I did not set out to make a cosy religious drama that would please everyone but a true film about the horror and blasphemy perpetrated against human beings by their fellow men in the name of Jesus Christ.'

Trevelyan passed on the letter to Harlech who was 'impressed by the obvious sincerity' of the director and by the extent to which 'he had co-operated with us by modifying the film in accordance with our suggestions.' However, the fault line between the examiners and Harlech and Trevelyan did not narrow when the whole Board viewed the cut version of *The Devils* on 8 April.

Harlech was actually seeing the film for the first time, as was Frank Crofts, who after joining the BBFC in 1948 succeeded Fleetwood Wilson as chief

Right Ken Russell directs Oliver Reed and Vanessa Redgrave on the set of *The Devils* (1971).

Below Flushing out the devils. The Inquisitor's underling (Max Adrian) induces hysteria in the enclosed order of Ursuline nuns during the notorious enema scene.

censor in 1950. So once the President had expressed his view that the film was 'deeply moving' and also 'basically acceptable for the "X" category', he invited Crofts to give his opinion. The chief censor immediately suggested further multiple cuts to Sister Jeanne's masturbation scene, also to the shots in which an enema is administered to her on an altar, as well as to various other sequences which he considered extraneous to the main story.

Then, for the first time in the memory of anyone at the Board, Lord Harlech lost his temper. As a Roman Catholic he declared he knew that Russell was sincere. He reminded everyone that Russell was a recent Catholic convert. (In fact Russell had converted ten years before and would soon relinquish his Roman faith.) But Crofts stood firm. He insisted that further cuts had to be made. 'Rubbish,' shouted Harlech.

After that, everyone left the viewing-room and Crofts's fellow examiners commiserated with him. They were shocked by their President's uncharacter-istic behaviour, but they also knew that Harlech's opinion would undoubtedly prevail. After all, Trevelyan had been in favour of passing the film from the beginning and he was the person who would decide the fate of the film.

Trevelyan asked for further cuts. Why he did so is not revealed in the BBFC papers. Maybe he thought that it was the only way to unite the Board before he retired. Maybe he was impressed by the strength of Frank Crofts's convict-ions. On the other hand, Crofts was about to leave the BBFC, possibly due to the behaviour of Harlech. Anyway Trevelyan wrote an ameliorative letter to Russell which hinted at, rather than insisted on, five more 'modifications'. Russell immediately wrote back, now desperate to hold on to the central theme of his film which seemed to be slipping through his fingers. The hand-written letter, hitherto unpublished, imparts a sense of Russell's frustration but it also conveys the trust that existed between this director and censor.

> Dear John
> I have cleared up the shit on the altar, slashed the whipping and cut the orgy in 2 – this last has achieved several things – the sequence is now much more restrained, no longer self-indulgent and most impor-tant of all *The Rape of Christ* concept is strengthened and the idea that the true atonement for Christ's sacrifice is the mass as celebrated by Grandier – clarified. That after all is what the Catholic Church is really all about – the rest is eyewash – and this eyewash is what power mad neurotics like Father Barre practise in its name to the detriment of the human race. And this is also what the film is also really about. I hope you don't feel tempted to tamper with this sequence as it now stands – at best there can only be a couple of shots in question, and if these go – the meaning would also go too!
> Christ must be debased and seen to be debased. At the risk of being boring I must just say again that to me the sequence is the crux of the movie and should, *please* stay as it is – for England, anyway.
>
> Yours Ken
>
> P.S. Please show to Lord H if you think it has any bearing . . .

Christ or Grandier was seen to be defiled but Russell had to carry out a fur-ther four cuts, the last one of which he fudged because he said it was impossi-ble to do for technical reasons. Altogether one and a half minutes was removed from *The Devils* and while it is difficult to say what was lost the director Michael Winner, who is one of the few people outside the BBFC to have seen the cut footage, said, 'it should not have been cut.'

John Trevelyan now retired and was succeeded in July 1971 by Stephen Murphy. After ten years at the BBC as a programme maker Murphy had become senior programme controller in 1965 with the Independent Television Authority, a post which also involved censorship. Like Trevelyan he was an ex-schoolteacher, a heavy smoker with a rumpled appearance, who was skilled in public relations. He also tried to conform to his predecessor's latter-day line in liberalism; but unlike Trevelyan he could not fall back on 'clubbable' charm when faced by adversity.

From his own experience in 1958, Trevelyan knew that the new Secretary would be at his most vulnerable at the beginning of the job. He therefore stayed on through July to act as a consultant to the Board. But nevertheless, as the ex-Secretary later recalled, 'Stephen Murphy soon had problems.'

In the interval between the conception of *The Devils* in the spring of 1970 and its British release in July 1971 a confluence of political circumstances had given weight to the arguments of the film's opponents. To begin with, the unexpected election of a Conservative government under Edward Heath a year before had signalled a turn to the right on social as well as political issues. Moral rearmament groups like Mary Whitehouse's National Festival of Light and Lord Longford's Committee on Pornography, with such members as Peregrine Worsthorne, Kingsley Amis and Jimmy Saville, came into being that spring, and the Festival of Light in particular quickly proved that they were well placed to exploit the sea change in the political atmosphere. (Their rally in Trafalgar Square on 25 September 1971 drew a crowd of 35,000.) Compounding the moral backlash, the troubles in Northern Ireland erupted during 1970 into virtual civil war, and the passing of the Industrial Relations Act in the spring of 1971 also led to fears of civil unrest. Violence therefore joined sex as an emotive issue in which human behaviour, in all its representations, would now be harshly judged.

Moral reform groups like the Festival of Light cannot however recruit large numbers without the aid of publicity. Needless to say *The Devils*, with its masturbating nuns and free-loving Christ, provided an ideal whipping-boy with which to solicit attention from the press. The campaign was co-ordinated and vociferously led by the Festival's chief spokesman, Peter Thompson, a public relations executive for the anti-trade-union group, Aims of Industry. Thompson, in fact, had been an avid proponent of film censorship before he joined the Festival of Light. In 1965 he had been committed for an indefinite period to Broadmoor mental institution for an attack on three au pair girls, an assault which had been caused by a nervous breakdown which, according to Thompson, had in turn been partly caused by watching sex and violence in films. More recently Thompson attributed his interest in censorship to seeing an 'X' trailer of the incessantly brutal *Soldier Blue*, which had mistakenly been substituted by the cinema for the normal 'U' version. A year later he joined the

Soldier Blue (1970) featured the scalping, decapitation and impaling of Indians as well as the rape and mutilation of whites. It is unlikely that it would be passed even today.

evangelical Festival because as he later revealed, 'it might be a chance to extend my censorship campaign.'

As soon as *The Devils* was released in July, Thompson called for the withdrawal of its certificate. At the same time he organised a letter-writing campaign against the film which he described as 'offensive, repugnant and likely to injure the moral standards of society'. But Murphy stood firm. Although he had not seen *The Devils* until late July he agreed with Trevelyan's positive decision and he also agreed with his predecessor's subsequent advice. He stonewalled the Festival's demands and replied politely to every single letter of complaint with the recommendation to 'go and see *The Devils* (it won't corrupt you).' Rebuffed, Thompson switched his attack to the GLC.

He asked the authority to arrange a viewing of the film specifically for the purpose of banning it. The GLC acceded to the first request, but in spite of being 'under some pressure to prohibit' they said that it was their policy 'to accept films passed by the BBFC' and 'not to take action against individual films', otherwise 'we would end up by having total chaos'. Other authorities disagreed, however; and although one or two councils had refused to certify BBFC-passed films in the past, never before had seventeen authorities disagreed with an individual decision of the Board. But what the censors would have found even more disturbing was the adoption by three councils of a policy which could only destabilise the Board: henceforth they would review all BBFC decisions relating to 'X' films.

As long as this loss of local confidence in the censorship system remained confined to a handful of rural watch committees it could be withstood by the

BBFC. If it spread, however, to influential city councils BBFC decisions would extend no further than its offices in Soho Square. Back in the twenties this had been the stumbling block upon which the newly established Board nearly foundered; and unfortunately for the BBFC, the Festival of Light and its cohorts had discovered that the system's vulnerability could be measured in direct proportion to the gap between the BBFC and the councils.

Meanwhile, as the battle between the BBFC and the moralists raged on over *The Devils*, the press recognised that film censorship had acquired news value. Inevitably the various newspapers were divided in their loyalties but in this instance it was not just along obvious political lines. While the right-wing papers were predictably supportive of the Festival's aims, almost without exception the film critics planted their colours in the opposite camp. Although they would not have considered themselves to be supporters of the BBFC, the critics were also emphatically not in favour of increased censorship. Yet as the spotlight continued to shine on film censorship, critical disapproval escalated against the BBFC: and the *agent provocateur* who completed this transformation of compliant pacifists into bloodthirsty rebels was the Californian film director Sam Peckinpah.

At a time when films were beginning to reflect the trauma of American losses in the Vietnam war, Peckinpah's *Straw Dogs* assaulted the audience with no quarter granted to the faint-hearted. Set in the Cornish countryside, where an intellectually fastidious young American writer (Dustin Hoffman) has come for 'the clean air and water', the film pits its reclusive hero against a horde of yokels who first lay siege to his home, then rape his wife (Susan George), before themselves being slaughtered in retribution by the diminutive but redoubtable author. In short, the film was a Cornish Western with yokels playing the Indians.

The BBFC's examiners totally misjudged the likely reaction to the sexual violence in this film when they viewed it on 3 November 1971. Ken Penry, who had just replaced Frank Crofts as chief censor, noted that he and his colleagues 'were equally agreed that it is tremendously enjoyable for the most part, and compulsive viewing'. Their only qualm lay in the length of the rape scene.

Fortunately the new Secretary had anticipated this problem. Two months before, he had made a point of seeing *Straw Dogs* in its rough-cut stage and he knew then that the four-minute rape scene would have a 'massive impact'; so, not unnaturally, he asked Peckinpah to reduce the sequence.

What transpired then is one of those awkward ironies when the requirements of the censor do not so much muddy the water as stir up a wholly new apparition. *Straw Dogs*' producers duly carried out Murphy's orders but what had initially appeared to be a vaginal rape in which the victim was taken from behind now looked like buggery. Complicating the issue even further, the

The censor's treatment of the rape scene in Sam Peckinpah's *Straw Dogs* (1971) turned a crisis into a drama.

examiners found it difficult in subsequent conversations about the scene to persuade their Secretary that sex from the rear was not necessarily sodomy. As a sop to his own dignity the distraught chief censor appended a face-saving note to his examiner's report bewailing the fact that it was now too late to re-cut the film; its editing had been completed, 'so I fear there is nothing we can do about it, save a show of righteous indignation when accused.'

Some years later James Ferman, the current Secretary of the Board, found himself presented with the opportunity to satisfy his own curiosity about this sexual slip when he was introduced to the film's 'victim', Susan George. What

201

exactly was Peckinpah's intention? he asked her. 'Buggery,' was the instant reply.

Nevertheless, Murphy's slip became the Board's catastrophic blunder. The critics rounded on the film, with Alexander Walker of the *Evening Standard* in particular pointing to the contribution played by the Board: 'What the film censor has permitted on the screen in *Straw Dogs* makes one wonder whether he has any further useful role to play in the cinema industry . . .To pass it on for public exhibition in its present form is tantamount to a dereliction of duty. For if this goes, then anything goes.' Rubbing salt into the wound, Walker then revealed that 'someone close to the film' had told him 'the monstrous indecency' of the buggery scene 'was not intended this way but has been made to seem like it by censorship cuts'.

Even the extremely *laissez-faire* George Melly took issue with Peckinpah, asserting that: 'Sex and violence are consistently equated in this film. The gun and the cock are interchangeable.' More damagingly still, Melly added his name to a list of thirteen leading film critics questioning the Board's judgement in the letters column of *The Times*.

Such concerted criticism could have been fatal for Murphy at a time when *Straw Dogs* had already been coupled with *The Devils* as an example of the BBFC's dereliction of duty by champions of government censorship. (A cinema manager was currently informing Lord Longford's Committee on Pornography that people had fainted and vomited during a showing of *The Devils* and greeted the rape scene in *Straw Dogs* with 'delighted howls'.)

But the criticism of the Board was not as straightforward as the letter in *The Times* would have suggested. In fact many of the critics were using *Straw Dogs* as a battering ram with which to force the Board to unban a film of which they approved. The object of the critics' affection was the latest product to be exported from Andy Warhol's 'factory'.

Unlike the critics, and for that matter John Trevelyan, Murphy and his examiners did not care for Warhol's amoral, deadpan depictions of Manhattan low-life and his 1971 film *Trash* did not make them revise their opinion. Like *Flesh*, it had been initiated by the success of another film, this time *Easy Rider,* which Warhol wanted to emulate in one of his day-in-the-life scenarios, spiced up by the added ingredient of drugs.

The examiners found it impossible to relate to an 'underground' movie which accepted the drug culture without sociological solemnity. They pored over problematical scenes involving syringes, the attempted fellatio of Joe by his transsexual wife (Holly Woodlawn) and the sexual relief she/he finds, in turn, through the employment of a beer bottle; but, incredibly, the Board remained unconvinced that it was an anti-drugs film. They enlisted the help of a government adviser on drug dependency, a university research department and the GLC, who refused to come to their aid by granting the film a London-only certificate. Not satisfied with the 'critically intelligent' response from people who saw the film at the London Film Festival in 1971, the Board held its own test screenings, and in an effort to find a 'random audience' they even bussed in a party of middle-aged housewives from a nearby housing estate. 'Again,' the Board reported, 'the results showed a majority in favour of showing the film.'

Although the examiners were now convinced that the anti-drugs message within *Trash* had been absorbed by their sample audiences, they were 'still concerned with questions of public taste and the film's offensiveness'. Finally, in August 1972, when the distributor Jimmy Vaughan and the film's director Paul Morrissey agreed to minor cuts to the three difficult scenes, the BBFC relented. However, the Board suddenly remembered that the Longford Report on Pornography was about to be published. Apparently this would provide 'an opportunity for a public discussion of some of the issues involved'. The BBFC therefore 'continued to decline to issue a certificate' until 9 November 1972.

Evidently the Board was running scared; but they had nowhere to hide because their opponents in the anti-permissive lobby never had to wait long for another tempting target to be handed to them by the 'irresponsible' film industry. Also, the moral pressure groups were on special alert, having been taken by surprise by *Straw Dogs* and even worse, having had their thunder stolen by the film critics. They therefore set themselves up on their hind legs in anticipation of a feast to come; it didn't take long and was rich beyond their furthest expectations.

When Joe (Dallesandro) won't do the indecent thing in Andy Warhol's *Trash* (1971) the transsexual Holly (Woodlawn) employs a beer bottle as a substitute.

As John Trevelyan later said, 'It was bad luck for Stephen Murphy that very soon after this film [*Straw Dogs*] the Board had to make a decision on *A Clockwork Orange*.' The viewing of Kubrick's film took place on 15 December 1971 in the presence of Harlech, Murphy, Ken Penry and Audrey Field.

Field had already expressed disquiet about Terry Southern's original 1968 script for Kubrick, particularly in relation to the Board's old bugbear: the incitement to juvenile crime. 'I think it presents an insuperable obstacle from our point of view if we still hold . . . that an unrelieved diet of vicious violence and hooliganism by teenagers is not fit for other teenagers to see. The dialogue is a specialised slang . . . but the general intention (crude violence and obscenity) is always plain.' Once she had seen the actual film, from Kubrick's own script though, she reversed her opinion and along with Penry and Murphy she agreed that it should be passed without any cuts.

203

Considering the straits that the BBFC was in at the time, this was a brave decision. Kubrick's bleak vision of a future Britain brought a character to the screen whose fondness for 'a bit of the old ultra-violence' must have set the examiners' nerves jangling. From the film's opening scene of an opposing gang being set upon by Alex (Malcolm McDowell) in company with his 'droogs', 'the red vino', as the feckless hero put it, 'began to flow'. The film is about the importance of man's power to choose; Alex, however, chooses violence laced with sex. His succession of brutal acts includes bludgeoning to death a keep-fit addict (Miriam Karlin) with a giant phallic sculpture, a near rape, a complete rape with full frontal nudity. Then, as part of Alex's aversion therapy, clamps are attached to his 'glozzies' while he watches a film of seven 'malechicks' being 'given the old in-out-in-out' to the musical accompaniment of his favourite composer, Ludwig Van (Beethoven). Finally he beseeches the doctors to 'Stop it, I beg you, it's a sin.' Such repentance, 'which of course contains a moral message' persuaded the censors that the film was a 'valuable contribution to the whole debate about violence'.

Passed uncut by a censor but banned by its own maker, Stanley Kubrick's *A Clockwork Orange* (1971) still cannot be seen in British cinemas.

Harlech, however, had his mind on other business during the viewing. He had just been appointed by the government to the Pearce Commission which, in a fortnight, was due to leave for Rhodesia on a fact-finding tour prior to that country's independence. He therefore had to leave before the film was over but he left the viewing-room under the impression that the more extreme moments of Alex's ultra-violence would be removed.

The press were alerted to *A Clockwork Orange* when Adrienne Corri, who played one of the rape victims, gave an interview to the *Sunday Mirror* which appeared two days after the critics' attack on *Straw Dogs* in *The Times*. Corri, presumably in an attempt to boost public interest in the film, revealed that she 'was scared to see it herself' as 'this was violence beyond anything I ever imagined would appear on screen.' The paper then asked, 'How much more violence, sadism and rape is British film censor Stephen Murphy going to let movie-makers get away with?'

Within days of *A Clockwork Orange*'s release other journalists piled into the fray, the most pungent and pithy being Peregrine Worsthorne, the deputy editor of the *Sunday Telegraph* who described the film as 'muck in the name of art'. On the other hand, the same paper's film critic, Margaret Hinxman, hailed the movie as 'a masterpiece'. Worsthorne, though, was a powerful player in the bureaucratic circles of censorship for he straddled two camps. As a member of Lord Longford's committee on pornography he acted as a mouthpiece for the moralists, while as heir apparent to the editorship of the *Sunday Telegraph*, a bastion of the establishment, he would have been particularly wary of a film suggesting that Britain was sliding into a police state.

Before the film opened Worsthorne had attended a specially arranged

One of the scenes that the current censor says would be cut if *A Clockwork Orange* were submitted for a video certificate.

screening – a print having been provided by a craven British film industry – for Longford's commission along with Peter Thompson and the curly, white, wing-haired peer. And although Worsthorne subsequently commented that this was 'a sick film for a sick society' both Longford and Thompson heaped praise upon Kubrick. Thompson even informed the production company that, 'to someone who has committed violent acts and who has been mentally ill, this film seems to have an awful lot to say to society.' Not surprisingly, his convictions soon realigned themselves and *A Clockwork Orange* was added to the

Festival of Light's black list, although this change of heart was less well publicised than Thompson's initial praise.

At last, the tide seemed to be turning for the Board, but then for the first time since the thirties the government intervened in film censorship, and the intervention did not favour the BBFC. Asked to comment on the connection between the rise in violent crime and violence in films, the Home Secretary Reginald Maudling replied that, yes, there probably was a connection. Film critics and historians have subsequently tried to explain away this response as 'rushed' or that Maudling was 'caught off guard', but the Home Secretary would have had time to collect his thoughts before he went on to tell the crowding journalists that, due to 'personal concern', he planned to see *A Clockwork Orange* – presumably for the purpose of examining it.

For a government minister to publicly single a film out for special scrutiny before it had even been released not only pre-judged *A Clockwork Orange* but, because of Maudling's responsibility for law and order, it gave the moral rearmament movement the stamp of political respectability. The local authorities needed no further prompting. In a reversal of their previous policy of not taking action against individual films, the GLC's vitally influential film viewing committee decided to examine *A Clockwork Orange*. They did not impose a London ban, but their chairman Mark Patterson did announce that his committee intended to 'keep a closer watch on controversial films, particularly those passed by the censor for public viewing'.

Then, in a latter-day echo of T. P. O'Connor's arguments in 1917 that the cinema should be a site of entertainment and not social comment, Patterson remarked that 'in the context of violent times' his committee 'had to consider the wide, general political and social implications of films, particularly those which reflected anarchy and did not provide answers'.

Until that moment the Board's mainstay, the British film industry, had held firm. They had ignored the warnings of MPs, the press, numerous councils and even a plan by the Festival of Light to set up an alternative censorship system. Now, however, when the battle was at its most intense, their unity broke. They could accept one or two films, such as *A Clockwork Orange* being banned by half a dozen councils; but if the GLC, after the Board the most important censor in the country, no longer followed BBFC decisions, then profits would fall in the ensuing chaos. A suitable offering to appease the righteous wrath of the moralists had to be found, then sacrificed, which in turn would restore the trust of the local authorities in the film industry. Their eyes fastened on the new Secretary of the Board, Stephen Murphy.

Nearly twenty-five years before this a Secretary of the Board had lost his job because he had antagonised the industry; but in 1972 Stephen Murphy had not only lost the support of the BBFC's main sponsor, it was also during his regime that the councils had swung the censorship system in their own favour.

Of course, it was not his fault that Trevelyan had woken up the municipal censors in the early sixties or that those censors felt pressurised to act by the myriad voices of the backlash. He just happened to be the censor in place who was, in the words of the distributor Jimmy Vaughan, supposed 'to reconcile the viewpoint of a London audience in Chelsea with that of a local councillor in Southend'.

But the time for reconciliation, of whatever kind, was already over. 'Murphy Must Go' screamed the front-page headline of the 11 March 1972 issue of *Cinema TV Today*. Below it the trade paper ran the following story: 'As the GLC calls for a Royal Commission into censorship Kenneth Rive, the showmen's President says "We've got the wrong man in the job . . ."' As President of the Cinematograph Exhibitors Association, Rive had in fact been a member of the committee which had unanimously appointed Murphy two years before. Now he remembered, 'the film industry appoints the censor,' but also, 'it's up to us to put our house in order by getting rid of him.' Murphy was too liberal and, according to Rive, too loath to cut. 'I think that films like *Straw Dogs* and *A Clockwork Orange* are brilliant pictures,' said the CEA President. 'But I don't think they would be any less brilliant with a little cutting.'

The members of various other film trade organisations agreed with Rive that, unlike Trevelyan, Murphy 'should be a categoriser and not necessarily a personality'. Trevelyan himself tried to save his successor; but while his support at this time was not irrelevant, what Murphy needed was the backing of the President. Harlech was a man who treated film executives with the same gracious tolerance he had meted out to his civil servants whilst in government. In other words, they were there to serve him and that was the natural order of things.

But Harlech was in Rhodesia and in the meantime other film executives backed Rive's call for a trade association meeting to elect a new censor. Alternatively those within the industry who did not endorse Rive's campaign for tougher censorship were nearly all mute because they did not want Murphy to be replaced by anybody, and especially not by a stricter censor. Also, by then the national papers had started to exploit the divisive fracas with articles under such headlines as 'Sack the Censor – We've had enough dirt thrown in our faces'. The beleaguered Secretary was undoubtedly proceeding apace to the BBFC's back door when, at last, David Harlech arrived back in England.

The President immediately expressed 'complete confidence' in his Secretary and called for a private meeting with Rive and all the industry's associations. As is often the way with political leaders, Lord Harlech subsequently granted the Board's antagonists almost everything they could have wished for and then proceeded to ignore the agreement. Henceforth, according to *Cinema TV*

Today, the President 'himself will deal with the local authorities' and he would also 'be more directly involved whenever censorship is under attack. Stephen Murphy will remain silent in public: Harlech will be the "front man".' Finally, in a further re-emphasis of the flip-flop within the BBFC's hierarchy the paper reported that, 'Murphy's position as censor will be reviewed at the end of his first year to see whether or not his contract should be renewed.'

In fact Harlech had no intention of spending his time with provincial censors discussing parish problems or arguing with the press about the minutiae of an individual film's censorship. As the film historian and current film censor Guy Phelps has observed, Harlech had neither the expertise nor the inclination to carry out those tasks, and even though the President had won over the industry by reminding them that without the BBFC there would be a government censorship, this was, in fact, an empty threat. In reality, any system in which politicians have to explain in Parliament why films are censored would immediately become bogged down by the setting of precedent, subsequent anomalies and the slowness of decisions. Nevertheless, the part-time diplomat had won the Board a reprieve. Unfortunately it did not extend to Stephen Murphy who now had to endure six months on probation.

In the meantime the same charge of incitement to crime that had been laid against films in the Edwardian era was now being levelled at *A Clockwork Orange*. But whereas kids in 1910 committed burglary because of the 'flickers', in 1972 teenagers blamed their urge to mug old people on Kubrick's film, and as before the magistrates and judges indulged the easy excuse rather than the complex explanation. Pundits, such as the Labour MP Maurice Edelman, claimed that a 'clockwork cult' was taking hold in the nation's thoroughfares. 'The phallic dress of the "droogs" with their cod-pieces, will, no doubt become as widespread as the sub-Western gear in the High Street imitated from the Western film.' More calculatedly, the Conservative MP Jill Knight alleged that a link existed between Kubrick's film, which had recently been shown in her Birmingham constituency, and a murder committed there soon afterwards by a juvenile.

The director himself, who had made his home in England since 1961, defended his film first with the words: 'I'm very pleased with *A Clockwork Orange*. I think it is the most skilful movie I have ever made. I can see almost nothing wrong with it'; then when the tirade persisted he delayed the film's general release, which meant that for over a year it could only be seen in one cinema in London. Once it had had its initial run, Kubrick took what can only be described as his own personal revenge upon his adopted countrymen – he banned his own film. Because he owns the British distribution rights to *A Clockwork Orange*, Stanley Kubrick had – and still has – the legal power to outlaw the film within Britain. And this he proceeded to do by withdrawing the film from circulation in the summer of 1973. Unlike a BBFC-banned film,

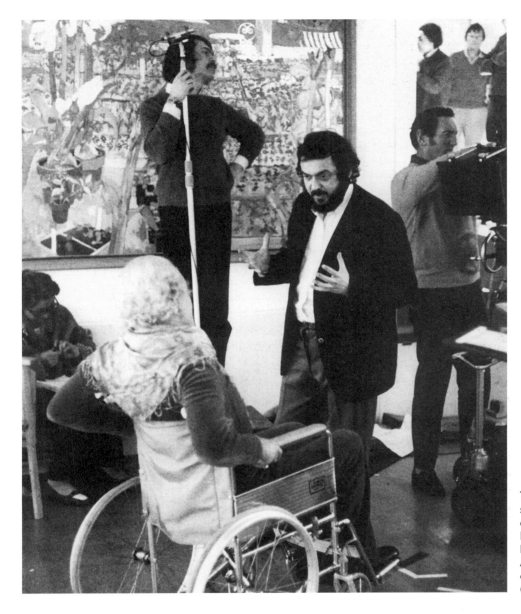

The film-maker and self-appointed censor Stanley Kubrick directing Patrick Magee as Mr Alexander on the set of *A Clockwork Orange*.

not even cinema clubs or film societies or media courses in universities or film schools are allowed to show this film. It is therefore the most effective banning in British film censorship.

Occasionally Kubrick's legal position is tested, most recently by the Scala Cinema which was fined £4,000 in the spring of 1993 for breaching Kubrick's copyright. In turn this resulted in the closure of the cinema, which, at the time, was one of only three outlets in London licensed to show non-certificated films. Thus the opportunity to discover what is being censored by the BBFC has been hindered by one individual's autonomous decision. For whereas official censors are occasionally, if rarely, called upon to explain their decisions,

209

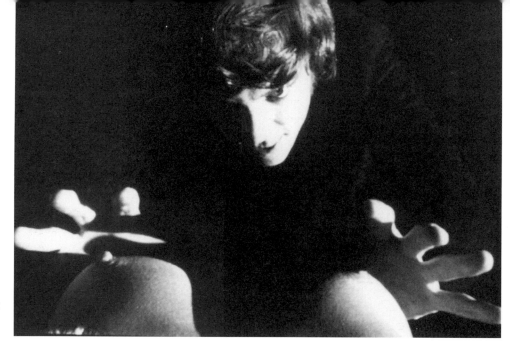

So near and yet so far: after Alex's aversion therapy in *A Clockwork Orange* (1971) he can no longer make contact with the opposite sex.

Kubrick's blackout has never been satisfactorily explained by the reclusive film-maker and censor. The listings magazine *Time Out* reported in December 1989 that Kubrick acted 'after he received death threats to his family and relatives'. But most film commentators think that a more likely motivation was provided by the politicisation of the film in which it was kicked between publicity-conscious MPs, a responsive press and the upholders of moral hygiene.

This cacophony of self-interest definitely distracted attention from the actual film, which, in the meantime, paradoxically still ticks away like a delayed-action bomb within the body of the BBFC. *A Clockwork Orange* is the most sexually violent film ever made for the commercial cinema. Just the single infamous image of Alex bearing down to sexually impale as well as physically destroy with the gigantic phallus would be rushed at with scissors in the feminist-friendly atmosphere of today's BBFC. In a confirmation of that policy the chief censor from 1975, James Ferman, has gone on record in asserting that he will cut 'deeply' into the film's two major rape scenes if Kubrick submits *A Clockwork Orange* for a video certificate in the foreseeable future.

Fortunately for Stephen Murphy, the submission of *Last Tango in Paris* (1972) took place after his position as Secretary had been re-confirmed. He must have been aware of the film's presence on the horizon. No other movie has caused the spilling of so much British newsprint, nearly all of which warned readers to expect a 'Marlon Brando shocker' which broke every 'permissive barrier' and wallowed 'in detailed perversions'. The plot was handily if simplistically summed up by the *Sunday Mirror* on 17 December 1972: 'Brando, hung up over his wife's suicide, meets sex-hungry colonel's daughter. Their minds click. He seduces her in five minutes flat. Then follows a series of blistering sequences to knock the bottom out of the back street porno market.'

When the BBFC's examiners viewed the actual film a month later they seemed almost disappointed by its lack of 'gratuitous nastiness'. 'The film is certainly not as pornographic as the pre-showing publicity would have us believe,' remarked one examiner. By now, though, the front pages of the nation's tabloids were presciently reporting the banning of a film which they considered 'unsuitable for English audiences'.

In fact, Bernardo Bertolucci's polemical depiction of a depersonalised sexual encounter provoked very little agitation from the Board. 'The sex is exercised with great restraint, a little too much in my opinion,' noted the new examiner, Tony Kerpel. 'Paul [Marlon Brando],' he added, 'seems to accomplish the most strenuous sexual athletics with his trousers on. It is language rather than visuals which seems to be the only real problem.' That verbal concern though only involved one line – when Paul orders Jeanne (Maria Schneider) to trim her nails and push her fingers up his anus, and even here the examiners were hesitant to cut, largely because the digital penetration is not seen but also because Harlech insisted that the line carried 'a point of importance in degradation'.

The remaining 'stumbling block', however, which the Board's examiners (along with Lady Harlech and Mrs Murphy) tried to step round was unashamedly illustrated on the screen. Paul's lubrication of Jeanne's anus with butter to enable him to sodomise her has since become the most famous sex

The most legendary sex scene in cinema: the ten-second cut from *Last Tango in Paris* (1972), of Marlon Brando smearing butter on Maria Schneider's anus, was supposed to satisfy the moralists – it didn't.

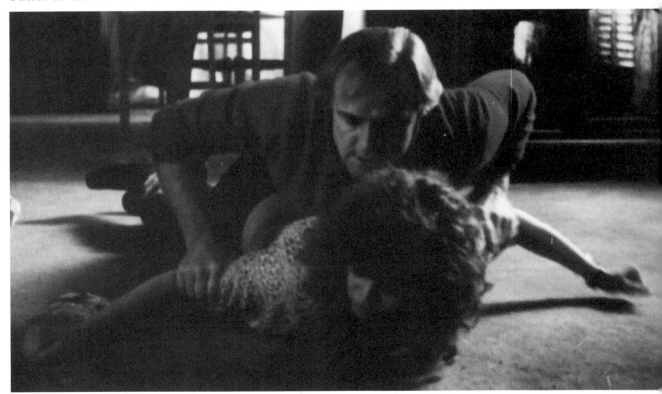

scene in the history of the cinema. In January 1972 it barely raised a flutter in the battle-hardened hearts of the BBFC's censors. Under the heading of 'the "butter and buggery" scene' it merited a single paragraph in one examiner's report. 'Except for the editing error in *Straw Dogs*,' wrote Newton Branch, 'we have had nothing like this and/or passed. The President thought it too long and [the] Sec[retary] is to go over it very carefully with the editor and script. (Brando's muttered dialogue here was very difficult to follow, amongst other things.)'

But, primed by the press, the moral watchdogs bellowed in outrage when on 16 February the Board announced that *Last Tango in Paris* had been passed with only a ten-second cut. James Ferman later admitted that the cut was 'a purely political decision', taken in an attempt to propitiate the Festival of Light. But, of course, a mere snippet of film did not satisfy the moralistic hunger of the ravenous God-botherers. Mary Whitehouse demanded the resignation of the whole Board as they had obviously all been overcome by 'collective madness'. The Festival of Light secured a copy of the script and sent underlined excerpts to sympathetic MPs like Maurice Edelman. They also unveiled plans to pressurise the councils and this last stratagem met with overwhelming success as no fewer than fifty local authorities banned *Last Tango* over the next three months. But, unlike with *The Devils* and *A Clockwork Orange*, this time the Board had prepared a defence. And unlike the row over *Straw Dogs*, the Board now enjoyed the crucial advantage of facing their moral opponents with the critics on their side.

Murphy circulated favourable reviews of *Last Tango* to all the leading local authorities and included helpful comments such as George Melly's pertinent advice: 'If you hope to be turned on, you'll probably get your money's worth better at *I Am Available* or *The Wife Swappers*'. He corresponded with sympathetic councillors and made himself available for town hall meetings. To some extent it was a losing battle, as many of the more malleable provincial censors were persuaded by the orchestrated letter campaigns of the Festival of Light to ban *Last Tango* without having actually seen it. But the Festival failed to win over vital councils such as the GLC, who had now decided that they had no business after all re-examining BBFC-certificated films. The Festival's campaign was also undermined by the popular, highly-publicised bus trips to neighbouring censor-free zones for those who wanted to see what all the fuss was about.

In spite of council bannings, the critical and commercial success of *Last Tango* in 1973 showed that the challenge from freelance censors could be withstood if the industry remained silent while the critics took on the role of defending a film that had been condemned to exclusion. In the latter part of that year, however, the Festival of Light decided to raise the stakes in their losing struggle against film-goers who 'followed Satan'.

On 7 January 1974, Edward Shackelton, a member of the Festival of Light's executive committee, brought a private prosecution under the Obscene Publications Act against *Last Tango*'s producers, United Artists. At the initial hearings the seventy-one-year-old retired Salvation Army social worker argued that 'the film was a record of obscenities practised by Marlon Brando and Maria Schneider and was not a fictional event' and that 'copulation near the beginning was so gross and performed in such a way that very few human eyes had ever been called upon to look at it.'

Never before had a film with a BBFC certificate been prosecuted under the Act and the very existence of the Board rode on a successful defence against the charge. If the Board was shown to be passing obscene material it would have failed in its primary responsibility to protect the British film industry from prosecution within the framework of civil or criminal law. At the beginning of March, after three sessions, the presiding magistrate concluded that there was a case to answer and committed United Artists to trial. Furthermore, this decision to bring cinemas within the scope of the Act was then upheld at the Old Bailey the following May by the Lord Chief Justice, Lord Widgery.

The edifice of Britain's film censorship was crumbling and Murphy desperately tried to shore it up with advice to the solicitors acting for United Artists. He supplied the defence with examples of sodomy in such films as Kenneth Anger's *Scorpio Rising* (1971), John Boorman's *Deliverance* (1971) and Pasolini's *Canterbury Tales* (1972), all of which had been passed by the Board. He pointed out that *Last Tango*, 'a genuine, serious film', had already been the subject of careful censorship. 'We felt that the film was a legitimate, if to some disturbing, exploration of the human spirit. At only one point did it seem to us to go visually beyond the bounds of decency we have so far accepted. This was in the famous "butter scene" where we felt that the point had been adequately made without the actual sight of butter being smeared.'

In fact, the defence was never called. On appeal Judge Kenneth Jones dismissed the charges because distributors do not 'publish' their films to an audience but to a cinema manager; therefore there was no case to answer. But if the Obscene Publications Act did not apply to film, surely another law could be turned to the purpose of God's work? Mary Whitehouse thought that she had discovered the appropriate implement when she prosecuted the Curzon Cinema for showing the GLC-certificated French film *Blow Out* (1973) under the Vagrancy Act. (The film was refused by the Board since the director, Marco Ferreri, refused to carry out suggested cuts.) Again the charge was dismissed as the Act did not apply 'within the closed walls of a cinema'. The presiding magistrate, however, provided Mrs Whitehouse with some consolation when he voiced his opinion that Ferreri's gastronomic attack on bloated capitalism did represent 'an indecent exhibition'.

Needless to say the moral policemen went in search of another film to haul

Overlooked by a portrait of super-aesthete Robert de Montesquieu, Ugo Tognazzi tries to choose between two delicacies in Marco Ferreri's 1973 hymn to excess, *Blow Out*.

before the courts on another charge. They could have pointed a righteous finger at *Uncle Tom* (1971), a racist 'inquiry' into the eighteenth-century horrors of slavery that dwelled in slow motion on the torture, mutilation and rape of blacks in the American South. The Board cut half an hour from this 'historical' study, but because it was released in the same week as *Last Tango in Paris* the attention of the morally concerned had become distracted by sex rather than violence.

The upholders of celestial retribution and their supporters in the press did try to fan the flames of moral indignation around one or two other likely film subjects such as Pasolini's *Canterbury Tales* (1972) and William Friedkin's *The Exorcist* (1974). In the latter case, the Festival of Light coupled Friedkin's manipulative horror movie with the recently reported suicide of a sixteen-year-old boy who had seen the 'X'-certificated film the week before his death but Murphy courageously refused to budge. Peter Thompson then reminded the BBFC Secretary that, 'in my recently published book *Back from Broadmoor* I advocate the setting up of a new certificate known as the 'Y' certificate that should be appended to certain 'X' films whose content is likely to cause distress.' Murphy replied that 'the public interest in demonic possession means that *The Exorcist* is more of a social phenomenon than a problem in censorship.' Any argument was then effectively ended by Dr Ramsay, the Archbishop of Canterbury: 'If there's an immense craze on the subject,' he pronounced, 'it is a sign of spiritual immaturity.' (Unfortunately, this kind of common sense would be conspicuous by its absence in the future video censorship of *The Exorcist*.)

Later in the year the Festival also attempted to dissuade numerous 'backsliders' from multiplying the box-office returns of *Emmanuelle* (1974); but by now the heart had gone out of the battle. The extra-censors had very little to show for their four-year struggle against the BBFC. None of the films that they had attacked had suffered commercial damage at the box office; a fact which was duly noted by a nervous film industry. The lack of susceptible films to denigrate for the delectation of the ever-eager press also led to a fall-off in numbers at the movement's morale-boosting rallies. Their influence over the local authorities was also dwindling and now extended not much further than the rabid sworn-in enemies of 'spicy' films. Even more disastrously, their one-time ally, the GLC viewing committee, had switched sides yet again and indeed had taken the offensive with a proposal to abolish film censorship for adults within London.

The Board could only claim a Pyrrhic victory, though. They had maintained the censorship status quo, but at a prohibitive cost to their own equilibrium. Murphy had grown weary from what he called 'constant sniping attacks' which, unlike Trevelyan, he found difficult to slough off. He lacked the emotional resilience which is so necessary for a successful censor. In a letter to George Melly, dated 22 November 1972, he confessed that 'the job has brought me little other than personal misery'; yet the put-upon Secretary was unbending in his support of certain films such as Nicolas Roeg's *Don't Look Now* (1973) and Dusan Makavejev's *WR – Mysteries of the Organism* (1972) both of which he refused to cut in spite of pressure from examiners due to the films' provocative sexuality. By contrast, he hacked at other less reputable films, crudely tearing out most of a sado-masochistic sex scene between Marlon Brando and Stephanie Beacham in Michael Winner's *The Nightcomers* (1972), a sequence from Liliana Calvani's *The Night Porter* (1974) in which Dirk Bogarde thrusts two fingers in and out of Charlotte Rampling's mouth, and most glaringly from Alexandro Jodorowsky's psychedelic Zen-Western *El Topo* (1973) which in spite of the plaintive advice from one examiner – 'might it be proper for the GLC to decide on this one?' – was greeted with open scissors by a bedazzled Board.

As for the state of film censorship itself, this was still threatened by the likelihood that the Festival of Light would eventually unearth a temporal law to censor the 'unholy image'. On the other hand, after 1975 neither the major studios nor their directors felt so inclined to tackle the twinned themes of sex and violence, and from now on this double-headed monster would only be treated by independent producers. In a sense films would no longer be designed for the purpose of destabilising accepted values or, more particularly, as a means of confronting the censor. In effect the flirtation between alternative values and the mainstream cinema was over. Film would now become a wholeheartedly commercial medium and in the years ahead censorship would be guided by that new adherence.

THE NECESSITY OF CENSORSHIP 13 ✂

In 1975 the British Board of Film Censors lay battered at the feet of its enemies. But before the coup de grâce could be delivered and the choicest morsels distributed amongst the local authorities and their moral rearmament allies, a white knight in the form of a new Secretary of the BBFC would ride to the rescue, scatter the righteous and pacify the provincials. And this brave new censor not only boasted a strong arm. He understood the legal framework of censorship and he would carry the faltering Board to the safest haven in the land – the law.

No sooner had the President of the Board, Lord Harlech chosen James Ferman to be the new Secretary of the BBFC than the unflappable peer knew that he had made the right decision. At lunch with his new Secretary on 11 June, Harlech told Ferman that the Board was in crisis. It had lost the confidence of the industry and the councils. 'Stephen [Murphy],' he said, 'has been making many good decisions but they've been badly presented. We now have to make our case and we have to explain our decisions.' Ferman replied that they should hold a press conference to announce his appointment. From that moment on, and at the time of writing, James Ferman has dominated film censorship in Britain.

Later that day at the hurried press conference the new Secretary told the assembled journalists that he would stay at the BBFC for five years as it would only take about that amount of time to 'modernise' the censorship system. The forty-five-year-old ex-New Yorker then intended to return to the 'creative heat' of TV film-making. There, ironically, Ferman had himself been the victim of censorship fourteen years earlier when his 1961 documentary for ITV on religious tolerance, *The Freedom To Worship*, had first of all been banned and then had seventeen minutes removed from it at the request of the Northern Ireland section of the Independent Television Authority.

Censorship of his own films, though, was a side issue for Ferman in 1975. At the time he was still a freelance film-maker with a young family to support, and because he did not hold a contract with any of the major television companies his appointment to the Board solved his immediate financial problems. But it also has to be admitted that the soft-spoken American citizen was far more qualified to be a film censor than any of his predecessors. As well as his personal experience of being at the wrong end of censorship, Ferman's documentary involvement in drug treatment, social welfare and community health care programmes brought a knowledge of social issues and professional expertise to the practice of censorship. Indeed, many of the BBFC examiners say that Ferman is at his most content leaning over a cutting-room table; and, crucially, it is this knowledge of the film-making process – together with a sanguine temperament – which has undoubtedly allowed him to react with calmness when faced by the orchestrated hysteria of moral pressure groups.

Back at the BBFC press conference, the *Evening Standard* film critic Alexander Walker suggested to the new Secretary that his job should remain empty. But Ferman had already realised that the barbs of recalcitrant anti-censorship campaigners could be laughed aside as liberal fancy. The actual battle lay elsewhere. It was more concrete, and it could be found in the legal power of local authorities to overturn the Board's decisions. Those authorities had to be put back to sleep again. Then the film industry could go about its business in a rational, organised manner without having to pre-plan for perpetual crises.

First of all, though, Ferman had to persuade the councils that the BBFC's new role was one of 'professional adviser' to the local authorities rather than the everyday reality of a wary, hesitant censor trying to protect the British film industry. 'John Trevelyan and Stephen Murphy,' says Ferman, 'used to describe themselves as "guardians of the industry". I told the authorities that we're not the guardians of the industry, we're the conscience of the industry.' In short, Ferman had decided to distance the BBFC from 'the industry'.

Yet the means with which the new Secretary accomplished this sleight of hand were extremely risky for the Board. In spite of opposition from amongst his own examiners, Ferman issued a monthly bulletin to all the councils, costing them £50 per annum which detailed the censorship of each individual film that the Board had passed or rejected over the previous month. After only one year the examiners' doubts had been justified. The Board's enticing revelations actually prompted the local authorities to call in more films than they had asked to see before the reports were published. The industry, in Ferman's words 'got the wind up' and screamed, 'What are you doing to us?' The patient Secretary could only reply, 'Trust me.'

Ferman now describes his 1975–8 bulletins as a 'teach-in' which showed 'how the job ought to be done'. More to the point, they demonstrated that the BBFC sentry was alert at his post, practised in the ploys of censorship appeasement, and, most importantly of all, that the bread-and-butter work of the Board is deadly dull. As the local authorities made the disillusioning discovery that the day-to-day work of the censor is more concerned with paperwork than pubic hair, subscriptions to the bulletin fell off, as did local interference in film censorship. By the end of the seventies the hydra-headed municipal censor had been lulled back into a netherworld and only came out to sniff the air when he sensed irreligiousness in *The Life of Brian* (1979) or sexual heat from *9½ Weeks* in 1986.

It must have been tempting at the time for liberal cinema-goers to applaud this vanquishing of provincial philistinism, but the cheers would have stopped in their throats when they realised that they had been outwitted by the new censor. Because Ferman had achieved more than the mere thwarting of provincial interference. He had centralised the very process of film censorship, which now reverted to the Board; once the monthly bulletins petered out due to local authority apathy the doors closed behind an empowered and once more secretive BBFC, and they remain firmly shut to this day.

One year after he became Secretary Ferman told a group of exhibitors, 'By being secret all we do is increase suspicion.' Nevertheless, covert film censorship would become Ferman's chosen method to disguise the Board's decisions. Henceforth from within the BBFC the history of British film censorship would be delineated and recounted by Ferman or his designated officers. Furthermore, this initial informal proscription of information would become official BBFC policy in January 1993. From that date onwards the Board's Secretary decreed that every report on a film which had been submitted to the Board after 1975 would now be made known to the public only at the discretion of the Secretary himself. Thus the knowledge of what films have been censored since 1975 and why they have been censored has only one source – Britain's chief censor.

In 1993, at a time when censorship boards in Europe were opening their doors for the first time to public inspection, Ferman offered the following explanation for his adoption of this 'internal policy': 'The Board's results are for public scrutiny, but we have to work with some sense that we are secure and that there is confidentiality within recent history. The date we have set, and it is quite arbitrary, is 1975.'

In fact some of the examiners did feel secure enough to reveal and explain their own decisions. But due to the legal obligations within their BBFC contracts they run the risk of legal action being taken against them if they betray confidentiality. This particular clause is similar to contracts signed by the employees of many private companies and it can be strictly enforced. It states that examiners are forbidden 'during the course of your employment, or thereafter, to publish or disclose to any person confidential or privileged information as to the Board's affairs or any other matter which may come to your knowledge in the course of your employment'.

Whether there should be privacy clauses in the contracts of those who serve in a public body is questionable. But further doubt is added to this issue of the BBFC's public accountability by the fact that the responsibility for withdrawing or extending examiners' contracts beyond their fixed term lies in the hands

219

of the BBFC management. That the head censor along with his designated nominees who make up that management should hold such power over the employees of a public organisation makes a mockery of their own accountability. Nevertheless for these reasons the circle of secrecy that surrounds British film censorship is legally impervious, and the comments here of examiners who have served at the Board after 1975 must therefore remain anonymous.

At the time, though, it was a surprise to the examiners that the new Secretary's forte as a censor initially lay not so much in an intimate knowledge of film as in a steady application to the kind of legal technicalities of censorship of which previous Secretaries had not been fully aware. In 1975 however, it was just such a legal question which the Board had been trying to avoid, but which it now had to confront. What laws should be applied to films?

The year before an Appeal Court had dismissed the prosecution of *Last Tango in Paris* because the judges decided that the film did not come under the Obscene Publications Act. Mary Whitehouse's Festival of Light then cast around for a more appropriate judicial means with which to quash the film of their choice. But this proved fruitless until one of their congregation brought a GLC-certificated Swedish sex education film called *More About the Language of Love* to the attention of the Director of Public Prosecutions in June 1975.

This time the DPP made the tactical decision to prosecute under the common law offence of indecency rather than the Obscene Publications Act. This meant that the film did not have to be taken as a whole; the jury only had to find a scene, or even a single image, to be indecent in order for the film's distributor to be found guilty. This they proceeded to do – within twenty minutes – ruling that one shot near the end of the film, illustrating the preliminaries to fellatio to be 'grossly indecent'. The distributor was subsequently fined and, not surprisingly, the British film industry yelled in alarm. If a properly certificated film was not immune to prosecution, what was the point of the BBFC's additional certification system. Admittedly, the Board had not passed this particular film; nevertheless from the point of view of sex-film distributors the BBFC's existence had now become superfluous.

One of the BBFC's examiners has pointed out that 'Jim Ferman might not know how to deal with people but he can write a brilliant legal letter', and towards the end of 1975 Ferman presciently recognised that the only way to disentangle film from the legal system was to take it out of common law and bring it within the Obscene Publications Act. A film could then be defended on the same grounds that applied to books, magazines or the theatre – in other words, either on grounds of context, public interest or artistic and educational merit.

In the meantime, a film was submitted to the Board that has been described by the critic Philip French as 'one of the most truly disgusting movies that I have ever seen'. Loosely based on the Marquis de Sade's novel *120 Days of Sodom*, Pasolini's *Salo* (1975) is set in the small northern Italian town of the same name during the closing days of the Second World War. There, the Fascist burghers inflict a series of ritualised sexual humiliations upon local villagers who have been chosen for their youth and beauty. The film finally erupts into a crescendo of orgiastic violence featuring sadism, masochism, coprophilia and sodomy which are all intertwined with a marriage ceremony in which the bride and groom are smeared with faeces. French also points out that *Salo* 'is beautifully photographed', but that would have probably been to the film's disadvantage if, as seemed likely, it was brought before 'twelve good Englishmen and true' on charges of indecency.

Bottoms up: Pasolini's whip-crackin' paean to sadism, *Salo* (1975) brought down upon the head of its British distributor the charge of 'keeping a disorderly house'.

Somewhat naïvely, Ferman thought that he could pass Salo because of its 'importance'. Harlech sided with the examiners and soon disabused his Secretary of that notion. Even so, Ferman felt that this 'remarkable picture', which was Pasolini's last film, should not be consigned to darkness. Therefore when *Salo*'s distributor Curtis Elliott, who owned the Cinecenta film clubs, came to Ferman and asked him to cut the film for an 'X' certificate, Ferman said, 'I don't think this is a film which should be cut. If I were you I would show it on a club basis.'

Within twenty-four hours of opening at the Old Compton Cinema Club in Soho, *Salo* was confiscated by police from Scotland Yard on the grounds that Elliott was 'keeping a disorderly house'. He immediately rang Ferman. 'What have you done to me?' he cried. 'We followed your advice and the film has been seized by the police. They visited my office. I've been showing sex films for years and I've never had the police in my office until I showed this film – which you said was reputable.'

In order to make amends to the distraught distributor, Ferman promised the DPP that the film would never be shown again until it had been shorn of any potential indecency. Supervised by two lawyers, Elliott's cutters mined the film for a legal offence which meant that *Salo* had to be torn apart and rearranged in a rough semblance of the original version. A prologue, with accompanying maps, was then added which legally 'explained' de Sade, the town of Salo and its role in the Fascist retreat up the Italian peninsula. But by the time this had been added to Pasolini's own prologue, which contained a list of suggested reading, so much text had been inserted into the film it not only looked unrecognisable, it looked not dissimilar to a book.

This rigmarole could have been repeated six months later when a British distributor wanted to submit Nagisa Oshima's *In the Realm of the Senses* (1976) to the Board. This sexually uncompromising Japanese picture, in which a pair of young lovers make the unfortunate discovery that strangulation maintains erection, still marks the outer boundary of what the British censor considers to be sexually acceptable. Finally passed in March 1991, after much deliberation, the film would have undoubtedly fallen foul of common law indecency fifteen years earlier. Fortunately for the film and its distributors, though, Ferman had by then persuaded the Labour government to incorporate films within the Obscene Publications Act. When Oshima's film was shown in 1978 at the Gate Cinema Club in Notting Hill it therefore came within the framework of a 'deprave and corrupt' clause rather than the more malleable 'likely to harm' test.

Ferman had brought films within a law which was exceedingly difficult to prove, and indeed no certificated film has been successfully prosecuted under the Obscene Publications Act. But the price of the reform was the withdrawal by the GLC from film censorship. Stung by the conviction of *More About the Language of Love*, and then reassured by the film's new protection, they disbanded their viewing committee in 1977. Not only did this deprive London film-goers of the chance to see BBFC-banned films, it also denied the BBFC itself of the opportunity to 'test the water'. Once again the overlooked side-effect of a liberal reform was the consolidation of power over film censorship within the BBFC.

Within those offices a new element now entered censorship whose influence is still felt today. At the beginning of 1977 the Board had three examiners, the ex-wing-commander Ken Penry, the Young Conservatives' ex-chairman Tony Kerpel, and Rosemary Stark, who had come to Soho Square from the National Film Archive. The men tended to rule by the book, cutting films according to

Eventually passed in 1991, Nagisa Oshima's *In the Realm of the Senses* (1976) still marks the boundary of what is sexually acceptable in the British cinema.

relevant BBFC policy. They also judged sexual violence not from the point of view of victimisation but according to previous rules relating to the amount of flesh shown on screen. But later on in the year Ferman recruited two more women, Maggie Mills, a clinical psychologist, and Margaret Ford, who also came from the National Film Archive. Both of them joined Stark in her opinion that jocular references to rape should no longer be sniggered at but should now be cut.

Ferman regarded himself as a pre-feminist even going so far as to tell one of his female examiners at a later date that, 'You don't understand, I'm a better feminist than women are.' In consequence one of his first acts as Secretary was to recall *Emmanuelle* (1974) so that a scene in which the eponymous heroine is gang-raped in an opium den, while her elderly protector looks on approvingly, could be cut.

Not surprisingly a BBFC blockade was therefore raised against the new imported sub-genre of psycho-sexual 'slice 'n dice' movies from Japan, Italy and the USA. At the time, critics ascribed the unparalleled increase in violence in such films to America's bitterness at defeat in the Vietnam war, or alternatively to a collective hangover induced by the sexual excess of the 'swinging sixties'. But, whatever the supposed sanction, the Board was suddenly inundated during 1976 by long, fixated scenes of violence against women. In that one year alone, no fewer than fifty-eight films featuring rape were submitted to the BBFC, nearly all of which were either cut or banned.

The American contribution to the recent marriage between horror and the sex movie, most infamously exemplified in *I Spit On Your Grave*, *Killer Nun* and the notorious *Ilsa, She-Wolf of the SS* cycle, were duly banned only to resurface on the black market during the video scare of the early eighties. The Italian variant – reputedly financed with Mafia money, according to Ferman, – along with insidious Japanese examples of sado-porn such as *Violated Angels*, which attempted to achieve a social sanction by intercutting the rape of a dying nurse with shots of the Japanese army on manoeuvres, were also summarily rejected. Alternatively, the Italian and Japanese versions of these rape fantasies suffered from minimal budgets and were so badly photographed they did not even fare well under the dustbin label of 'video nasty'.

Milder conflations of sexual violence divided the examiners along gender lines. Interminable rows split the Board throughout the late seventies whenever Stark, Mills or Ford tried to differentiate in favour of violence to property, as opposed to violence to people. Because they had the support of Ferman, however, the women were usually able to enforce this distinction. For example, in 1974 Bertrand Blier's *Les Valseuses* was banned because two wandering louts (Gérard Depardieu and Patrick Dewaere) rampage through a holiday home and a shop without being interrupted by the police. After 1975, though, this type of film received more sympathetic treatment. *Death Weekend* (1976), in which a housewife (Brenda Vaccaro) is offered as a sexual prize to a marauding gang by her desperate husband, featured an 'appalling orgy of

Ilsa, She-Wolf of the SS (1975), a tacky American exploitation movie, inspired by the career of the concentration-camp commandant Ilsa Koch, resurfaced in the early eighties as a 'video nasty'.

destruction' according to the August 1976 Bulletin; but because the leader of
the gang falters just as he is about to rape the heroine and vents his frustration
upon her furnishings instead, Ferman only demanded eleven seconds of cuts.

The Board's censorship of this particular film, however, does lend itself to
other interpretations. Before its submission *Death Weekend* had already been
attacked in the British press for its 'gratuitous violence' and as a result Brenda
Vaccaro personally visited Ferman during the summer of 1976 to plead for a
certificate. And because her character slaughters the gang one by one at the
end of the film the female examiners argued that unlike *I Spit On Your Grave*
– which contains a similar but more sexually suspect plot – *Death Weekend*
was 'acceptable even justifiable' as it upheld 'not so much rape-and-revenge as
rape-and-survival'.

Such niceties unfortunately did not apply across the board. Films containing
female violence towards men, whether it was treated seriously as in Barbet
Schroeder's exploration of sado-masochism *Maîtresse* in 1976, or slightingly,
as in John Waters's *Desperate Living* (1978), were either swept under the
BBFC carpet as 'ahead of their time' or, as in the latter case, they were greeted
with a po-faced solemnity that almost rivals the humour in Waters's original
'travesty'.

While the Board conceded that certain film-goers would be amused by
Desperate Living, 'perhaps as a holiday from a world where standards really
matter', the overall verdict was that it was a 'coarse, mocking, deliberately vulgar' film in which 'disgust and decadence are rampant'. When the gay mother,
Mole, wins a lottery and has a penis transplant, only to cut it off because her

The reticent
husband begs the
gang in *Death
Weekend* (1976) to
take out their anger
on his wife instead.
The film won favour
with the Board
because it featured
violence against
property rather than
people.

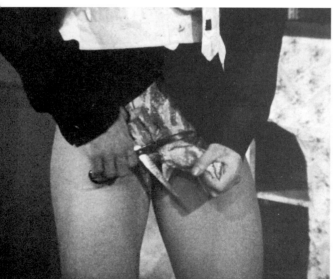

girlfriend Muffy is less than enthusiastic, the Board sniffed that 'lesbian love is grossly paro-died'; and as for the sequence in which Peggy Gravel encourages her gigantic gay black maid Grizelda to sit on her suburban husband, Mort, and smother him to death, this was merely a con-firmation of Waters's 'cynical contempt for cur-rent values'. Unbelievably, this camp comedy was banned in August 1978 because the BBFC declared that it sought 'its laughs by doing dirt on life'.

Predictably, the film-maker most bloodied by such earnest, bloodless piety was Russ Meyer, the 'King of the Nudies'. The critic Kim Newman says that in Meyer's later films 'nothing leads anywhere except to more sex, violence and showy technique'. Yet even the early work of Meyer, such as *Fanny Hill* (1965), *Faster Pussycat Kill Kill* (1966) and *Vixen* (1968), was either banned, not submitted or, in the last instance, reduced to half its original length.

The two Russ Meyer films that came before Ferman's Board are *Supervixens* (1976) and *Beneath the Valley of the Ultravixens* (1979) and perhaps inevitably, their comic-strip violence won the disapproval of the women exam-iners and the Secretary. The episodic *Supervixens* only suffered from a relatively short three minutes of cuts, but these included the film's climax in which the villain stakes out the heroine on a mountain top with a stick of dynamite protruding from between her legs. The villain then overcomes the escaping hero and dumps his unconscious body on top of the hapless heroine. Her attempts to revive him as the fuse slowly burns down carried 'sexual overtones' according to a thunderstruck censor; so once again the Board attempted to separate the cocktail of sex and violence with a pair of scissors and once more the deliberate absurdity of a film-maker was unintentionally added to by a sanctimonious censor.

But this did not mean that the Board tolerated Meyer's pneumatic sex. Among the examiner's details of the ten-and-a-half minutes amputated from Meyer's most recent film, *Beneath the Valley of the Ultravixens* (1979) are the following: 'Lavonia riding Rhett in a lake', 'a back-lit shot of pubic area as Lavonia performs fellatio' as well as 'a shot of Lavonia kicking La Marr in the crotch and his penis falling out of his trousers'. There was even a surreal cut of Lavonia sitting astride a 'pointy mountain'.

Russ Meyer asserts that *Ultravixens* 'originally ran for 94 minutes, yet it was cut down to 55 here'. For his part, Ferman rebuts that charge as 'nonsense'. The solution to the missing footage probably lies in self-censorship. Up until the arrival of videotape, film distributors often pre-cut their sex titles in anticipation of the Board's wishes and it was not uncommon for whole reels to be removed by nervous film salesmen. Whatever the cause, Russ Meyer is one of a handful of movie-makers who does not allow his films to be shown, either in the cinema or on video, if they have been cut. For that reason, with the exception of *Beyond the Valley of the Dolls*, none of his films can be seen in Britain unless they are shown under club conditions.

The hapless heroine (Shari Eubank) is about to have a stick of dynamite placed between her legs – and that signalled one more cut to Russ Meyer's *Supervixens* (1976).

Evidently the films of John Waters and Russ Meyer were submitted to such tough censorship as a result of the Board's particular brand of strait-laced feminism during the latter half of the seventies. In most cases the Board has ruled that unreal, stylised violence deserves more lenient treatment than the unglamorous realism of protracted death. Yet Waters and Meyer, as well as other directors of black comedies, such as Paul Bartel and Roger Corman, were cast out of this redemptive circle simply because their humour had yet to be legitimised by convention – in fact their films were the forerunners of the new wave of darkly exaggerated British comedy which was to emerge in the early eighties

227

and find its way into the mainstream via television programmes like 'The Young Ones'.

The BBFC's reliance on selective judgement when confronted by screen violence was underlined at the beginning of 1981 when Ferman explained why he had released one of the first mainstream examples of the 'stalk 'n slash' cycle, *Friday the 13th* (1980) unscathed. 'The murders were so far fetched,' he said, 'with knife blades coming up through beds into somebody, that it was clearly unreal.' He then added, 'The nice thing about fantasy is all the time you can keep reminding yourself, "I can't get hurt, no one's going to get hurt, it's just make believe."' On the other hand, 'If you present it [violence] realistically, it impinges on your feelings, you haven't got that suspension of disbelief.' So what was 'worrying' about the most famously violent film of its time, *The Texas Chainsaw Massacre* (1974) – which Ferman banned twice – 'is how good it is. It's very persuasive all the way through, and you do feel you are watching reality.'

Such statements are, in fact, an echo of the BBFC's perpetual attempt to remove social comment from films because the Board believed – and still believes – that the cinema should be a place for entertainment. But in the same

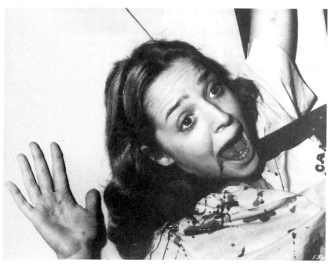

Friday the 13th (1980). The acceptable face of violence, according to the BBFC's Director, James Ferman.

interview, Ferman then shifted his ground to point out the danger of entertaining, rather than realistic, violence. 'We are experiencing more violence now,' he said, 'and the danger is that by showing that as entertainment you can normalise it, or legitimise it, which is something we are not prepared to do. Violence in society,' he added, 'should always be presented as unacceptable.' Of course, if films which present violence as real and unacceptable were less, rather than more likely to be censored than those which present it as entertainment, the contradiction would be resolved and the use of double standards could be ignored.

As recently as 1992, the Deputy Director of the BBFC, Margaret Ford, summarised the Board's enduring policy towards sexual violence on the screen. 'What we are concerned about,' she said, 'is the violent attack on a woman in which the prize for the audience is an eroticised thigh or a breast being exposed or knickers removed. You can see either the attack or you can see the sex but you can't see both.' In practice, neither was allowed to cinema-goers of the late seventies, even if the sex was divorced from the violence.

The most bizarre, if not the most important example of censorship in this period mixed sex and violence in roughly equal proportions. Yet both were cut from *Caligula* (1979). Initially the film was based on Suetonius's *Lives of the*

Caesars but its financier, the *Penthouse* publisher Bob Guccione, felt that something was lacking in both Gore Vidal's original screenplay and the subsequent footage directed by the exploitation movie-maker Tinto Brass. Additional hardcore scenes of sexual violence, according to the hirsute publisher, would provide the missing ingredient, and these he proceeded to add in 'glorious Technicolor' close-ups.

Mysteriously forewarned by the magpie-eyed Mary Whitehouse, the British customs sequestered *Caligula* upon its arrival in 1980 from America. But the film's distributors requested a classification from the BBFC anyway, and, due to the Board's 'professional relationship' with the customs authorities, this was acceded to, but on two conditions: the film would not be allowed to leave the Board and secondly, if cuts were made those cuts had to be carried out on the Board's premises; also the out-takes had to remain in the building.

In an attempt to sidestep the Obscene Publications Act the modifications were overseen by a battery of Guccione's lawyers who, along with Ferman and an editor, crammed themselves into a tiny cutting-room that had previously served as the Secretary's cloakroom. Ferman was now in his element, splicing and slicing into Guccione's two-and-a-half-hour, multi-million-dollar folly. The lawyers recommended about ten-and-a-half minutes of cuts, which ranged from the Empress Livia bathing her face in a bowl of semen, sequences of actual sex, and bestiality involving a woman and a horse, to a bizarre brothel scene which had to be cut under the Protection of Children Act as it showed babies being trained for their future profession by sucking phallic-shaped bottles. Ferman now concedes that 'Ten minutes is a lot of footage', but in 1980, when the abridged film was viewed by a group of customs officials, they showed their appreciation of the Secretary's doctoring skills by declaring that, 'It's rather a good film.'

But from the point of view of granting a BBFC certificate, Ferman was still not satisfied. So he went back to work in his cloakroom where he found another four minutes to excise from this dwindling epic. This largely comprised more female genitalia, which although 'not very explicit was not the sort of thing you saw in magazines at W. H. Smiths'. Not surprisingly, therefore, 'the most controversial film of the eighties' caused a lot of disappointment and very little fuss when it finally opened at the beginning of 1981.

Yet the censorship of *Caligula* does raise an important issue. Opponents of the BBFC, such as the media lawyer, Geoffrey Robertson, have suggested that film censorship should be left to the courts. The disadvantage of such a system can be seen in the dissection of *Caligula* where, in addition to BBFC examiners demanding deletions, the lawyers had to cut a film so that it could jump through a legal hoop. A similar reading of the Obscene Publications Act had destroyed a more serious film, *Salo*; but in addition there is another law whose effects the BBFC has had to anticipate and be equally aware of, which has

229

The imperious Emperor (Malcolm McDowell) exercising his *droit de seigneur* over a newly married couple in *Caligula* (1979). What started out as an historical mess was reduced by censorship to a staccato farce.

affected numerous films, namely the Protection of Children Act.

Under the 1978 Act, which is far more stringent than any other equivalent law in the western world, it is illegal to show a sexual image of anyone below the age of sixteen. Context does not provide a defence and it is the one offence relating to the media where indecency still applies. Ferman first became aware of its implications when he was told that Louis Malle's *Pretty Baby* (1978) would have to be re-submitted to the Board because it had a shot of Brooke Shields lying naked on a *chaise longue* with her legs slightly apart. Once the film had been viewed again the problem was all too apparent. The twelve-year-old actress had no pubic hair and her vagina was, therefore, clearly visible.

Before Ferman's time the scene would simply have been removed, but censorship had advanced during the seventies in tandem with the technical progress of the film industry. In the early sixties, the critic Alexander Walker complained that the cuts demanded by the BBFC had made a film 'jump as if the cameraman had been kicked'. Now the cutter could smooth over these rough edges with sophisticated optical tricks such as retouching the film. This device was not so effective in the case of Brooke Shields's crotch, however, which as a result of intricate adjustment ended up looking as blank as the

And Oscar no longer makes three. Due to the Protection of Children Act Oscar (David Bennent) can no longer appear in the same picture that his parents are making love in. This picture has therefore had to be changed.

featureless figleaves displayed in nudist magazines during the fifties; as the BBFC examiner, Ken Penry later put it, 'The print was toned down so that the actual cleft was not visible.'

The dilemma posed by parliamentary laws for censorship is that the lawyer and the censor always have to anticipate their effect. They therefore cut deeply to make sure that there's no room for doubt in the minds of a potential jury. This wreaked havoc in the censorship of Volker Schlöndorff's *The Tin Drum* (1979) where the young hero witnesses various relatives and friends making love. As with *Pixote* (1982), the legal problem lay in whether the child-actor had actually witnessed the 'indecency' while the film was being made. This kind of judicial quandary, which is difficult to disprove, meant that *The Tin Drum* came close to being banned in Britain. In the event, Ferman demanded many cuts from a film which was left untouched in the rest of Europe, but which in Britain was graced with a stutter.

More recently the Act has taken a toll on Martha Coolidge's *Rambling Rose* (1991) because of a scene in which a fifteen-year-old actor (Lukas Haas) seduces Rose and then, crucially, masturbates her to orgasm. Film-goers had to be compensated with the fact that in Ferman's opinion: 'The scene we had

231

to trim was one of the best actor's scenes anybody here can ever remember.' In contrast, the fourteen-year-old actress Fairuza Balk was allowed to show her backside in her role as the virginal Cécile in Milos Forman's *Valmont* (1991) since the bottom in question did not belong to Ms Balk but to a body double, 'who was well over sixteen years old'. Even more importantly, the scene was so carefully staged, according to the Board, that Ms Balk never actually appeared in the same shot as her so-called 'stunt butt'.

Curiously, this Act was also responsible for literally one of the most delicate of cuts ever applied to a film. In Oshima's *In the Realm of the Senses* a pivotal scene shows the female lover looking after two pre-school children. As the little boy and girl dance naked around her she reaches out, grabs the boy by the penis and yanks. The boy pulls away and the penis stretches in the woman's hand. The boy bursts into tears, then the little girl also starts to cry and the scene ends. As Ferman points out, this would constitute 'genuine, unsimulated sexual abuse'. On the other hand as the cineaste-censor also asserts, the scene is crucial 'because that's the moment when the audience realises that the woman is unbalanced'. Also, 'having identified with her the audience now has to pull back from her because she's done something that's appalling by anybody's criteria.'

Ferman spent nearly eighteen months between August 1989 and the beginning of 1991 attempting to resolve this problem. When the film was shown at the Gate in Notting Hill during 1978, the cinema's owner had cut the penis yank on the advice of his lawyer Geoffrey Robertson, but the scene then made no sense as the film cut away when the children were dancing. Intrigued and determined to preserve the film's 'emotional fulcrum', Ferman sought the permission of Oshima to try out an 'optical zoom'.

He gave the film to the most advanced optical house in London where they stopped the film at the appropriate moment and removed the bottom fifth of the frame for about eight seconds' running time. The editors then very slowly zoomed in on the remaining four-fifths of the film and blew it up so that the whole frame was filled. As a result the audience sees the top of the woman's arm reaching out and then sees the boy's face darkening, or, as Ferman puts it, 'You see her intention but you don't see contact.'

When later faced by the comment that such intricacy merely removes the censor's fingerprints, the Secretary replied, 'We are part of the whole process of film production, distribution and exhibition.' He then added, 'I also don't think that the industry would be very happy if we announced our presence.'

Whether Ferman liked it or not, in 1977 the Labour government decided to investigate that presence through the setting up of a committee to report on film censorship and obscenity. At the outset this commission, which was placed in the well qualified hands of Bernard Williams, a sociology professor from King's College, Cambridge, declared its intention to 'establish censorship on a more rational and deliberate footing'. Understandably, the Board had a lot to fear from such words. Also, the inclusion on the committee of liberal writers such as the film critic David Robinson, the psychotherapist Anthony Storr and the social affairs journalist Polly Toynbee suggested that the committee's final report would question the necessity of adult film censorship.

Ultimately, though, the only conclusion that can be drawn from the Williams Committee was its sheer unpredictability. In their two years of deliberation the committee heard the Festival of Light line up alongside the Association of Metropolitan Authorities in favour of ending local censorship; they listened to the BBFC defend local authority interference as 'a safety valve'; they noted the GLC's request for state censorship; and heard a spokesman for film exhibitors argue that, 'the cinema should have parallel treatment to the theatre; there should, in other words, be no prior restraint and films which are challenged should be able to fight for their rights before a jury in open court.'

Apart from the rebuke to the BBFC, this statement by the General Secretary of the Cinema Exhibitors Association, Robert Camplin, throws a rare light on the relationship between the film industry and film censorship. The CEA had been the main proponent and supporter of the BBFC at its birth and in its infancy. Now, in a forecast of the industry's attitude to the video scare seven years later, a trade magazine replied to Camplin's remarks in the same terms that the CEA itself had used at the 1917 Commission on Cinema when it wanted to outlaw independent distributors. 'Perhaps,' the editorial suggested, 'it is not unkind to conclude that there is a breed of exhibitor who would be

This still from *In the Realm of the Senses* (1976) has been censored in the same way that the scene was in the film that was shown within Britain.

233

delighted to have a green light on showing hard-core porn because he believes he will make a great deal of money from so doing, while relying less on existing distribution companies and more on his own initiative.' In other words, stay in the existing censorship system or you will be treated as a renegade.

After weighing up a great deal of conflicting evidence the Williams Committee finally published its conclusions at the end of 1979, and on first reading, their recommendations appeared to be extremely radical. 'Censorship imposed by local authorities on the basis of their powers to license cinemas should be ended.' 'A statutory board should be set up to take over the censorship powers of the local authorities and the functions now exercised by the British Board of Film Censors . . . The Board should be known as the Film Examining Board and should comprise about twelve members chosen to represent a range of interests, including the film industry and local government, and relevant expertise.' To everybody's surprise a liberal committee set up under a socialist government had, in effect, recommended state control of film censorship.

The Williams Committee, however, proved to be incapable of even performing this ideological *volte face* without shooting itself in the foot. Two clauses later it recommended the appointment of 'a Chief Examiner of Films and . . . a small staff of film examiners to take decisions on individual films.' Williams, presumably, wanted to preserve the existing day-to-day operation of film vetting. Nevertheless, with the exception of the BBFC's President and Secretary being replaced by a committee, the committee had simply stated that film censorship should now have the force of law with no means of appeal. Even Ferman, who was fearful that the committee would not recognise the necessity of any kind of board, baulked at the prospect of so much power being put at the service of censorship.

By the time this exhaustive survey had been published a Conservative government under Margaret Thatcher had come to office and it would have seemed a natural, if not an ideologically appropriate, step for it to have seized the opportunity to centralise the legal authority of film censorship. Yet, since the origins of the BBFC in 1912, governments of all persuasions have taken an ambivalent attitude towards an institution that brings controversy as well as political control. Apart from the question of overseeing the cinema, however, the Williams Report had arrived at the politically unacceptable conclusion that the link between films and the 'deprave and corrupt' test had not been proved – their implications being that the causes of corruption amongst the nation's youth could be found in the environment rather than on the cinema screen. The findings of this well argued but politically ill-timed report were therefore quietly buried.

On the other hand, the Williams Committee, acting on the advice of the Board, did set in motion a train of events, which, ironically, very nearly led to the bankruptcy of the BBFC. The first event which set this surprising process in motion took place when the Board provided a viewing for the committee of the same collection of film cuts that it usually showed to suspicious councillors or interested observers of the BBFC's work. Ferman then suggested that the committee visit Soho's sex clubs where they would be able to make comparisons with the sort of films from which the cuts had come. The outraged members thus came to the conclusion that these sex clubs should be restricted since they showed films which 'served no purpose other than to sell the idea that it is highly pleasurable to inflict pain'.

It was subsequently decided that the best way to close this censorship loophole was to dissolve the sex clubs' use of twenty-four-hour membership and in that way bring all film clubs within the ambit of the same local licensing laws that applied to other cinemas. Furthermore, Williams also recommended that from this time on these licensed clubs should only be allowed to show titles which had been passed by the BBFC. But at the same time that he wanted to incorporate clubs into the BBFC system Williams also recommended that a new category which his report referred to as 'Restricted 18' should be adopted. This new classification, taken from the French censorship system, would allow non-violent pornography to be exhibited in those new specially licensed cinemas.

At the time Ferman took – and continues to take – a liberal attitude towards consensual sex on the screen. He therefore acted upon the Williams suggestion for a new category as it would 'enable us to pass a few films each year which we believe to be legal and harmless but which are rather beyond what most local authorities are today prepared to accept in the adult cinema.'

He hoped it would also benefit the Board's finances. Then, as now, the BBFC's income was solely dependent upon the fees charged for the classification of films. In 1982, however, the supply of films being submitted to the Board was drying up due to the effects of the recession on the American and British film industries. Earlier that year, with film submissions dwindling to their lowest figure in the Board's history, Ferman had been forced to reduce two of his five examiners to a one-day week. The Secretary therefore eagerly anticipated the 'flood of sex films' which the Williams Committee had helpfully pointed in the direction of the expectant Board. Surely, the examiners told themselves, the Board would now be saved by the public's incessant demand for cinematic sex?

As for Williams's suggestion that local licensing laws should be applied to the new BBFC 'R18'-certificated sex cinemas, this happily coincided with the government's current 'return to family values' and the proposal was therefore implemented under the Cinematograph Amendment Act of 1982. Thus the stage was set for a brave step forward into a future where consensual soft pornography would be brought out into the open and made available to local cinema-goers. No longer would the Board's examiners be splitting pubic hairs trying to make up their minds as to whether they should excise the third buttock, delete the fifth pair of breasts or blank out inappropriate genitalia. Ten years after America and the rest of Europe, unbridled love-making would finally be seen in British cinemas.

Unfortunately the sex films never arrived at the BBFC. This was on account of the yawning chasm between the intention and the actual effect of Williams's ill-fated recommendations. The reason why these films never appeared was because there was nowhere to show them once they had been classified. Almost without exception the local authorities demurred from Ferman and Williams's invitation to grant licences to 'R18' sex cinemas within their own precincts. Moreover, in Soho, the ruling authority at Westminster not only refused to grant any applications for new licences, they took advantage of the Cinematograph Act to close down most of the existing cinemas that catered to the 'raincoat brigade'. So after a brief gulp of air the pornographic film industry was once more driven underground where it continues to flourish to this day.

As for the 'R18' category itself, that was consigned to limbo where it has now become a source of censorship by classification, since any film or video which is so designated is restricted to a handful of cinemas or licensed video stores. Once the international sex film distributors had absorbed that lesson they no longer bothered to submit their titles to the Board, with the consequence that the BBFC still faced bankruptcy.

Thus in one stroke Ferman somehow managed to minimise as well as maximise the power of the Board. He helped to bring sex cinema clubs within the orbit of the Board, but at the same time he destabilised a part of the industry which might be regarded as immoral in some quarters, but which nevertheless contributed over a third of the BBFC's annual income. On the other hand, by 1983 Ferman had stabilised the political position of the Board. He had gained the support of influential liberal opinion-makers on cinematic sexual violence; but, even more importantly, he had had luck on his side. None of the films which were submitted during the first part of his tenure contained the same explosive mixture of controversy and popularity which had ignited under the censorship system in the early seventies.

Also he did not suffer from the sort of interference that constantly hounded his predecessors. In the summer of 1979, Mary Whitehouse and the Festival of Light tried to whip up public indignation over Monty Python's *The Life of Brian* which they attacked as 'sick, its story veering unsteadily between sadism and sheer silliness'. Repeating their tactic against *Last Tango in Paris*, the evangelical activists again circulated an excerpt from the film's script (the Hermit scene) to various MPs and other potentially susceptible public opinion-makers. But once the actual film opened very few people took *The Life of*

Behold the Messiah.
Graham Chapman in
the title role of *The
Life of Brian* (1979),
which Mary White-
house attempted –
unsucessfully – to
prod into
controversy.

Brian or the Festival's campaign against it as anything more than an amusing
example of British eccentricity at its best.

In the same year various local authorities felt that they 'had to be seen to
take a strong line' against Walter Hill's *The Warriors* due to pre-publicity surrounding its depiction of gang warfare on New York's subway system. But, in
fact, Hill's treatment of stylised violence owed more to *West Side Story* than to
The Wild One – most of the cast were ballet dancers – and once more a film
did not accord with press predictions. In a genuflection to the past, rather than
the present powers of provincial censorship, Ferman felt that he ought to make
deletions to the film; but he then discovered that there was nothing to cut.
Moreover, he realised that if he did remove anything he would break up Hill's
visual fluency and give the audience an unexpected jolt. So, as a sop to the
councils, he raised the film's category from 'A' to 'X'.

Regrettably, a lack of controversy and conflict, and even the consolidation
of power over film and its outlets, did not make up for a shortage of funds
with which to run the BBFC. Yet, within one year, the Board would expand
from its unpretentious offices on the second floor of 3 Soho Square to occupy
all five floors of the Georgian building; and from his own refurbished office
overlooking London's film district Ferman would feel ever more secure in the
knowledge that the BBFC's influence was spreading into areas that his predecessors could never have dreamed of. That gap between the threat of imminent
bankruptcy and a future of prosperity and empire-building would be filled by
the emergent new film technology popularly known as video.

VIDEO GAMES 14 ✂

The emergence of video provoked exactly the same response as the birth of moving pictures at the turn of the century. It was a runaway success; but, like film eighty years before, it was viewed with acute suspicion by the political establishment. While the immediate anarchy surrounding the sales of videos attracted opportunists, the reaction from the more respectable side of the film trade also echoed that of Edwardian film distributors: the business had to rid itself of vulgarity; it had to be made respectable if it was to enjoy the custom of the middle classes, which in turn meant that irresponsible elements had to be cast out for the sake of a rational, well organised, responsible industry. The final immersion in Edwardian waters was performed by politicians who inevitably and immediately scented a bureaucratic vacuum in the chaos which accompanies any new industry. In the arena of censorship where film meets politics, the contemporary age would now fulfil the first rule of this self-restraining institution: political control is applied in direct proportion to the popularity of a new medium.

Thus the invention of video provided opportunities for all and it was with that premise in mind that the nascent industry sought self-regulation. The industry did not lack the means to tell potential customers what videos contained; that was all too apparent on garish covers of axes embedded in skulls and drills bursting through eyeballs. On the contrary, what the major distributors wanted was a system whereby easily offended customers could tell conventional, mainstream film videos from the exploitation tapes on offer from the 'merchants of menace'.

In November 1981 the British Videogram Association entered into negotiations with the Board of Film Censors. Within a year the two organisations had drawn up a code of practice similar to the film censorship system, and by 1983 many of the major distribution companies were submitting their titles to the Board for classification. At the time, Ferman said that he wanted to reinforce the voluntary system with the use of sanctions against renegade retailers who sold uncertificated titles. But such a step would have been unnecessary; for the compliant distributors would have undoubtedly repeated the early history of film censorship when the less responsible exhibitors were forced into line by the major distributors' monopoly of available films.

Opposite Hooked on you: passed by the GLC in the year of its release, *The Texas Chainsaw Massacre* (1974) won new fame in the mid-eighties as a 'video nasty'. But by that time this classic horror film had already been rejected by the Board three times.

239

History, though, was not permitted to repeat itself. Britain jumped instead into a state system of film censorship that it had successfully avoided for almost seven decades. Admittedly the censorship of celluloid had quickly become voluntary in name only, but the delegation of power over videotape to the government during 1984 meant that from then on a separate and statutory certificate would be needed for a video release. This would now be added to a film's initial BBFC classification. Yet the introduction of a second certificate for video brought with it the most secretive and pervasive measure of media control that Britain has ever imposed upon itself. From the point of view of film history, not to mention freedom of information, one question naturally occurs: how did this happen?

It is not an accident that, in the early eighties when video was still in a legislative vacuum, Sam Raimi's frenetic comic-chiller *The Evil Dead* (1983) was the biggest selling title on the video market. The new medium was perfectly suited to the marketing of horror films. The audience for them is young and therefore the quickest to adapt to a new technology but, as from time immemorial, juvenile taste in the early 1980s upset 'ordinary people'. And it was this eternal difference that was seized upon by Mary Whitehouse when she showed a compilation of highlights from horror videos to Conservative MPs at their party conference in the summer of 1983.

Whitehouse had labelled the new medium, with its mixture of skull-splitting, eye-crunching and tongue-skewering, the 'video nasty'; but the term actually covered a multitude of films, ranging from the irresistible to the unbearable, from Wes Craven's adaptation of Bergman's vengeful *Virgin Spring* (1959), *Last House on the Left* – which had been banned by the BBFC back in 1972 – to more recent, so-called documentaries like *Faces of Death* (1980) which, in this instance, turned mortality into a freak show. But, of course, any cinematic distinction between fast-moving, innovative examples of the horror genre like *The Evil Dead* and the static dismemberment of women or animals which distinguished other 'nasties' was lost in the hot-house atmosphere of a government party conference; so, not surprisingly, Mrs Whitehouse's indiscriminate compilation provoked the desired response.

Also, and even more to the point, those Conservative MPs faced an election in a few weeks' time and their image as the party of law and order appeared dishevelled. The first recession of the eighties had led to riots in Toxteth, Southall and Bristol; maybe a promise to rid the country of the new film curse so prevalent on the nation's high streets might distract the electorate's mind from any link between urban riots and the government's chosen policies.

For nearly twenty years both film censors and their opponents had been able to withstand the moral reductivism of Mrs Whitehouse because the infinitely indignant housewife had not been able to win over mainstream opinion to her cause. But now a holier-than-thou alliance was forged between the moral minority and the Conservative Party, and together they would bring about Britain's first film censorship law.

Before this could be done, however, a moral panic had to be induced with the 'nasty' nailed to the masthead. In the ensuing furore that blew up over the easy access which video provided for the unrestricted viewing of horror films, the salvationists and their sympathisers in the Conservative Party enjoyed three crucial advantages. Film critics who would normally have opposed censorship had yet to appreciate the potential of horror as a film subject; those who did recognise the merits of the revived genre in the work of such directors as David Cronenburg, George Romero and Abel Ferrara were too young for their views to be considered relevant; lastly, and most importantly, the video proscribers could direct and dictate the terms of the argument to a massive audience through the prurient sections of the tabloid press.

As the handmaiden of Conservative Party opinion, the *Daily Mail* led the self-fulfilling campaign on its editorial pages with the constant coupling of 'nasties' to those who sold them. 'How much longer,' the paper asked on 30 June 1983, 'will the Government dither and Parliament blather while our children can continue to buy sadism from the video-pusher as easily – and almost as cheaply – as they can buy fruit gums from the sweetie shop?'

Through the Director of Public Prosecutions the government acted on this heavy-handed hint and followed the *Daily Mail*'s accusing finger all the way past the distributors and copyright owners of video nasties directly to the video retailers, where the police then carried out wholesale confiscation of tapes. Such leapfrogging over more established opponents was an astute tactic by the DPP, for the video traders were the weakest link in the industry due to their lack of financial resources. Unfortunately, the police lacked what BBFC examiners called 'film literacy' and as a result during that summer they tended to stray away from their remit. In Slough they impounded copies of the Dolly Parton musical comedy *The Best Little Whorehouse in Texas* (1982) from a newsagent, while a week later in August their colleagues in Manchester swooped down on Sam Fuller's war film *The Big Red One* (1980) which, to the surprise of the local constabulary, owed its title to the director's Second World War battalion.

In an attempt to snare more appropriate videos, Superintendent Kruger of the Metropolitan Police sought the guidance of the DPP, with the result that a list was drawn up in the latter half of 1984 of approximately sixty potentially obscene titles which became known as 'the DPP's big 60'. It included some risible examples of depravity such as Francis Ford Coppola's Vietnam war film *Apocalypse Now*; nevertheless prosecutions under the Obscene Publications Act went ahead, although convictions tended to depend on the area in which trials took place.

That did not pose a problem, however, for the government, as the Obscene

Publications Act does not actually apply to obscene materials, but to the 'distribution' of such material. Therefore the DPP office could – and did – repeatedly prosecute particular video dealers until it got a conviction. On the other hand, because the new industry provided such quick profits, convicted retailers were soon replaced by eager newcomers. Under the prompting of Mary Whitehouse the government therefore decided to switch tactics and prosecute a video distributor; and the 'obscene material' that this particular company was accused of distributing was Sam Raimi's *The Evil Dead*.

Billed by Mary Whitehouse as 'the number one nasty', *The Evil Dead* (1983) propels five innocent young students on a roller-coaster ride through zombie-lore and so much 'gore-fest' that even the normally phlegmatic James Ferman described it as 'over the top in its special effects'. Although the film's college humour violated the BBFC's Achilles heel concerning black comedy, Ferman was initially in favour of passing the film version. He told the distributor, Stephen Woolley of Palace Pictures, that Raimi's first feature had been made with 'a great deal of talent' and that it was 'almost a parody of horror'. Therefore he 'could probably let it through uncut'.

At the film's actual examination in front of the Board, Ferman and one of the examiners soon gave way to howls of laughter at 'the enormous gunk coming out of the walls and the blood spewing everywhere in all different colours'. The other examiner present, however (Ferman refused to identify either of them), remained ominously silent and once the film was over she vented her feelings. She was 'nauseated', it had 'affected her physically'; in fact her 'bodily integrity had been attacked'. Ferman decided that, 'if the film was going to have that sort of effect on some people' he had better 'take it down a little bit'.

The most specific criticism that the Williams Committee voiced against Ferman at the time of their Report in 1979 had been the Secretary's tendency to practise 'quantitative censorship'. In other words, as the committee asked, 'Will the third glimpse of a bloodied face or a third twitch of buttocks change the quality of what has been allowed twice?' Nevertheless, it would be this method of censorship that was applied to *The Evil Dead* in 1983.

One minute of footage, including a pencil being twisted into a leg and the surviving hero being hit repeatedly over the head with an iron girder by a female zombie, was removed. 'According to Jim [Ferman],' one anonymous examiner was later to comment, 'wiggling the pencil twice was completely unacceptable, whereas wiggling it once was all right.' Stephen Woolley also points out that the reduction from five to three blows in the girder scene rendered the effect more horrific not less, because 'by the fifth hit on the head the audience is laughing and saying how ridiculous it all is; whereas, with the cut, the violence is sudden and much more shocking.'

For the DPP, however, this was an 'obscene' videotape which Palace Pictures was accused of distributing, even though it had been passed by the film censor.

Opposite Sam Raimi's *The Evil Dead* (1983) – hailed by horror fans but branded the 'number one nasty' by Mary Whitehouse.

Presumably for that reason, on 7 November 1983 the jury at Snaresbrook Crown Court returned a verdict of 'not guilty' against Palace. In an immediate response though to that decision the junior Home Office minister David Mellor revealed the government's plans to transfer the site of its battle against the 'nasties' away from the quicksand of the Obscene Publications Act, in which the effect of a film or video has to be taken as a whole, to the firmer ground of video classification. 'The classic simplicity of the bill,' the minister told the House of Commons, 'is its proposal that the only matter of concern to the courts will be whether a video has a certificate.'

Consequently, the certificate issued by a government-delegated authority would replace the courts as the means to decide whether or not a video was 'nasty'; and thus the possibility of 'astonishing decisions' would be removed, along with the right to an impartial open hearing in which video distributors and retailers could present evidence.

The actual 'simplicity' of the resulting Video Recordings Act lay in the test of what would now contravene the law. If a video was sold without an approved certificate the seller of that video would be liable to a £20,000 fine. The contents, therefore, of a video no longer mattered; what was at issue was whether or not the cover of the video bore the government's stamp of approval. The immediate disadvantage of such a system was the fact that it had to be compulsory and all-encompassing to be effective. Unlike cinema-goers, who can see banned films in specific cinemas such as the National Film Theatre or the Institute of Contemporary Arts, under this act video buyers would not be provided with the opportunity to see what the censor had removed or rejected.

Once the Video Recordings Act was fine-tuned, furthermore, in the bill's Standing Committee, the disadvantages would multiply. In the meantime, while the law was being formulated, Parliament had to decide who the video censor would be. Of course only one practical choice presented itself; but, nevertheless, the Conservative side of the House of Commons poured scorn on the BBFC's qualifications: one examiner worked part-time at a Rape Crisis Centre, and therefore, according to the backbench MP Sir Bernard Braine, she was an 'ultra-leftist'; another was a reader at the publishers Jonathan Cape, and was therefore 'trendy'. Inevitably, the only censor on the Board who passed muster was Ken Penry who, according to Braine, possessed the all-important credential of having been an RAF wing-commander.

Before the BBFC could be officially designated as the video censor, however, the man who had done most to effect that delegation of authority to the Board died in a car accident. The President of the BBFC, David Harlech, had held the confidence of the government front bench and especially that of his friend the Home Secretary William Whitelaw. It was Lord Harlech who instructed James Ferman in the ways of Westminster, who pointed out to the American-born censor that the 'arm's-length principle' of delegated authority had sustained the Board for seventy years, and that it would now win for them the plum of video. 'Don't you understand,' he told his colleague, 'that for a practising politician to be able to say, "don't look at us, look at them", is a crucial advantage? For that reason they'll be happy to have someone who is independent of the government.' And, as Ferman himself added more recently, 'that's what happened.'

With Harlech's untimely death, Ferman lost his principal adviser. According to the examiners, the Board's Secretary was 'stunned', 'devastated', and 'lost'. 'As soon as Lord Harlech realised,' Ferman remembered, 'that I was prepared to do that press conference on my first day at the Board he coached me in being confident, in how to give interviews; in when not to say too little and when not to say too much.' Moreover, the death of this popular censor would also affect the rest of the Board. 'He was a court of appeal,' says one censor, 'because if he approved or disapproved of a film he would quite often have the last word; and although he was sometimes peremptory we all trusted him completely. He was not Jim's creature. You must remember that he had appointed Jim, so it was a respectful relationship.'

A vacuum had now been created at the head of the Board and it had to be filled quickly because of the exact legal nature of the BBFC's new authority to censor video. That authority was not delegated by the government to the BBFC as a whole, or even to Ferman but specifically to the new President and to the two new vice-Presidents – whose office had been created under the Video Recordings Act 1984 (VRA). In theory these three Presidents would be the most powerful members of the Board. The BBFC would act in their name and they would be responsible to Parliament – and the public – for the carrying out of the VRA. In order for them to retain any kind of power in practice, however, they would have to demonstrate a knowledge of film and BBFC bureaucracy that was equal to Ferman's, and this, the new President, Lord Harewood, and his two deputies, Monica Sims and Lord Birkett, failed to do. So it would be Ferman, not them, who decided what films should be viewed by the public's representatives on the Board. On the relatively rare occasions when the head censor has requested the presence of the Presidents in the BBFC viewing room it has to be a matter, however, of some doubt whether the public has been well served. For their designated officials have literally been sleeping partners. 'If the Presidents stayed awake during the viewing of films, it would help,' one examiner commented.

It is unlikely, however, that the Home Office's initial nominee for Harlech's replacement as BBFC President would have proved an improvement on the actual appointment. For Ian Trethowan, the government's first choice to head the Board, was selected purely on the grounds of his known sympathy for the Prime Minister's policies. Not since 1972, when the Conservative minister

Reginald Maudling had insisted upon visiting the Board to see *A Clockwork Orange*, had a government so blatantly interfered in the administration of film censorship. Curiously, James Ferman happened to be on holiday in Crete at the time of the proposed appointment, so it was left to his deputy, the redoubtable wartime pilot Ken Penry, to turn back this attempt to pack the Board. Fortunately Penry had the support of his colleagues, who threatened to resign en masse if the Home Office imposed Trethowan by dictat. The government therefore withdrew its nominee.

With the actual passing into law of the Video Recordings Act it soon became apparent to most members of the Board that the government had buried a cluster of time bombs within the bill – which the BBFC then had to administer. The first fuse had been laid when the Standing Committee's unofficial adviser Mary Whitehouse tried to have a 'deeming list' inserted into the bill which would have demarcated 'those elements of violence and obscenity which should be deemed illegal'. Such absolute terms, however, proved too difficult even for the acquiescent MPs on the committee. So instead the dogged Whitehouse persuaded Sir Bernard Braine to insist upon the inclusion of the famous clause requiring that classification must have 'special regard to the likelihood of video works . . . being viewed in the family home'.

The subsequent adoption of these words could be taken to mean that any video image which could upset a child old enough to recognise what was on the television screen should be banned. Thankfully, the Board's examiners did not take the clause in this light. In fact they were oblivious to it. 'Some of us,' said one censor almost a decade later, 'were at great pains to point out that less than a third of homes have children under sixteen in them; therefore the whole audience could not be censored down to the level of a "PG" certificate.' Another examiner put it even more bluntly. 'The phrase is nonsense because I, as a censor, cannot police the home; that's not my job, yet that was what the Standing Committee claimed the Act was all about. In fact it was a cosmetic exercise to get a government into power because in the final analysis it does not matter what I classify a video as, since that is entirely dependent upon those who either sell it, hire it or the homes in which it is seen.'

A decade later, in 1993, Ferman also admitted that the impossibility of enforcing the clause constitutes 'a major problem'. Also, when asked if there was a contradiction in the classification system for videos, since they are given certificates for different age groups while, at the same time, they are supposedly being censored for children, the chief censor replied, 'Yes, there is,' and then finally conceded that the categories 'are simply consumer advice'.

Nevertheless, Sir Bernard Braine's impractical phrase does affect film censorship because Ferman argues that, 'we do have to take seriously the idea that certain images will be seen in the home.' In particular it has meant that one of the most popular videos in the world has yet to be certificated in Britain.

'The central character in *The Exorcist* [1973],' Ferman explains, 'is a twelve-year-old girl, and because she is possessed and this voice is coming out of her saying these outrageous obscenities we had to bear in mind the "suitability" test. Also we had to ask ourselves, 'If this film is seen by any under-age kids, would it be so terrifying that it would seriously disturb them?'

The answer is presumably yes; because Warners, the distributors of *The Exorcist* have repeatedly asked Ferman for a video certificate. But before a video – or a film – can even be considered for classification it has to gain permission from the Board to be submitted. Although this particular film was never deemed by the DPP to be a 'video nasty', Warners tactfully delayed their video submission to the Board until the publicity surrounding the Video Recordings Act had died down. The patience of the distributors held up until 1988, presumably because they did not want to release a cut version of the movie. By the spring of that year, however, they had prepared all the attendant publicity for an imminent release of their biggest-selling title. At the last minute, though, Ferman scuppered that plan by citing recent cases of child abuse, and a year later in 1989, reports of satanic child abuse provided an even more appropriate excuse.

Setting aside the censor's perennial habit of coupling films to successive social problems, the censorship of *The Exorcist* highlights the constant likelihood

Passed in every country to which it has been submitted, *The Exorcist* (1973) is banned on video in Britain.

of collusion between the censor and the censored. Ferman has admitted that he has regular telephone conversations with Warners about the status of *The Exorcist*, but he is ambiguous about their content. 'I don't think,' he said 'that it has ever been submitted officially because that film and *Straw Dogs* are the two titles that I have constantly said would give us difficulties.' The Secretary then revealed that, 'There are two scenes [including Regan's notorious masturbation with a crucifix when she screams, "Fuck me, fuck me"] that might have to be cut in *The Exorcist* for the home. But on the other hand' says Ferman, confirming Warners' wishes, 'does one want to cut a film as famous as *The Exorcist*? It would be better to pass it uncut.' The deadlock continues.

One of the requisites of censorship, according to James Ferman, is that it should reflect public opinion; and although the chief censor concedes that it is difficult for one decision on an individual film to incorporate the multiplicity of opinions at large in society, nevertheless the Board can, in the last resort, reverse earlier conclusions. 'Bear in mind,' the head censor advises, 'that we can always come to a different decision five, seven or many years later. If we drop a clanger we can put it right.'

But this safety net, as the film commentator Mark Kermode has revealed, does not apply to video. Under the terms of the Video Recordings Act, Ferman is unable to reverse video decisions whether or not they accord with public opinion. Once a video category has been assigned by the Board that classification is permanent, and this immutability is the second and most crucial fault line running through the 1984 bill.

Evidently, at the time of the Act's passage through Parliament none of the legislators took into account the effect of time on film censorship; for there is no provision within the Act to say that once a video has been classified the same version of that title can be granted anything other than the certificate it was given at the time of its original submission. In other words, unless a tape is 'substantially' altered between submissions the certificate – or the refusal of a certificate – cannot be changed.

The root of this problem lies with the Home Office, because it is their guidelines on the meaning of the VRA that bracket the Board's video decisions. In an attempt to thaw this ice-bound system, Ferman asked the government if he could reconsider video decisions and reinstate cuts. But the Home Office's reply merely restated the 'suitable for home' test. 'Once a video has been passed,' they told Ferman, 'it is out there on the shelves,' and therefore, 'it cannot be controlled in the same way that a film is in the cinema.'

This argument is predicated not only upon the assertion that video buyers are beyond any form of social control, but also that public attitudes are locked into stasis. Ferman himself acknowledges his imposed impotency. 'We cannot rescind decisions. That's it,' he says. But he must also be aware that this policy which has been foisted upon him will have increasing repercussions on the credibility of the Board. Because many of the BBFC's decisions, some of which at the time of writing were already a decade old, will become more and more irrelevant with the passage of time.

The other inconvenient residue left behind by the VRA was unintentionally outlined by its sponsor, Graham Bright, when he brought his Bill before Parliament. 'Some of the worst tapes,' he complained, 'have been caught by the Obscene Publications Act, but there are a large number whose context falls short of the strict test of obscenity in that Act.' The MP need not have been concerned, though; a video only had to be put on the DPP's list, and not necessarily prosecuted, for the BBFC to regard it as problematic. The Board has no choice about this because their decisions always have to be taken in the light of relevant laws. In theory the Board has to check whether a particular video has been convicted for obscenity but if the DPP thought that the title was impoundable then it is safe to assume that the Board's subsequent treatment of the film will be affected – even if there has been no conviction.

As a result of the stigma attached to being on the DPP's 1984 list even less obviously cruel video nasties, such as *The Burning* (1980) and *The Evil Dead*, have to be altered 'significantly' before they can be granted a certificate. In the former film a series of killings featuring garden shears had to be severely trimmed. (Shears are included in the Home Office's video nasty guidelines under the heading 'everyday implements'.) In the latter case the DPP's designation meant that another minute, made up from the arboreal rape scene – 'initially we did not think that anybody would identify with a tree,' says Ferman – had to be whittled off the already censored film release version of *The Evil Dead*.

In fact, less than half of the video nasties on 'the DPP's big 60' list have currently been granted BBFC certificates. At the time of the video scare in 1982–4 it was argued by others, besides the censors, that the screening of the detailed rape and mutilation of women as well as the actual killing of defenceless animals in films such as *Cannibal Apocalypse* (1980) and *I Spit On Your Grave* (1978) should not be allowed to gain a profit for their creators. Indeed, it is difficult to agree with the restaurant customer in the so-called documentary *Faces of Death* (1980), when he asks, 'If I can get closer to "Gawd" by eating monkey brains, why not?' But the atmosphere engendered by such tawdry examples of the cinema also tarred other very different films with the 'nasty' brush.

'The only gore movie genuinely to approach art,' says the critic Kim Newman, 'is Abel Ferrara's *Driller Killer*.' The branding, however, of this fast-paced, 1980 punk-style movie as a member of the 'nasty' species has billeted it in an uncertificated limbo ever since 1984. Exactly why the DPP chose this particular exploitation film for prosecution is mysterious. It does not pander to the sexist rape fantasies so common in films of its type. Instead, with the

The white man's burden. *Cannibal Apocalypse* (1980), a conventionally over-imaginative horror chiller featuring 'POWs in captivity . . . starved in captivity . . . released with a taste for human flesh!' was caught in the 'nasty' net.

Opposite With its title and eye-catching cover, Abel Ferrara's *Driller Killer* (1980) became an obvious target for exorcism during the video scare of the early eighties.

illogical logic of a psychotic, its protagonist (played by the director) kills Bowery bums out of a fear common to natives of New York – downward social mobility. But Reno kills those he does not want to join with an electric drill (doubtless categorised as an 'everyday implement' by the Home Office). Under the Obscene Publications Act, a film or video has to be judged as a whole; yet undoubtedly it is this one moment, in an otherwise obliquely violent picture, when Reno's power drill enters a vagrant's eyeball that removed any doubts from the minds of many a juror.

Like other videos of the time, *Driller Killer* also suffered from its own publicity. The very title and its 'most appalling eye-popping cover,' as Ferman described it, propelled the film beyond the redemptive touch of the censor. Moreover, the conviction of a video as obscene had a knock-on effect in which the film version suffered from the same stigma, even if it had not been officially outlawed. For this reason no distributor has bothered to submit Ferrara's directorial debut to the censor for either a film or video certificate; but after informally examining the picture, Ferman's deputy Ken Penry revealed that *Driller Killer* 'was cuttable. We could have taken out that particular [eyeball] shot, but the distributor lost interest. From their point of view if they don't keep the goodies, it's just not worth progressing.' But this inimitable censor also admits that, at the time, he was not an admirer of Ferrara's fluent, low-slung, hand-held camera technique. 'Now and again,' he snorts, 'you get clever dicks who say, "Aaah, this is art. This is bigger than it seems." But I think of Joe Bloggs who's going to the Odeon on Saturday night who's not on that

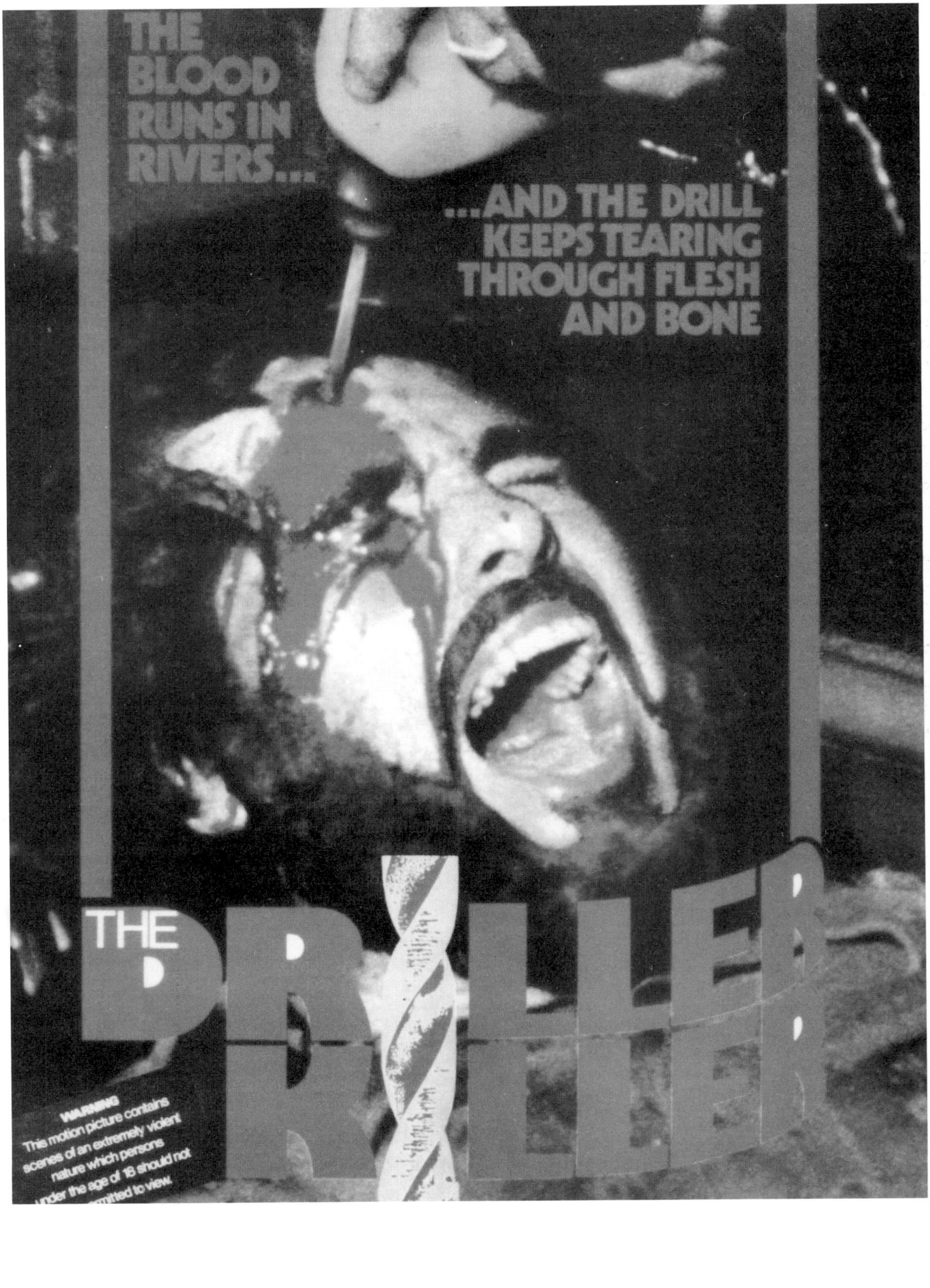
THE BLOOD RUNS IN RIVERS...
...AND THE DRILL KEEPS TEARING THROUGH FLESH AND BONE
THE DRILLER KILLER
WARNING
This motion picture contains scenes of an extremely violent nature which persons under the age of 18 should not
mitted to view.

Just as Hitchcock's *Psycho* (1960) revived the chiller in the sixties, Tobe Hooper's ground-breaking *The Texas Chainsaw Massacre* (1973) rejuvenated horror in the eighties.

wavelength. He's going along seeing it literally as it's presented and I always keep that in mind.' Summing up, the no-nonsense adjudicator pronounces that, 'Joe Bloggs is the majority and film censorship is for the majority.'

In the gap between the initial popularity of video during 1982, and its censorship by the BBFC in 1984, a relatively old film seized the imagination of young horror fans; probably because this time the contents of a film lived up to its name. Made in 1973, *The Texas Chainsaw Massacre* is loosely based on the macabre exploits of Ed Gein, the Wisconsin farmer whose incident-rich life also provided the source for Bob Clark's *Deranged* (1974) as well as Hitchcock's *Psycho* in 1960. In Tobe Hooper's 1973 version, two young couples and a crippled friend wander into the home of four unemployed slaughter-house workers who have been transformed by Hooper into an outrageous, inverted parody of that all-American institution the family. Led by doddering Granpaw – 'the best killer there ever was' – as the pater familias, and featuring the chainsaw-wielding, bewigged Leatherface as an overworked Mom, this disturbing clan pursue their filial motto, 'our family has always been into meat', at the expense of the unsuspecting visitors.

According to Ken Penry, *The Texas Chainsaw Massacre* 'was rather unique because it did not have particularly outrageous visuals; but it was so well made it had this awful impact all the way through. It was a revolting film, and I still think so.' Although it relied so effectively upon suggestion rather than depiction, the bloodless picture was nevertheless banned when it was originally submitted to the Board in March 1975. The film did gain a London certificate from the GLC at the time; but the distributors still hoped for a wider general release so they retraced their steps to the BBFC's door two years later, by which time James Ferman had become Secretary.

'*The Texas Chainsaw Massacre* seemed like the pornography of terror,' the Secretary later commented. In an astute stratagem, however, the distributors appealed to Ferman's better nature. 'They asked me to come and work with their editor to see if we could make it more palatable.' The team removed the obvious violence, such as a shot of one of the female victims hanging up on a meat-hook and they even knew where the 'main problem' lay; nevertheless they also realised that they were trying to pin down an elusive target.

What these particular film doctors discovered was the impossibility of censoring intangibles such as a 'macabre atmosphere' or 'mental terrorisation'. Yet there was one slow-moving scene in the film's high-velocity viciousness that could possibly be tinkered with. Here, in fitting homage to the family heritage, Granpaw is given the honour of delivering the *coup de grâce* to the last survivor with the same ball-peen hammer that he used to stun cattle with. Yet even here the censor found his scissors blunted by Granpaw's decrepitude because the hammer keeps glancing off the victim's scalp. Admittedly this does not stop the old man from attempting repeated blows, but the intended victim's endless screams do not help his aim.

Everybody on the Board watched the cut version and, as the editor manqué remembers nearly ten years later, 'at the end, they all said, "it hasn't made any difference at all; it's exactly the same film. Taking out those moments of explicit violence has not helped."' 'The problem,' they now realised was 'psychological torture'. Heaving a sigh, Ferman then declared in the tone of a hunter bemoaning the one that got away, 'We tried.' And he was to try again three years later, but once again he was defeated by the fact that, unlike the co-accused in the 'nasty' dock, Hooper always cuts away from gaping eviscerations and leaves the audience instead with the sound of an approaching chainsaw. If a film is censor-proof, though, the censorious do not question themselves. They merely remove the evidence of their failure.

Not surprisingly, the greatest repercussions of the Video Recordings Act were upon the Board itself. The immediate difference was economic. The fees from the backlog of videos which now had to bear the BBFC's stamp would pull the Board back from the brink of bankruptcy. What was an unsteady trickle of submitted films became a flood of tapes, and the promise of continued supplies meant that the Board itself could now afford to splash out on a facelift. From one dingy floor of 3 Soho Square, the BBFC colonised the whole building which was then remodelled, carpeted throughout and decked out in chrome. In a simultaneous acknowledgement of corporate aggrandisement the BBFC renamed itself in the middle of 1985 the British Board of Film Classification and the Secretary was re-cast as the Director. This, however, was not merely Orwellian newspeak; the function as well as the face of the BBFC had irrevocably changed.

From an intimate little group of four examiners and the Secretary classifying under 400 films in 1984, the Board would grow to seventy-one people processing 4,000 films and tapes every year. What one of the examiners described as the 'cosy pleasantly unpretentious' atmosphere of a senior common room transformed itself into a factory where the conveyor belt never stopped belching out a stream of video cassettes.

To censor the backlog of 6,000 video tapes, which had to be classified by the end of 1986, the BBFC for the first time in its history publicly advertised for new examiners. Once the applicants had been winnowed out by Ferman and his deputy Ken Penry, the Board found itself with six male university graduates, one of whom boasted a PhD in German cinema. This group, which came to be known as the 'Soho 6', were now trained by the senior examiner, Margaret Ford, to become what Ferman, in his first days at the Board would have called 'professional advisers to the film industry'.

First of all they studied how to 'read' a film in order to distinguish the difference between the film-maker's and the audience's point of view. Then they learned how to separate and analyse their own responses, and lastly, and most importantly, they learned how to sense whether a film was trying to 'sell' them something. As for actual censorship: 'if we wanted a cut,' one of the recruits recalls, 'we had to justify it in writing as well as in conversation to the other examiners. If we wanted to reject, we had to make an argument which suggested no other possible decision.'

Suddenly Board meetings which had been sedate, mutually supportive little gatherings became argumentative, cerebral and highly personal. Ferman was intrigued. This was a world far removed from that of Ken Penry's censorship in which 'Joe Bloggs' decided, and in which reports could end, 'Give me Rambo any day.' The Soho 6's reports might lack Penry's personal touch, but they were film literate, more reasoned and much more sharp.

Nevertheless, videos were being censored more than films, especially in the adult categories. From September 1985 to December 1986 under a tenth of all video features were cut, but in the combined adult categories of '18' and 'R18' that figure rose to nearly a third over the same period. Admittedly, many of these titles were forgettable sex films. But also adding to their number were another seventy videos which were purposely not submitted to the Board, either because they were on the DPP's 'nasty' list or because they had been rejected already as films. 'Deterrence,' according to the Board, 'had thus played a role in controlling the level of violence allowed into the public domain in Britain.' Nevertheless many members of the same Board did not agree with those decisions because they simply did not see the point or the necessity of censorship for an adult audience.

In the meantime, at the instigation of one of the Soho 6, various examiners decided to follow up on the lessons imparted by their training. Then, they had repeatedly been reminded that their decisions had to be justified either in writing or at meetings; but where was the means to examine the Board's own final decisions? The examiners sought Ferman's permission therefore to introduce a system of checks and balances in which differing decisions would be referred to a committee and from there to an even bigger committee if an agreement could not be reached.

Ferman's curiosity now began to slowly transform itself into concern. On the one hand he was proud of the reviving, rumbustuous, intellectual approach the Soho 6 had brought to the BBFC; at the same time, however, he was becoming less and less interested in the day-to-day decisions of the Board, and becoming more and more interested in the Board's external links to legislators and other opinion-makers who could affect film censorship. Again it has to be emphasised, though, that the chief censor preferred, and still does prefer, combative examiners to silent gainsayers. But above all, as 1986 drew to a close, nothing, not even democratic decision-making, could be allowed to slow down the processing of those uncertificated videos which always seemed to be banking up against every available wall.

The Director played for time, but the majority of other examiners repeated back to him his own mantra, 'If we can't justify it we shouldn't be doing it.' When the subject refused to bury itself Ferman finally gave in, but at the same time he built a bureauocratic wall around himself, made up of what the writer Tom Wolfe has, in a different context, called 'flak-catchers'. These internal trouble-shooters comprised his new deputy, Margaret Ford, the Assistant Director, Guy Phelps, and a varying number of Assistant Principal Examiners. From behind this managerial line-up Ferman would alternately stonewall, agree with, concede to and override the decisions of the examiners. The Director would later call this era from 1975 onwards 'the golden age of censorship'; but others in the Board would call it an age of 'expanding empire under the control of an autocrat who was revealing dangerous symptoms of one-man censorship.' The new battle lines for today's film censorship had been drawn.

In some respects, the eighties was indeed a golden age of progress for the Board. Yet, along with the vanquishing of his most recent enemy the video nasty, and the triumphant return to a newly fortified BBFC with the priceless plunder of purified video, Ferman had also brought back with him a disease which exposes and then eats away at the nerves of censors. Accountability, which had once been his ally, would now turn on him. In the days ahead, when everybody else would think that peace had come to the arena of censorship, the struggle between the Director and his examiners would resound from within the sound-proofed walls of 3 Soho Square, occasionally escaping to the world beyond.

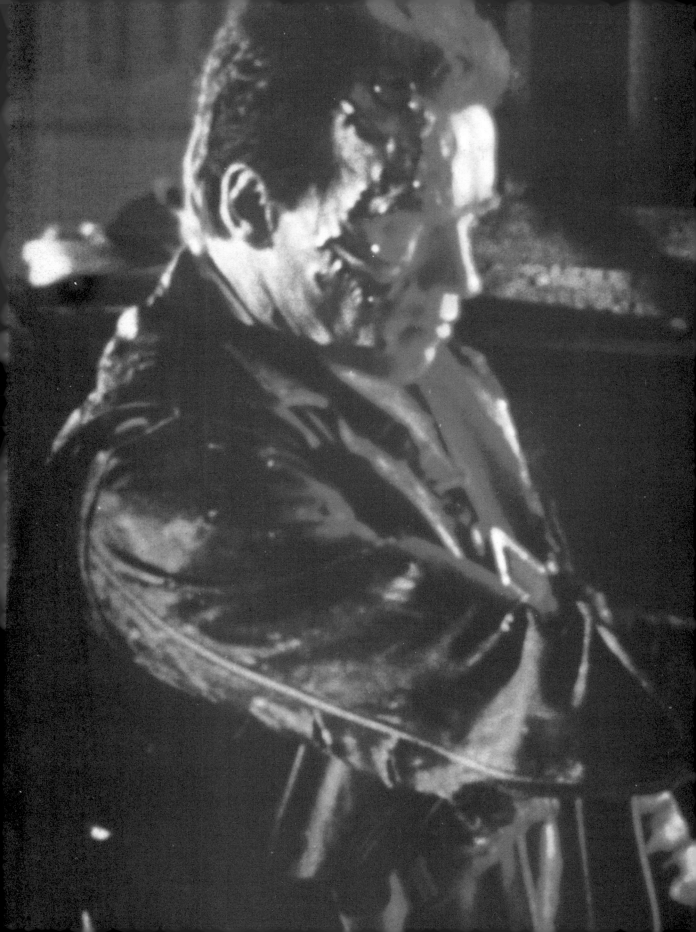

FIGHTING THE GOOD FIGHT

15

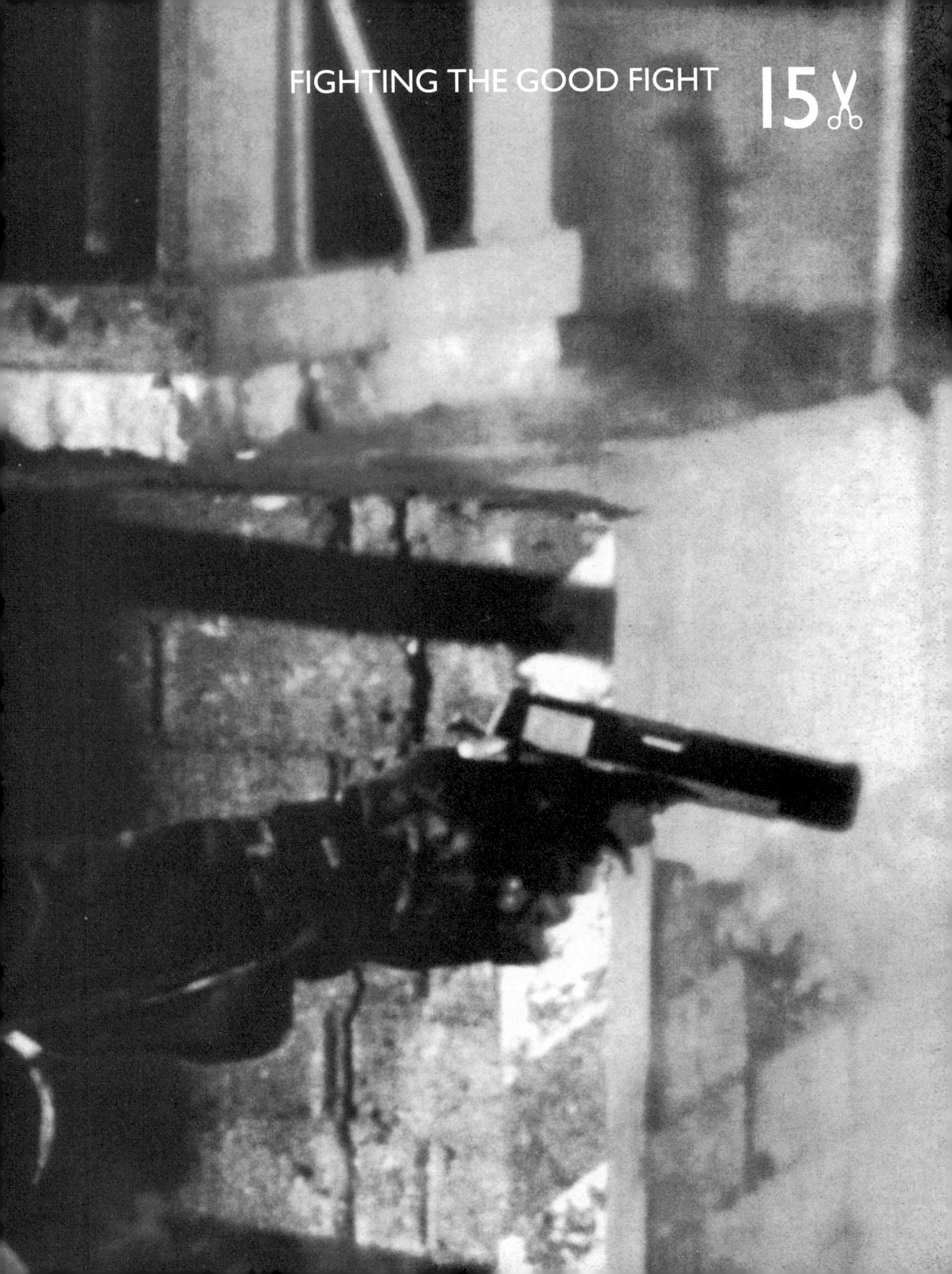

British film censorship had never been healthier than it was in 1986. Its opponents on the left saw television as a more relevant background in which to struggle for free speech, and its extreme proponents on the right had been appeased by their victory over video 'nasties' in 1984. As for the institution which presided over that censorship, it was now blooming under the sunlight provided for it by fees from classifying videotapes. At its head, James Ferman enjoyed unparalleled power for a film censor. Video had given him the resources to employ twenty-one examiners, commission papers on film subjects, organise international conferences and generally supply himself with the wherewithal to enforce one of the strictest systems of film vetting in the world. Paradoxically, these very reasons for success would now factionalise the BBFC and lead to an autocracy in which one-man censorship under 'the Director' would prevail.

Very few films are banned in Britain today. This is not due to any upsurge of liberalism within the BBFC; on the contrary, it is largely because the kind of sex and horror films which in the past would have been rejected by the Board are now submitted by censor-conscious distributors only as videos, and therefore are subject to a different, more stringent, process of control. For film, however, which is not subject to the 1984 Video Recordings Act, the ban has been almost completely replaced by the cut. Classification has become the deciding factor in what a film can or cannot contain, and this change in emphasis was reflected in the Board's re-emergence as the Board of Film Classification in 1985.

As a result, films are now liable to be cut to fit in to their intended category; and the reason why this kind of film censorship currently makes up much of the day-to-day work of the Board can be found in the complex, commercial configurations which circumscribe Hollywood's own censorship system.

Unfortunately, from the point of view of convenience, the classifications of the Motion Picture Association of America's vetting system do not directly correlate to Britain's categories. For instance, in the upper-age bracket America has an 'X' certificate for soft and hard porn of various sexual persuasions, none of which is even submitted to the BBFC, let alone passed. On the other hand, the MPAA's nearest equivalent to the Board's '18' certificate is a '17' which therefore tends to be stricter; so that, for instance, the sex scenes in 9½ *Weeks* and Ken Russell's *Crimes of Passion*, which could be seen in Britain, were reduced for their American '17'-certificated release. But, ironically, it is the lower-age brackets of America's censorship system which impinge more closely upon the BBFC.

A large proportion of the American films which dominate the British box office are rated 'PG13' under the MPAA's classification. But these movies are not necessarily made with that category in mind. Quite often they could be granted an American 'U' certificate. Ironically, though this proof of innocence has to be avoided at all costs by Hollywood producers trying to attract the widest possible audience. For, according to these producers, the all-important American teenager does not like to see films which are available to his or her younger brothers and sisters. Therefore, in order to hoist up a 'U' to a more commercially viable 'PG13' a single sexual swear-word or a piece of violent action is injected into otherwise innocent films.

Thus Will Scarlett's rousing cry of 'Fuck me!', as he sees Robin of Locksley flying over the Sheriff of Nottingham's battlements in *Robin Hood: Prince of Thieves* (1992) became 'Blimey!' in its British version; or a scene from *Mrs Doubtfire* (1993), in which the eponymous nanny, played by Robin Williams, precipitated BBFC cuts due to his/her use of sexual innuendo. In this instance a rare explanation for a classification decision was provided by the head of the Board: 'Maybe there is a trend towards allowing jokes about vibrators and sexually transmitted diseases in family films, but I don't think most ordinary parents would approve.' Such parent-conscious censorship has affected numerous films from a single cut to *Edward Scissorhands* (1990) and *The Witches* (1989) to eleven for *Robin Hood: Prince of Thieves* in 1992 (all from its opening scene) and, in what must be a record for the 'PG' category, twenty-five cuts to *Indiana Jones and the Temple of Doom* (1984), also from its opening scene. In comparison, the removal of a 'fuck' from the Australian film *Crocodile Dundee* seems a small price to pay for its box-office success.

But the struggle to attain this favoured category is sometimes of no avail. Citing his own example of a failure to achieve a 'PG' for his film *The Frog Prince*, the producer David Puttnam was told by James Ferman that it 'had been awarded a "15" for the cinema because the story dealt with an under-age girl losing her virginity.' 'The girl in the film was eighteen,' points out the producer, 'there was no really bad language and absolutely no nudity.' Puttnam then explained that the coming-of-age film had been made for an audience of twelve- to eighteen-year-olds and 'at a stroke, the silly decision meant that half the audience was unable to watch the film.'

A similar reason for classification in the '15' category was proffered to Stephen Woolley for another coming-of-age film, *Shag* (1990). This time a non-sexual scene of a girl in bed with a boy provoked Ferman into an extraordinary assertion that 'there is now evidence which shows that young women who sleep with men can catch cervical cancer'; and therefore Woolley 'should not be producing films that encourage this'.

Moving up a category, the same producer enjoyed better fortune, however, in his pursuit of a '15' certificate for his otherwise ill-fated 1986 musical *Absolute Beginners*. Woolley first became aware of an incipient problem when the BBFC rang him with the news that his leading star, Patsy Kensit, had inadvertently revealed a nipple during the film. 'I thought this was crazy,' recalls the producer. 'No way would she have shown her nipple. In fact I had to spend the whole film covering her up because she had made such a big deal about not showing her body.'

In an echo of Ingmar Bergman's quest for Eva Dahlbeck's nipple in his 1955 film *Smiles of a Summer Night*, Stephen Woolley now went in search of its modern counterpart. But whereas the Swedish master was able to find at least half a nipple, Woolley could find none. 'They have this machine at the BBFC,' which slows the film down to a frame so that you can see everything minutely,' he explains. Yet in spite of a painstakingly close inspection which was spread out over two hours, the renegade nipple could not be located, and the suspicious censor had to be satisfied with Woolley's word that the elusive aureola was a product of the BBFC's over-active imagination.

Within the confines of the '15' bracket, the classification quandary faced by producers of sequels to blockbuster movies relates to a young audience's increasing expectations from formula films. Usually this is supplied by an increase in the violence quotient. Thus *Die Hard II* (1990) and *Terminator II: Judgement Day* (1991) boast a combined body count of over 400 corpses. The BBFC, however, does not question the level of these numbers, so much as the manner in which the bodies are treated en route to disposal. What the censors are attempting to avoid in such films is an awareness of violent death, and therefore the shorter the death throes the less likelihood of BBFC interference.

The intended category for these replicant movies is '15', but the equivalent rating in America, 'PG13' allows far more of what James Ferman calls 'personalised violence'. What the Director means by this phrase is the kind of violence which is inflicted on a character known to the audience, rather than de-personalised violence against a faceless victim, such as is seen in war films. According to some of the current examiners, 'personalised violence' is a particular obsession of the Director's; and it has therefore resulted in multiple cuts to hundreds of action adventure films. To give only a few of the examples from this popular genre: *Lethal Weapon II* (1989) – cuts of bloodspurts and gunplay; *Terminator II* – kneecapping; *Die Hard II* – heavy punches; *The Punisher* (1991) – needle insertion; *The Bodyguard* (1992) – karate blows; *Under Siege* (1993) – eye gouging and knife stabs to the groin and armpit; and most recently the Sylvester Stallone vehicle, *Cliffhanger* (1993) which, according to Ferman, 'was cut quite drastically' due to its featuring of headbuts and repeated kicks to Stallone's midriff and head.

Whether this kind of violence is personalised or not, such cuts usually qualify for what the 1979 Williams Committee called 'quantitative censorship' whereby one from a series of actions, such as punches, will be arbitrarily selected by the Board for deletion. Yet this same criteria is also applied by the Board to the wider genre of '15' certificated thriller films – including such critically approved examples as Kathryn Bigelow's *Point Break* (1991), which suffered from multiple small cuts of body blows totalling twenty-five seconds; or

Quentin Tarantino's *True Romance* (1993), in which various violent scenes were cut, in this instance, for an '18' certificate, as well as Wolfgang Peterson's *In the Line of Fire* (1993), in which a neck-break administered by the villain (John Malkovich) was cut because it happened to be the second violent death within the same scene. Moreover many '15' certificated films are then subject to language cuts. Again, Ferman asserts that 'It is quantity more than individual words'; and finally, yet another sliver is very likely to be sliced off when the films are transferred to video.

Over the last five years, at least 10 per cent of '15' certificated films have been cut; yet that figure is doubled for the upper category of '18' (which had changed from 'X' in 1982). Normally such a high proportion of cuts could be accounted for by sex films trying to escape from the 'Restricted 18' for licensed sex cinemas into the more commercially viable '18'. But in 1991 this only applied to six 'adult' films. The discrepancy can be explained by the extraordinary range of conditions imposed by the BBFC on adult-oriented films.

For instance, the censor-prone producer, Stephen Woolley was confronted once again in 1989 by the Board with evidence that one of his films displayed a private part. This time, however, the BBFC presented incontrovertible proof.

'Presidential' robbers hold up a bank in Kathryn Bigelow's *Point Break* (1991) – as with so many other thrillers it was quietly cut by the BBFC for violence.

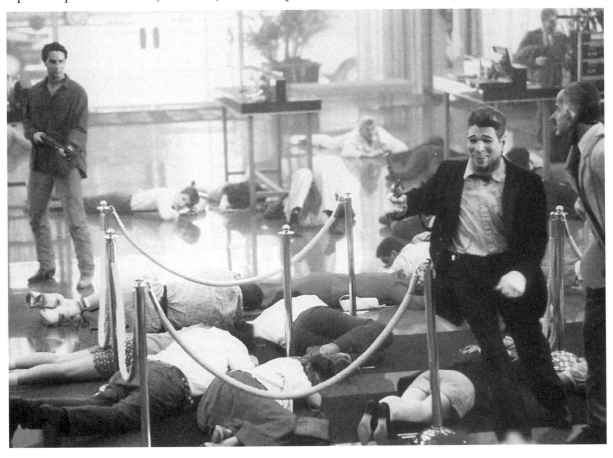

The intended category for Michael Caton-Jones's film about the Profumo affair, *Scandal* (1989), was an inevitable '18'. In the Cliveden-set orgy scene, however, an unmistakably erect penis stood up for all the audience to see. What's more, on this occasion the penis could not be explained by a censor's wishful thinking or even by a trick of the light, because it was moving in and out of somebody else. 'There was a woman,' says Ferman, 'sitting astride a man's lap, bouncing up and down.' Also 'it was shot from below, looking up between the woman's legs.' Brooking no doubt, the Director asserts that 'it definitely looked like a penetration shot. It was hard porn in fact.'

Woolley was genuinely flabbergasted. He had been unaware that actual sex was being performed on the set of his film so he could only splutter, 'it was a candle. I swear it was a candle.' But by this time Ferman was no longer interested in excuses. The chief censor and editor extraordinaire had become intrigued by the problem of how to snuff out the 'candle'. The blemished film was therefore sent to an optical house where technicians diffused the light coming from a lamp in the foreground so that it cast a fuzzy glow over any errant thrusts. The satisfied censor could now issue an '18'.

At the other extreme, which demarcates the difference between rejection and acceptance as an '18' certificated film, prurience can be transformed into genuine controversy. For, of course, the fact that the Board rarely rejects films does not mean that would-be censors outside the BBFC would not like exceptions to be made for certain examples of their own choosing.

The BBFC received 1,870 letters and petitions in favour of banning Martin Scorsese's naturalistic 1988 film *The Last Temptation of Christ*. (No other film has inspired so much BBFC correspondence since Bruce Lee's numerous British fans protested to the Board that all of their idol's more damaging blows had been removed from *Enter the Dragon* in 1973.) Remembering the advice of his predecessors in similar circumstances, James Ferman politely fobbed off all these requests with replies to every single letter. The chief censor knew, though, that a circular letter, however graciously expressed, would hardly be sufficient to quell the concern that was currently being declared by the redoubtable religious campaigner, Mary Whitehouse. For the unstoppable moralist had threatened to invoke the blasphemy law if she thought that the subsequent film would require such a step. (She had brought such a prosecution to a successful conclusion against *Gay News* in 1977 for publishing a poem with a homosexual interpretation of the Crucifixion.)

Normally Ferman could have gone ahead and simply sacrificed the film, but in this instance aesthetic considerations came into play. The film critics might not have been given permission by their editors to raise a bleat over the blanket banning of video nasties, but even the most ignorant critic would have no choice but to howl for Ferman's blood if he deleted a single frame from the oeuvre of America's most prestigious living director.

For once the tactically minded censor found himself with very little room to manoeuvre. He therefore decided to buy some insurance in the form of twenty-eight assorted priests, deacons and bishops who were inveigled into the BBFC's viewing-room to watch *The Last Temptation of Christ*. Ferman remembers that none of them actually liked the film. However, they were prepared to tell their congregations that Scorsese's liberal retelling of the Gospel was not afflicted by blasphemy. And in spite of Cardinal Basil Hume's advice to the Catholic community not to see the film, a controversy which had torn America apart failed to stir more phlegmatic British souls.

The Last Temptation brought with it something else, though, which distanced it from controversy. Once the film was actually released it failed to summon up much public interest. In contrast, when John McNaughton's *Henry: Portrait of a Serial Killer* was submitted to the BBFC on 7 January 1990, everybody on the Board knew that this film would not quietly disappear in a welter of public apathy.

Henry took more time to censor than almost any other film in modern times, and its censorship highlights the BBFC's adoption of the language of psychology and psychiatry as a means to determine who is most liable to be

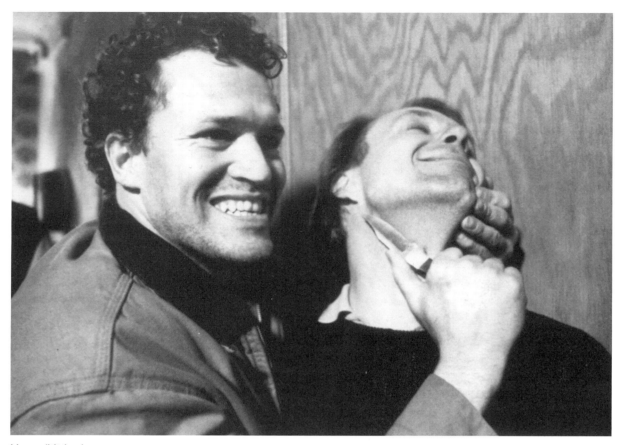

Henry (Michael Rooker) – with the assistance of writer-director John McNaughton – stays in character on the set of *Henry: Portrait of a Serial Killer* (1989).

affected by a film. Yet in spite of the Board's new rationale, by the time *Henry: Portrait of a Serial Killer* had been certificated on 16 April 1991, the film's own moral questioning of violence had exposed the more frail and easily accommodated morality with which censorship disguises itself.

Based on the self-confessed crimes of Henry Lee Lucas, who killed his prostitute mother at the age of fourteen, McNaughton's narrative picks up its psychopathic hero's murder trail during a stopover in an unnamed, indistinguishable American industrial city. Here Henry (Michael Rooker) is joined in a killing spree by the even more degenerate Otis (Tom Towles), who possesses an equal propensity for violence, but who betrays signs of nervousness when the victims have to be disposed of. 'What'll happen?' he moans, as Henry hefts the bodies of two women into a trash bin. 'Nothing . . . absolutely nothing.' And he is proved right. Unimpeded, Henry leaves the city and once again goes on the road. And it is this lack of closure, of retribution, along with the film's unrelieved depiction of how arbitrary violence can be, that set the BBFC alarm bells ringing. Yet *Henry* could have been even more testing for the censor. In the original uncut version, shown at the Scala Cinema in London (where many of the examiners first saw it), McNaughton's film opened with a montage of stills showing Henry's victims in rigor mortis. Amongst them is a woman slumped on a toilet with a broken-off bottle embedded in her neck and blood running down over an exposed breast. That shot was removed for the British film-goers courtesy of the owner of the European rights to the film.

'It seemed to me such a prurient, exploitative shot of a female corpse,' recalls Ferman, 'the sort of thing that I was used to in a very different kind of movie. That scene predisposed me to expect the worst from the rest of it.' The chief censor's suspicion was then confirmed by a video sequence in which Henry and his buddy Otis film the murder and subsequent rape of a woman (Henry props the camera up on the ground), as well as the killing of the rest of her family.

The violent details of this scene, such as the woman's and the boy's necks being broken, did not pose a particularly difficult problem for the Board. What actually concerned the examiners was the way in which the scene had been treated, or more precisely the angle from which Henry himself filmed it. For this shot looking up the legs of a struggling woman as her pantyhose are torn off is a staple of rape scenes in exploitation movies. (A similar shot of wriggling legs was cut from Hitchcock's *Frenzy* (1971), despite the fact that the uncut version is regularly shown on television.)

According to Ferman, the generally agreed position taken towards this scene was summed up in a rare glimpse into one of the examiner's reports which stated: 'The effect of a film within a film here is not to distance it but rather through the home movie feel, give the impression that this could be located anywhere, including one's own home. Added to that the woman is totally de-personalised. The camera gives us no lead-in to the assault from her viewpoint and therefore no feel for her as a person. Otis and Henry we already know, however, and, accordingly we see her through their eyes. Conventions from the standard repertoire of filmic sex and violence also operate here, such as the positioning of the woman towards the camera. By these devices viewers are invited to participate, to see the titillatory nature of such cruelty and the film is therefore truly exploitative.'

Whether the film should have been made from the viewpoint of the murderer or his victim, these remarks, as in so much film censorship, are merely a confirmation of the director's intentions. For, in his review of the film for the *Evening Standard*, Alexander Walker pointed to the opposite conclusion with the comment that the director 'poses the problem of killers like Henry so directly and unhysterically that the film is far more disturbing than titillating'. The critic then closed in on the central truth of *Henry*'s 'moral blankness', which Ferman, in particular, tried to avoid: 'Film censors either have to ban the film or abandon any hypocritical effort to detect the morally compensating values they usually rely on finding in order to protect the trade they service from the affronted feelings of the public.'

Initially, James Ferman did want to ban *Henry*, but he did not have enough support amongst influential examiners to enforce his wishes. One of these examiners says that the reason why she thought that the film should not only be released but released unscathed was, 'no killer wants to look like, live like or be like Henry. On the contrary I think that these sort of people want to look like Hannibal Lecter [from *Silence of the Lambs* (1991)].' After endless discussions, rows and repeated showings of the film, Ferman, the examiners and the President finally agreed to split their differences and remove just over a minute from the rape scene. Soon, however, the Director was presented with another opportunity to chip away at the film when it was submitted on videotape in the latter half of 1991.

Earlier in the year James Ferman had declared on Barry Norman's 'Film '91' TV show that he would never pass *Henry* on video. Possibly the unprecedented censorship of *Henry* which followed is explained by the adamancy of this remark.

At this stage, the evidence of the two psychiatrists who had been consulted by the Board was considered to be of special relevance. Although this particular medical team had a limited knowledge of film, nevertheless they believed that the playback capability of video could be employed by murderers to endlessly rehearse a killing; and, once primed, the potential killers would be ready to go out and 'do the real thing'. Moreover, this is a belief that is held by Ferman and many others on the Board. According to Margaret Ford, the Deputy Director, the two psychiatrists reported that the murders in Henry could indeed 'disinhibit the guys with the eggshell skulls, the ones who you don't have to go very far to arrive at their psyches'.

Ferman's belief that a film's fantasy gradually becomes reality for potential criminals was therefore vindicated and as a result another fifty-two seconds were cut from the video version of *Henry*. 'All the material we cut,' he says, 'was violence connected with sexual abuse of a victim. Therefore it could have got past the guard of the audience. Once you're into sexual images,' this censor warns, 'you can turn people on because whatever one part of their mind is telling them, another part is telling them something else.' Thus the censorship of *Henry* supposedly acted both to remove the 'disinhibitors' which affect those people that 'the Board is most worried about', and also to put a stop to anybody else's involuntary sexual arousal at the sight of rape.

Of course there is a confusion in Ferman's words between the deliberate moral blankness being presented in a film, and the assumption of an audience's moral susceptibility which is then used as a basis to justify censorship. But in fact the video censorship of *Henry* did not just concern itself with the moral vacuum supposedly occupying the minds of cinema-goers, because it also consisted of cuts to a scene in which Henry batters to death a male TV salesman with one of his own television sets. But once again the film-maker's stated

Henry with his sidekick, Otis (Tom Towles), confronts the owner of a (stolen) television store at the beginning of a scene which would be cut for the film's video release.

intention to force the audience 'to question their own attitudes to murder as entertainment' was censored by Ferman for the very reason that the scene was not offered to the viewer as formula entertainment.

Yet even after this cut the chief censor was not satisfied. For he was still worried about the effect of the family murder scene upon a video audience. For his part McNaughton felt that this sequence was the pivotal point of the whole film: 'That's really the key scene of the picture. We set it up so you see Henry and Otis about to enter the house and then you see the image on TV. And because you know that they have a video camera, you think you're seeing them murder the family as they're taping it. But then you realise that you're watching it on the cinema screen, just as they're sitting there watching it on video. And that's where the whole picture turns inside out, where it says to you: "You think this is graphic, but you're sitting here watching it, waiting to be entertained. Now what do you think about yourself, and what do you think about watching this kind of violence on screen?"' In other words, any vicarious pleasure for the audience is cut short by the creeping realisation that Henry and Otis are watching the same scene at the same time as you, the viewer.

Indeed McNaughton's intention is confirmed because the scene ends with a shot of Henry and Otis on a sofa watching the video. But Ferman still believed that the sequence carried an inherent danger. 'The principle we followed in cutting the scene was to cut out the masturbatory pleasure. We were worried,' he said, 'about the sexual turn-on element for solitary men watching at home.' As a result, the cuts for a video release were taken out of Otis molesting the woman while her son looks on. But then this censor stepped outside his job description by adding to, as well as subtracting from, a film. In an attempt not so much to forestall psychopathic behaviour as interrupt onanism, Ferman inserted the later shot of Henry and Otis watching their video on television into the actual scene as shot by Henry's video camera. Thus the concentrated continuum needed for masturbation would presumably be interrupted by the sight of Henry and Otis's faces. Leaving aside the fact that John McNaughton's permission to alter the order of his film was not sought it must be a matter of conjecture whether Ferman's intervention had the desired result. The *Time Out* reporter Nigel Floyd who unearthed this extraordinary example of a censor's presumption wrote at the time, 'This radically alters the structure of the scene: by pre-empting the crucial moment at which our guilty complicity is exposed, Ferman's version subverts this moment of subversion.'

The chief censor, in turn, might argue that such intervention is in response to a question he posed to himself during the censorship of *Henry*: 'How does one get the audience to take a properly moral view about the violence that's shown on the screen?' Ironically, this implies that Ferman did indeed understand McNaughton's attempt to open a moral trapdoor under *Henry*'s audience. Because in common with a small band of other films which feature hard, personalised violence *Henry*'s audience is forced to acknowledge its role in the fulfilment of a wish it barely knew it had: it is both victimiser and victim.

Above all, what the censors and the two psychiatrists were looking for in the cut scenes, as well as all the others in the film, was McNaughton's repugnance for Henry; and because the director refused to provide the audience and, more importantly, the censor with that sort of familiar reassurance, his film lost just under two minutes. Like so many other films of note which have suffered at the hands of the BBFC, *Henry* was simply censored because of its unfamiliarity to the censor.

James Ferman has an affable, relaxed manner. There is no hint of his American origins in his pleasant BBC style of speaking and even when closely questioned the only sign of unease he betrays is a tendency to fiddle with his fingers. From behind a large desk on which stands a miniature film director's canvas chair doubling up as a paper-clip-holder, the head censor looks out over the garden of Soho Square. Now in his mid-sixties, with the etiolated complexion common to censors, the BBFC's Director possesses the confidence of a man who is used to being listened to.

It is tempting to assume that a man who is in charge of running what he calls 'the strictest censorship board in Europe' must be an unthinking reactionary. But in fact Ferman has been in accord with, and sometimes ahead of, liberal opinion during his tenure at the BBFC. His stand on sexual violence has won increasing support from women. To balance that restriction, in 1982 he tried to introduce consensual pornography into the cinema through the ill-fated 'Restricted 18' category; and he still might succeed in this aim by pulling soft-porn films through the back door propped open by sex education videos. Ferman's character also echoes this paradoxical combination of strict liberalism. BBFC examiners say that their Director is 'manipulative', 'Janus-faced', and 'autocratic', but they also describe him as 'committed', 'charming' and 'intelligent'; and inevitably his censorship and more particularly his own campaigns within that censorship, have reflected those strengths and weaknesses.

After his ongoing attempt to outlaw sexual violence from British cinemas, Ferman's longest-standing crusade has been against certain kinds of weaponry. This started, as these sorts of proscriptions usually do, with a mixture of common sense and curmudgeonly chiding at film-makers who 'ought to know better'. The first object designated for special care was the 'nunchaku', or Chinese rice flail, more familiarly known in the west as chainsticks. To begin with, the BBFC noted the 'astonishing skill' of the Hong Kong star, Bruce Lee, with this weapon. 'Indeed,' a 1978 report breathlessly revealed, 'it is said that the film company had to slow down his sequences in order to make the weapon visible to the audience, while later exponents of the art have had to have their combat scenes speeded up in order to compete with the legend.'

What had been permissible for the great martial arts master back in the early seventies was denied, however, to his less nimble successors, and their attempts to thwack opponents were consequently removed. For in the meantime, the national press had picked up local stories of the weapon being used aggressively by British youths. 'Thugs,' said a police spokesman in February 1974, were 'being influenced by kung-fu mania'.

The next weapon to join the BBFC's forbidden list had been caught up in the backlash released by the Hungerford killings in the summer of 1987. The press traced links between Michael Ryan's random shootings of bystanders in the Berkshire market town and the incessant gunplay of the first two *Rambo* films. In fact Michael Ryan was not a member of his local video club and he never admitted to seeing either of the *Rambo* movies, although statistics show that they were the most popular films of the time which contained violence. Yet in spite of the insubstantial evidence of any connection between a Rambo's militaristic psychosis and Ryan's random killings, the Board began to give more attention to the 'fetishisation of weaponry'.

The Board also set great store by its belated discovery that the 'Rambo knife' or as it is more commonly known, the Bowie knife, was 'already being

269

The first two *Rambo*s were passed uncut by the BBFC but the censorship of *Rambo III* in 1988 coincided with the Michael Ryan killings at Hungerford – so a minute of footage was removed.

sold by many weapons shops in Britain to teenagers whose lifestyle owed little to military discipline'. As a result, and despite the fact that the first two Rambo films had been released untouched, just over a minute of footage was taken out of *Rambo III* in July 1988.

Presumably due to its lack of military sanction, if not its legality, the Rambo knife then joined what was a growing list of prohibited weapons on the screen. These now comprised Ninja death stars, spiked knuckledusters, metal claws, butterfly knives, lighted aerosols, crossbows and telescopic catapults. But what had begun as a reasonable as well as a politically sensible response to actual incidents in which people were harmed, now entered the realms of the surreal.

It first became apparent that Ferman was suffering from a nunchaku obsession when a scene from the police comedy *Dragnet* was cut in 1989. The actual frame, which was lifted out of this film, featured an otherwise harmless conversation between Dan Akroyd and his partner, Tom Hanks. But what Ferman had noticed was the presence of a poster in the background upon which Bruce Lee was brandishing a pair of chainsticks.

The following year the crusade to rid the screen of this weapon reached even

The dreaded chainsticks as demonstrated by their peer, Bruce Lee in *Enter the Dragon* (1973).

more outrageous lengths when a sequence from *Teenage Mutant Ninja Turtles* (1990) had to be sanitised because one of the anthropoids called Michaelangelo was swinging what looked to Ferman suspiciously like a pair of the infamous nunchaku. Out the scene came, and it was not even reinstated when one of the examiners pointed out to his boss that in fact Michaelangelo was swinging a string of sausages.

In an attempt to swerve the Director from his chosen path of non-nunchaku, an examiner now decided that extreme steps had to be taken. Halfway through one of the Board's meetings on weaponry he reached into his pocket and slyly produced a pair of the dreaded chainsticks. He then started to swing them around above his head but unfortunately the chain immediately got caught around his neck and the examiner nearly strangled himself. But even after this peerless demonstration of the weapon's self-destructive capability in the hands of an enthusiastic amateur, Ferman was still not persuaded to desist. Finally, in exasperation, the examiners told him that there was no evidence from the police or the courts that the weapon had been used for years. 'Aaah,' replied the imperturbable Director, 'that shows the success of my policy.'

This character trait of sticking his head in the sand has undoubtedly affected

271

Ferman's censorship. On the general level of film appreciation it influences the Director because he has very few interests outside the BBFC. He rarely leaves his office before nine or ten o'clock in the evening. He occasionally goes to the opera or to the theatre, but he never goes to a public cinema except for Royal Film Performances. He therefore has very little understanding of the way an audience complements a film through its response to cues or, alternatively, its groans of approbation. This is particularly relevant, furthermore, to an appreciation of horror films which invariably employ innovative visual triggers to surprise a youthful audience already wise to the ways of the genre.

On a more specific level, Ferman's obduracy has played a hand in the classification of certain films. The Director's own cinematic taste veers towards such emotive movies as *Terms of Endearment* (1983) and *Madame Sousatzka* (1988). In any other context the choice of somebody's entertainment is incidental to their professional capability, but inevitably in the case of censors their taste tends to guide the direction of their scissors. For instance, John Trevelyan told George Melly that he 'censored whatever turned him on'.

In Ferman's case the marriage between his taste and his obduracy led to a campaign in which he sought a '15' certificate for Oliver Stone's 1986 Vietnam war film *Platoon*. In this instance the violence of war is presented and then resolved within the personal conflict between a good American (Charlie Sheen) and an evil American (Tom Berenger), and presumably for the head censor, the triumph of humanity over destruction provided a guide for teenagers with which to demarcate different factions within a war.

A member of the Board recalls that, 'Jim fought and fought hard for that certificate although a majority of the examiners wanted to make it "18". Yet in spite of a high quotient of "fucks" and "motherfuckers", as well as drug scenes in the film he would not budge from a "15".' This display of tolerance, however, was in direct contrast to the treatment accorded to Stanley Kubrick's depiction of the same war in *Full Metal Jacket* the following year.

Opposite (above)
Oliver Stone's Vietnam war film *Platoon* (1986) and **(below)** Stanley Kubrick's Vietnam war film *Full Metal Jacket* (1987). One was classified '15', the other '18' – but it could just as easily have been the other way round.

In what one examiner calls 'an orchestrated campaign' Ferman insisted that an '18' certificate be attached to this film. 'Jim,' this examiner reports, 'felt that Kubrick's approach to the war was cold and intellectual while Stone's was personal, because unlike Kubrick he actually fought in Vietnam. But whichever way you cut it,' this censor says, '*Platoon* doesn't loathe its war.' The same censor thinks that the roots of the differing decisions lie in Ferman's background. 'He cited his stance as a liberal. I would just cite it as American.' In the light of his future censorship of *Henry: Portrait of a Serial Killer*, it has to be assumed that Ferman did not think that the conventionally emotive violence of *Platoon* would be imitated by young cinema-goers, whereas the analytical, depersonalised, fatalistic violence of *Full Metal Jacket* would inspire copy-cat behaviour.

At the even more important upper limit of '18' classification, where films are

more likely to be rejected, the Director's obstinacy has resulted in the exclusion of one particular bête noire. For nearly a decade Ferman has insisted that *The Exorcist* should not be granted any kind of video certificate. One of the censors explains how the Director has accomplished this lengthy boycott: 'The film has never been officially submitted to the Board because the distributors are always being told by Jim that this is not the right time to pass it. But without that submission we cannot discuss its suitability for a certificate. In that way the film has been denied a hearing and kept under wraps.' In response to this stratagem one examiner declared at a Board meeting that, 'to let it appear that it was the industry that was withholding the work to collude in a lie'. 'It is a form of one-man censorship,' another examiner concludes.

Following repeated requests from the public as to the film's whereabouts on video the examiners have pestered Ferman for a release date. One asked the Director why he was refusing to pass a film for video which had been revived with great success in the cinemas. Finally another examiner asked Ferman, 'What do I say when someone asks me why the film is not in the stores?' 'You tell them,' the chief censor replied in exasperation, 'that the Director of the BBFC is not going to pass it because the Director says so.'

It has to be pointed out, though, that there are limits to James Ferman's one-man censorship. Unlike his post-war predecessors, the present chief censor has to act within the constraints imposed by a huge bureaucratic organisation. The checks and balances within the Board's various review committees usually – but not necessarily always – winnow out the more wayward decisions of examiners as well as those of Ferman himself. While many of the thirteen examiners complain that their painstaking judgements are overruled, Ferman has recently bowed to pressure within the Board to relax his weapons policy and there have even been intimations that *The Exorcist* will finally be released on video.

Nevertheless, the BBFC now occupies an area of censorship which was not open to the Board in the past. Video censorship has not only offered the Board the opportunity to control the content of a new medium, it has also allowed the censor to determine the way in which that medium is presented to the public.

When the Video Recordings Act was passed in 1984, no provision was made for the censorship of video covers. Quickly noticing this bureaucratic lapse, Ferman advanced into the overlooked territory. A Video Packaging Review Committee was established in 1987 which included distributors and senior examiners from the BBFC. Ostensibly this is a voluntary scheme, but a logo indicating an approval of the VPRC is compulsory for all distributors who have chosen to submit their covers to the committee. The BBFC, in the person of Margaret Ford, will only say that membership is 'highly recommended', but Norman Abbott, the Director General of the distributors' body, the British Videogram Association, told the film journalist Julian Petley: 'I've no doubt that the BBFC has penalised people who haven't gone into the scheme, by holding up their material. But if you play ball with the system, accept the Board's judgement and don't make a fuss, then you get better treatment.'

Such remarks would carry less significance if the committee did not carry out its work so comprehensively. For instance, the cover of *Hellraiser* (1987) originally had a hook pulling dessicated flesh to the edges of its sleeve, in order to give the impression that the whole cover was made of skin. But this effect was then ruined by the VPRC because they insisted that the red blood seeping along the edges be in green. Indeed all blood on video covers is toned down; naked bodies are covered up and any sight of a meat cleaver carries automatic rejection.

The extra-legal censorship of the packaging committee does not stop with the design of covers, however; it also determines their text. In hindsight, the removal of the word 'chainsaw' from the title *Hollywood Chainsaw Hookers* (1989) might seem inevitable, but the deletion of the line, 'The worst violence since *I Spit On Your Grave*' from the cover of a recent British horror film would have brought a smile to the lips of Orwell's Big Brother. For the members of this committee suggested – to no avail in this instance – that this phrase could not be used because the Board had not passed the earlier film and therefore the public could not be reminded of its existence.

More significantly, the setting up of the VPRC has helped to change the overall structure of the video film industry. Norman Abbott explains the first step of this transformation which the censorship of video covers has brought about. 'If the distributor comes up with some controversial packaging and the VPRC say "No, we don't like that, there's far too much blood on the axe" or "You can't have that woman tied to a tree", it has to go back to the applicant, more artwork has to be done, and then it's resubmitted. All this causes delay and expense.' As a consequence, the smaller independent distribution companies incur more losses than their bigger competitors because they rely on strong images to create an impact with their packaging. By contrast, 'The majors', according to Colourbox's Robert Starks, 'have all the well known titles – they could put out a big title in a white sleeve and still do well.'

Censorship has also abetted the monopolisation of the video industry due to two effects of the Video Recordings Act, one of which is unseen, and the other unintentional. First of all, the sex films which the independent companies distribute are more likely to be banned under the Act's 'suitability for the home' clause; and secondly the cost of certificating a video, which is between £500 and £600, has a disproportionate effect on the smaller companies because many of their titles will only sell a limited number of copies. The BBFC's fee will therefore take a far greater percentage of their profits than it would from one of the majors' big-selling titles.

Thus the censorship of video in all its different forms has led to the kind of overhaul that the film industry went through after the introduction of celluloid censorship in 1912. In other words, the smaller companies have suffered from a new industry's attempt to win a respectable middle-class clientele. 'I felt that there was a conspiracy amongst the majors to push out the independents and bring in a sanitised environment for them to make a profit in,' says Stephen Woolley of Palace Pictures. 'And,' he adds, 'they succeeded a full 100 per cent.'

Far from being a useful guide, though, for the BBFC, film censorship that is carried out at the behest of respectable public opinion is just as liable to be rid-dled with anomalies as any other form of screen-vetting. The most recent instance of this kind of public demand for intervention was understandably encouraged by the murder of the two-year-old Liverpool boy James Bulger in February 1993. (Also the connection between screen and violence seemed to be emphasised in this case by the fact that the key evidence of the crime was contained in fuzzy images caught by a video surveillance camera.) In any event, a moral crusade was then fuelled by the appearance of the critic Michael Medved's examination of screen violence in his book, *Hollywood vs Civilisation* which was published by the owner of Twentieth Century Fox, Rupert Murdoch, and then serialised in one of his British newspapers in the same month.

In the subsequent hurried search for an immediate explanation for social violence even the Prime Minister John Major subscribed to the belief that films can brutalise. But what was the actual effect on film censorship of all the demands for a reduction in the violence that was 'seeping into the nation's living rooms'?

At the time that James Bulger's body was found and that particular moral panic erupted, four violent films were poised for cinema release. More by luck than judgement the British distributors of one of these films, the anti-neo-Nazi thriller, *Romper Stomper* (1992) first submitted their title solely for video release, and when the Australian film gained publicity for its fight scenes it was then submitted for a cinema certificate. In the second instance, the distributors of the Belgian black comedy, *Man Bites Dog* (1992) submitted for a video and film certificate at the same time. When the row over film violence in the home began to gather momentum after James Bulger's death it was therefore too late for the BBFC to prevent either of the films from being given a video release.

But this was not the case, however, with the two other films earmarked for release. Quentin Tarantino's *Reservoir Dogs* (1992) and Abel Ferrara's *The Bad Lieutenant* (1992) both gained an uncut BBFC '18' certificate before they were submitted for video classification. 'There is very little violence shown in *Reservoir Dogs*,' claimed Ferman at the time, 'and what there is is context-ually justified.' Similarly, the chief censor praised Ferrara's *Bad Lieutenant* as

Opposite (above) The Australian vigilante movie *Romper Stomper* (1992) was classified on video because it was submitted to the BBFC before the James Bulger killing. **(Below)** Quentin Tarantino's thriller *Reservoir Dogs* (1992) is banned on video because it was submitted afterwards.

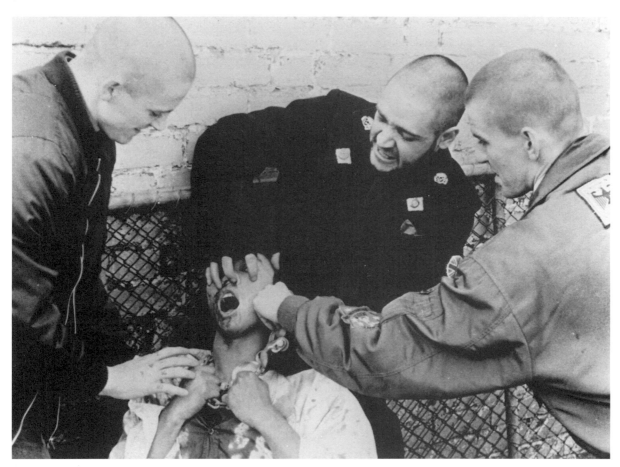

'a study in Catholic redemption' in which Harvey Keitel's corrupt cop redeems himself through the intercession of a nun who insists on forgiving the teenage boys who raped her. 'He's transformed at the end,' commented Ferman, 'and I think it's necessary to go on this journey with him from one extreme to the other.'

By the time, though, that these two censor-approved films had been submitted for video classification the BBFC could not be seen to be putting any more violence into the nation's living rooms. Two films, therefore, which in Ferman's words, 'simply happened to be around', and which incidentally refused to indulge in the popular Hollywood device of reducing violence to its barest components and then inflating it with hot stylised air, were consigned to a video limbo – from which they will not be released until public opinion is appeased.

Today film censorship is largely devoted to film classification and what one examiner calls 'hacking through the grunge'. By this he means cutting sex films on video. Soft-core exploitation tapes, however, could soon be liberated by the advent of the sex education video. Towards the end of 1993, the sexual parameters of what was or, what was not, allowed on British screens was changing with the submission of almost every sex education title. In short, sex on the British screen was in flux and still is.

Next to sexual violence, gay male sex used to be the most proscribed area of film censorship. Refreshingly provocative homosexual films such as Frank Ripploh's *Taxi Zum Klo* (1980) either had to be cut heavily to gain classification or be withdrawn from censorship – which, in this case, is what Ripploh decided to do until 1992 when he received a belated certificate. Narrative gay films are usually censored at source by producers, and therefore are rarely made. But, increasingly, gay soft pornography is coming before the Board on video. The more liberal examiners want to pass these tapes uncut but until recently they were opposed by Ferman. That opposition could be open to question, however, because of the Director's decision in 1993 to classify such titles as *Getting It Right* and the *Gay Man's Guide to Safe Sex* series. These particular sex education tapes featured male anal sex as well as fellatio and so for the first time a realistic depiction of gay sex is available to the British public.

The BBFC's unwritten rule precluding the sexually unconventional does, however, apply to other forms of minority sex including troilism or group sex, infantilism, sado-masochism and coprophilia which are only allowed in their most oblique forms or, as in the last case, excluded altogether. On the other hand, far more leeway is allowed to more conventional heterosexuality. Blatant erections have been passed in such art-house pictures as *The Adjustor* (1992), *Les Amants de Pont Neuf* (1992) and *In the Realm of the Senses* because these films are tailored to a specific, liberal middle-class audience.

The precise whereabouts of the penis, though, is carefully circumscribed by the BBFC. While it can be touched by hand – male or female – it is only allowed to receive this sort of attention in sex education films. In this format, penetration into the vagina or a woman's mouth has also recently been passed, most notably in ground-breaking heterosexual sex education tapes such as *Orgasm Workout* (1992) and *Kama Sutra 2* (1993). Ejaculation or the 'money shot' as it is known in the exploitation industry, has yet to make its appearance, however, on the British screen.

Like the penis, the depiction of the vagina, at present, constitutes a bureaucratic minefield for the censor. Within the '18' category for exploitation titles, pubic hair can be seen, but the hair must not be parted by spread legs. If it is then the film becomes a 'Restricted 18'. What the censors call 'digital distension' in which fingers are employed to reveal the labia is only allowed in sex education or the exclusive 'R18' category. Alternatively, a man or a woman can go below the frame for oral sex but if he or she is seen by the camera, the category once again changes from '18' to 'R18'; and even within this classification the tongue is only permitted to approach the general area of the genitals alongside the thighs and never allowed to lick the penis or enter the vagina. As for the actual engagement of penis and vagina, they are not allowed to approach each other but brief glimpses can be shown within the 'R18' category of penile motion and the meeting of the pubic hair once penetration has been achieved. The full exchange of genitalia is again confined to sex education tapes.

Normally, this arcane world of sexual film censorship is closed to British film buffs. A leaked report, however, which was published by the *Guardian* on 18 February 1994 provides a rare public insight into the stringent anatomical exactness with which BBFC examiners apply themselves to sex on the screen. One of the films under scrutiny was *Satin and Lace – an Erotic History of Lingerie* (1992) which was discussed at a Board meeting on 15 May of that year. The examiners said that this type of exploitation came under the so-called ILOOLI rule which declares that 'inner labia is out but outer labia can be in' and their final judgement in this case was that 'glimpses of cleft and labia . . . are acceptable, but a clear distension of labia would still be cut for '18'.

BBFC policy, the leaked document revealed, declared that 'invasive, intrusive, internal labial vaginal shots', were unsuitable for '18' but acceptable for 'R18'. It then emerged that over the previous three years these meetings followed a familiar pattern: conscientious analysis of aroused penises, exposed labia, or sado-masochism, followed by a row with Mr Ferman. After lunch there would be more erect penises, and the sniping would begin again.

At one point in another meeting, Geoffrey Wood, a university anthropologist, had argued that the examiners' objective was 'to move the Board into the twentieth century'; and later on at a further meeting the censors attemped to draw a distinction between soft porn and sex education tapes. Apparently this

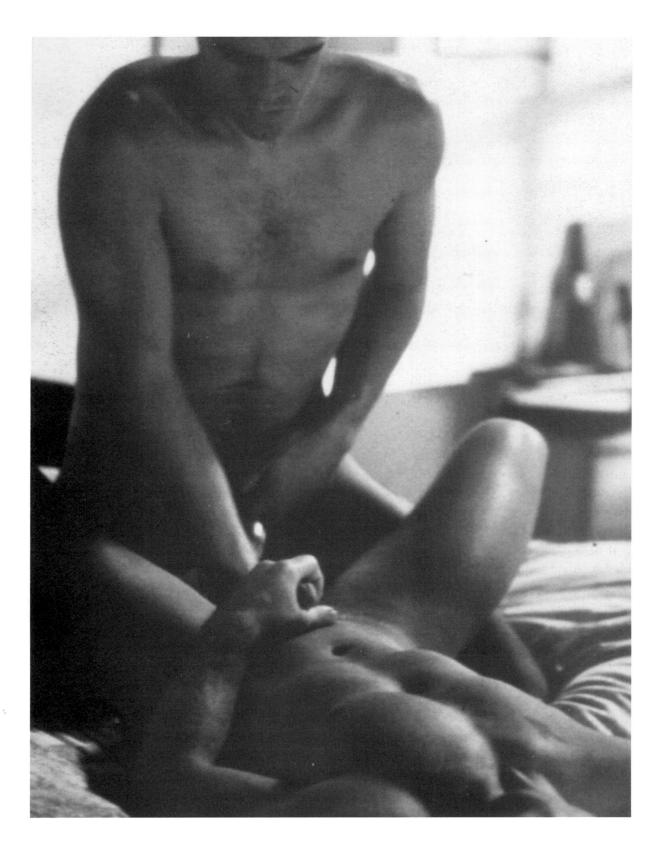

related to the examiners' repeated attempts – vigorously opposed by the chief censor – to abandon 'R18' because, since there were so few outlets for the category, the use of the classification was therefore censorship by default. Jeremy O'Grady, a sociological researcher, then pointed out that exploitation producers were using sex education 'to get around the ludicrous standards we impose on sex'.

It also came to light that the examiners had expressed doubt about the Home Office guidelines on sex and violence and the government's definition of what reasonable people might accept in soft porn. A woman examiner believed that the function of perversions for their practitioners was 'a way of staying alive, almost as essential as breathing'. This particular discussion then ended with a colleague posing the question, 'What about the Clapham omnibus woman who likes "château fuck" films?'

Unfortunately for the Board's management, if not its employees, any clearly delineated line through interlocked limbs and intertwined pubic hair is in imminent danger, however, of being removed by the transmission of pornography direct into British homes via satellite. That the presence of such material on British screens obviously contravenes the BBFC's sexual censorship rulings seemed to have been overlooked when the government signed the European Directive on Transfrontier Broadcasting. The government's decision in April 1993 to outlaw the decoders which unlock such transmissions is probably only a short-term stratagem, as the transmissions themselves are legal. On the other hand, by the time the legality of decoders is resolved, the government is presumably hoping that it will have excluded Britain from the option of receiving hard-core pornography.

The other threat that impinges on the future of film censorship will also be decided by the precedence accorded to one of two laws. In theory, European trade agreements allow individual British citizens to bring into this country any kind of film or videotape for their own consumption which does not contravene laws such as the Obscene Publications Act. In practice this is opposed by the customs law which clearly states that goods entering Britain do so by the 'gracious permission of her Majesty the Queen'. The customs authorities are therefore acting within their rights if they confiscate pornographic videos being brought back from a holiday in an EC country. Presumably a precedent will be established through a test case in a courtroom.

The current popularity of sex education videos and their lack of controversy has given the courts and the political establishment room to manoeuvre. But this is a paradoxical opportunity. For the success of these videos suggests that, for the British people, sex on the screen is acceptable within the privacy of the home, but unacceptable in public on the cinema screen. Support for pornography, whether soft or hard, would therefore be foolhardy in the public arena of politics.

By the end of 1993, both the BBFC and James Ferman had arrived at a forked road. At the time, the contracts of most of the examiners were due to be renewed. So it now became a matter of some concern to those outside, as well as inside, the Board as to who exactly would be retained and who would be pruned. In other words, would Ferman hive off the examiners who questioned his decisions?

On 6 December 1993, Ferman told the *Evening Standard*, 'There is no truth in the rumour that the BBFC has dismissed any examiners. The fact is that throughout this year, the Board has been planning to reorganise with effect from the beginning of 1995.' In fact, he had already sent letters to each one of the examiners informing them that their contracts would not be renewed. From 1 January 1995 nine examiners would be employed by the Board, five of them would be newcomers to the BBFC; the remaining four would be selected from amongst the previous examiners. In a subsequent interview the Director pointed out that the Board had recently given an undertaking to Parliament that 'we'll have a changeover'. But he also said that it was 'coincidental that the changes have been announced at the time of the Bulger case'.

Both comments appeared, however, to be red herrings. For two months later, the *Guardian* reported that on 19 January 1994, the dispute had come to a climax when nine of the Board's examiners met the President and the two Vice Presidents to make a final appeal against their dismissals. There the examiners argued that the changeover to nine full-time examiners would lead to a closed system, less responsive to changing social standards on sex and violence, and it was for these reasons of hermetism that Stephen Murphy had abandoned such a system twenty years before. But the Presidents – colloquially known within the BBFC as the 'Three Blind Mice' – were sceptical about the examiners' fears and felt that it was not their role to interfere in employment matters. A woman examiner then addressed the Presidents: 'Given that censorship here is not a democratic process, we all feel that some checks and balances in ensuring the representation of people's freedom are required, not just in the public domain, but here in the privacy of the Board and its internal working. What is it,' she asked them, 'that you do that produces checks and balances on what many of us here would see as James Ferman calling the shots?'

For his part, Ferman dismissed newspaper suggestions that he was introducing the changes in order to make his position more powerful. 'That's nonsense,' he declared in the *Daily Telegraph* on 19 February 1994. 'I am extremely powerful and keep an extremely tight grip on standards. If I disagree overwhelmingly with the Board about a film, I can overrule their decision subject to the discretion of the Vice Presidents.' The chief censor also pointed out 'the need to have a smaller, more committed group of officers. Having semi-detached Board members no longer works,' he said. 'Some of the examiners have been here too long. We need fresh faces.'

In the light, however, of his on-going battles with examiners over accountability within the BBFC for classification and policy decisions another interpretation has to be attached to these dismissals. It is more than likely that Ferman will now take advantage of this opportunity to rid the Board of what he has called its more 'vexatious' members. The new examiners will 'be easier to manipulate', a censor observes, 'because they won't have the independence of mind that comes with experience and outside interests'.

The five new full-time examiners, this censor believes, will be more conducive to arguments for the retention of 'R18' and against the liberalisation of sex for the more available '18' classification. Moreover, when the changeover is coupled with the government's current pressure on the Board to tighten controls on violence due to the Bulger case, it is doubtful, this examiner says, that any calls will be voiced in the future from within the Board for a more reasoned, accountable system of censorship. Thus, the future of the BBFC will be similar to its immediate past: a painstaking advance in sex, but only in sex education; progress in violence if the film-maker possesses an artistic reputation; and overall retreat in the face of government and tabloid pressure.

One other explanation that Ferman gives for the BBFC's wholesale redundancies is that most of the other European Boards constantly 'turnover' their censors and that there should be consistency in the administration of EC film censorship. But most of those Boards also change their head censors at regular intervals. However, this sixty-four-year-old head censor, who does not have a contract with the Board, has given no sign that he intends to give way to a successor in 1995 when he reaches the normal retirement age for BBFC employees. In fact, he disclosed in his letter of dismissal to the examiners that he intended to administer the BBFC 'alongside the new team which will see the Board through into the next century'.

The Director says that in the years ahead he would like to tackle the problem of bridging the gap between the different standards that apply to film censorship in EC countries. To do this he will have to persuade the other EC Boards to raise their limits on sexual violence while Britain lowers its own on consensual screen sex. This has already been partly achieved due to the current classification of consensual soft pornography on sex education tapes; whether that tolerance is extended in the future, however, to exploitation sex films is unlikely because of the ousting of liberal voices within the Board. Also any movement on the other side of the international bridge appears to be equally doubtful because, as Ferman himself has remarked, the European Boards jealously guard their own policies and they are not likely to give them up for Britain's convenience.

Britain's chief censor, on the other hand, possesses considerable experience on the international stage of film censorship. He has hosted two world conferences on 'Standards in Screen Entertainment', with leading experts giving talks on 'Protecting the Young', 'The Shock of Reality' and 'Freedom of Expression'. Unfortunately, Ferman has also introduced subjects into these well attended seminars which have provoked indignation as well as bemusement amongst foreign censors. Many of them expressed astonishment at the end of an illustrated lecture on child pornography given by Superintendent Hames of the Obscene Publications Squad which showed scenes of children being forcibly penetrated since this kind of material has never been part of their agenda. More to the point, Ferman must have also been aware that child pornography has never been submitted to the BBFC. In fact the British sex exploitation industry knows the requirements of the Board so well that their main editing house in Soho often does not have to re-cut films after they have been submitted to the censor.

Leaving to one side the belief amongst European head censors that their British counterpart tends towards eccentricity, it is tempting to believe that Ferman's leadership of the BBFC has been an oddity in the history of Britain's film censorship. Certainly Ferman himself believes that he stands out from his predecessors. But with the exception of Stephen Murphy in the early seventies, James Ferman's decisions have on balance, been no worse and no better than those of any of the other previous heads of the BBFC. Like John Trevelyan he has repeatedly told the press that he applies an aesthetic slide-rule to films but

like Trevelyan he has made exceptions – in Ferman's case to a vulva image on a TV screen during David Cronenburg's 1983 film *Videodrome*, as well as to Martin Scorsese's *Taxi Driver* (1976) in which the sound of Jodie Foster pulling down Travis Bickle's (Robert de Niro) fly was cut. Again, unlike Murphy but like Trevelyan, he has sailed with the wind of public opinion but retreated when blasts of controversy have been unleashed by newspaper furores. The actual difference between the present and past chief censors has in fact been difficult to discern because the change in emphasis has not been so much moral as pragmatic; for Ferman is more invulnerable than his predecessors.

How the chief censor achieved this was largely due to his astute exploitation of circumstance. Up until 1984 the make-up of the Board roughly remained the same (it was the films that changed). But then the BBFC became the only practical choice for the censorship of videos. The government, however, does not pay anything towards the administration of the Video Recordings Act; while the film industry which does, relies on the BBFC to protect it from newspaper campaigns for more censorship. That influence over the industry has in turn been concentrated upon Ferman because of the confidentiality clauses within examiners' contracts and also because the length of those contracts is ultimately his responsibility. On the other hand, if the government wanted to sack Ferman, they could not do so because the delegated authority to censor videos is not his legal responsibility. And assuming the government did decide to withdraw that authority from the Presidents of the Board Ferman would still head the BBFC's film censorship arm. It is these bureaucratic skills which forged such an invulnerable position that finally separate this particular censor from his predecessors.

Even James Ferman's political dexterity will soon be tested, however, by a question which could render all suppositions about the future of censorship redundant: how will the viewing of films be affected by current advances in home entertainment technology? Within a decade video films will merge with video computer games and, undoubtedly, such interaction with the viewer will then be extended to violent films, sex films and presumably sexually violent films. As James Ferman confirmed on Radio 4 in October 1993, 'The possibilities are endless.'

The present chief censor has pointed out that the progress of home entertainment technology could not only determine the course and the content but also the very survival of film censorship. 'It may well be that in the twenty-first century,' he believes, 'that it simply becomes impossible to impose the kind of old-fashioned regulation which the Board exists to provide, on films that come out of the stratosphere from a satellite that is over the mid-Atlantic and outside any national territory. After all,' he concludes, 'what's the point of cutting a gang-rape scene in a British version of a film if that film is accessible down a telephone line from outside British territorial waters?' Alternatively, any future government will only have one institution in place to turn to if they wish to challenge what the chief censor calls 'a very perplexing and rather daunting future' – and that is the BBFC.

In the history of film censorship one voice has rarely been raised: that of the British public. Censorship is done in its name, and, without its agreement cannot function. But film censorship has functioned for over nine decades: and paradoxically it owes its existence to a denial of public multiplicity and plurality.

Thirty-five years ago the surrealist film-maker Luis Buñuel said, 'The real responsibility for the spiritual stagnation of the cinema lies with the amorphous mass, routinary and conformist that makes up the cinema.' There is more than a grain of truth in this simplified statement. But the dice have also

Opposite Front pages like this instigated the Alton amendment which introduced two new tests for video censorship – 1) films which contain 'inappropriate role models' for children, and 2) films which are likely to cause 'psychological damage' in children.

THE Sun

Friday, November 26, 1993   **20p**   Audited daily sale for October 3,778,312

20P

Brave Roy's cancer is back

By NICK PARKER

TV star Roy Castle is battling cancer again —15 months after he thought he had beaten the killer disease.

The 61-year-old Record Breakers host went for new medical tests after feeling breathless.

His worst fears were confirmed on Tuesday when doctors revealed that cancerous cells had returned to his lungs.

He has been given chemotherapy tablets to

Roy . . . 'I'll beat it'

keep the cancer in check while more tests are carried out.

And he has pulled out of a variety show in Blackpool to have "a complete rest."

Non-smoker Roy, who lost his hair during radiotherapy last year, said last night: "I didn't want this to be known too soon because I didn't want cancer sufferers in my position to lose hope.

"I certainly haven't — and I'm determined to fight this disease and beat it again. I will battle it all the way."

His wife Fiona, 53, said at their home in Gerrards Cross, Bucks: "Roy won't have to go back to hospital.

"Doctors said it would do more harm than good if he went through all the treatment again.

"It's obviously a set-
Continued on Page Seven

FRENCH KEVOLUTION

Kevin is now the most popular name for baby boys in France, ahead of Pierre or Francois.

For the sake of ALL our kids...
BURN YOUR VIDEO NASTY

By CHRIS PHARO and ALAN MUIR

A VIDEO chain boss yesterday torched his entire £10,000 stock of tapes linked to the James Bulger murder.

And last night The Sun launched a nationwide campaign to get all other copies of Child's Play 3 burned. If you own one yourself, burn it safely. If you have rented one, take it back to the shop and ask the dealer to destroy it.

Last night Liverpool MP David Alton praised The Sun's campaign.

He said burning was the answer to the "gratuitous nastiness" of the video, which may have been seen by Jon Venables, one of the killers.

The boss who burned his Child's Play tapes — including 300 copies of No 3, featuring evil doll Chucky — is Imtiaz Ahmad, 52. He is marketing director of Azad Video, Scotland's biggest chain.

And as the nasties went up in a bonfire at Glasgow he said: "As soon as I saw The Sun report I ordered the shelves in our 80 stores cleared. I'm not having that kind of stuff in my shops. Child's Play 3 is spine-chilling, really nasty."

Liberal Democrat Mr Alton — MP for Mossley Hill, Liverpool, where the murder happened — said: "This video is a piece of
Continued on Page 11

PLAY £26,000 SUN BINGO AND £48,000 NOUGHTS AND CROSSES – PAGE 40 been loaded. For the range of social controls which has divorced the British public from the cinema encompasses an empowered press, an entrenched class structure, and a political system which is incapable of responding to its diversity. Since 1912 these institutions have been telling the cinema audience that, for their own well-being, an intermediary or censor should come between them and the film-maker. That persuasion is now almost complete. The vast majority not only accept an undoubted need to protect children from traumatic images, but they also wish to protect their fellow adults from such images. They have therefore accepted the safety net within the pre-judgement of films which the censor brings, and which free expression would remove.

Yet ironically Britain's film censorship has a dubious basis in law. Its Edwardian origins were only sanctioned by parliamentary legislation in 1953. Before that date it was simply co-opted by local government. But film censorship has only survived because it has aligned itself closely with public opinion. Briefly in its infancy and during the early seventies it lurched away from its public moorings, but the price cinema nearly had to pay was the imposition of a more tightly controlled system of censorship, rather than the system's dissolution.

Admittedly, the pre-planned frenzy behind the moral panics induced in those particular years, as well as that of more recent times, can be understood as an inchoate expression of barely understood fears that the screen might expose. As those social fears have changed so they have been successively manacled to the cinema. The belief that films could affect juvenile crime, then class conflict, then patriotism, then misogyny and sexism, and finally violent crime, has repeatedly sanctioned censorship. Yet the evidence collected in the continuous supply of reports from the first Cinema Commission in 1917 up to today's briefings by current practising psychologists, states that films can emphasise and reinforce, but they do not instigate, human behaviour.

The most recent of these reports was commissioned from the Policy Studies Institute by the BBFC and the BBC in order to compare the viewing habits of juvenile offenders with those of non-offenders of the same age. On the Radio 4 programme 'Kaleidoscope' on 9 October 1993, Tim Newburn of the PSI revealed that 'There is not much difference' in what the two groups are watching. 'With reference to horror movies or movies with a sexual content or slasher movies,' he concluded that, 'far from being a predominance, there is relatively little evidence that those kids [offenders] are spending much of their time watching them – certainly no more time than children of that age generally do.'

Many would argue that such reports are not conclusive and, surely, the protection of children should have precedence over freedom of expression for adults? For children have a right to be protected from harm, and parents have a right to expect help from those in authority. Of course a balance between freedom and responsibility is constantly sought and enforced by parents. Children are 'censored' every day, but once that power is extended to a political institution like film censorship then any intricacies of choice are lost in the necessity to satisfy either one principle or the other, because both cannot be contained within one censorship decision.

Alternatively, if censorship is to survive and retain its political sanction, it has to exploit demands for social intervention. Of course those demands have to be valid, but even more importantly, they have to enhance the power of the censor. In other words they have to ask for more censorship. Also, in this way, one social demand which supports censorship can be adopted at the expense of another demand which opposes censorship; hence the present head censor's remark on the Channel 4 programme 'Right to Reply', transmitted in the spring of 1993: 'We can't have freedom for adults in this country, because we can't trust adults to protect children.'

Above all it is the spurious use of legitimate concerns which underlines censorship's dependency on moral absolutes. This has, in turn, placed an impossible burden on cinema's greatest value – its plurality. For if the cinema cannot oppose as well as sustain our values it will have no roots in reality. If, on the other hand, we continue to accept film censorship and its attendant reductivism, then Shakespeare's wise dictum will no longer have currency: 'the web of our life is of a mingled yarn, good and ill together: our virtues would be proud if our faults whipped them not; and our vices would despair if they were not cherished by our own virtues.'

SELECTED BIBLIOGRAPHY

Introduction
Hooligan: A History of Respectable Fears by Geoffrey Pearson (Macmillan, 1983).

Folk Devils and Moral Panics by Stanley Cohen (Oxford, 1980).

Chapter 1
A Pictorial History of Sex in the Movies by Jeremy Pascall and Clyde Jeavons (Hamlyn, 1975).

Dirty Movies, an Illustrated History of the Stag Film, 1915–1970 by Al di Lauro and Gerald Rabkin (New York and London, 1976).

Came the Dawn by C. Hepworth (Phoenix, 1951).

A Million and One Nights by Terry Ramsaye (Simon & Shuster, 1926).

The History of the British Film 1896–1906 by Rachel Low and Roger Manvell (Allen & Unwin, 1949).

Chapter 2
The British Board of Film Censors: Film Censorship in Britain 1896–1950 by James C. Robertson (Croom Helm, 1985).

Annual Reports 1913–1937, British Board of Film Censors.

Film Censors and the Law by Neville March Hunnings (Allen & Unwin, 1967).

Cinema, Censorship, and Sexuality 1909–1925 by Annette Kuhn (Routledge, 1988).

Notes on the Origin and Development of the British Board of Film Censors 1912–1952 by Sidney Harris (London, 1960).

The Lord Chamberlain's Blue Pencil by John Johnston (Hodder & Stoughton, 1990).

Celluloid Sacrifice by Alexander Walker (Michael Joseph, 1966).

Chapter 3
The War, the West and the Wilderness by Kevin Brownlow (Alfred A. Knopf, 1978).

Behind the Mask of Innocence by Kevin Brownlow (Alfred A. Knopf, 1990).

The History of British Film 1914–1918 by Rachel Low (Allen & Unwin, 1950).

The Cinema: its Present Position and Future Possibilities, Report of Cinema Commission of Inquiry, July 1917.

Picture Palace. A Social History of the Cinema by Audrey Field (Gentry Books, 1974).

Chapter 4
BBFC Scenerio Reports 1931–1939 British Film Institute.

The Age of the Dream Palace: Cinema and Society in Britain 1930–1939 by Jeffrey Richards (Routledge, 1984).

The Censor, the Drama and the Film by Dorothy Knowles (Allen & Unwin, 1934).

The Political Censorship of Films by Ivor Montagu (Gollancz, 1929).

Nothing Sacred: Selected Writings by Angela Carter (Virago, 1982).

Chapter 5
The Hidden Cinema. British Film Censorship 1913–1972 by James C. Robertson (Routledge, 1974).

Caught in the Act. Sex and Eroticism in the Movies by David Shipman (Hamish Hamilton, 1985).

'The First Reality: Film Censorship in Liberal England' by Nicholas Pronay in *Feature Films as History* edited by K. R. M. Short (Croom Helm, 1981).

'The British Board of Film Censors and Content Control in the 1930s' by Jeffrey Richards in *Historical Journal of Film, Radio and Television*, Vols I and II.

Chapter 6
Filming as Subversive Art by Amos Vogel (Random House, 1974).

The Erotic Arts by Peter Webb (Secker & Warburg, 1975).

Goldwyn by A. Scott Berg (Hamish Hamilton, 1989).

Hollywood Babylon by Kenneth Anger (Arrow Books, 1975).

Chapter 7
'Movies and Mandarins : the Offical Film and British Colonial Africa' by Rosaleen Smith in *British Cinema History* edited by James Curran and Vincent Porter (Weidenfeld and Nicolson, 1983).

The Indian Film by P. Shah (Motion Picture Society of India, Bombay, 1950).

Film Censorship in India (Kino, Calcutta, 1964).

Screening History by Gore Vidal (Andre Deutsch, 1992).

Chapter 8
Film and the Working Class by Peter Stead (Routledge, 1989).

'British Film Censorship and Propaganda Policy During the Second World War' by Nicholas Pronay and Jeremy Croft in *British Cinema History* edited by James Curran and Vincent Porter (Weidenfeld and Nicolson, 1983).

'British Film Censorship Goes to War' by James C. Robertson in *Historical Journal of Film, Radio and Television*, 1982.

Michael Powell. A Life in Movies. An Autobiography (Heinemann, 1986).

Chapter 9

The People's Peace: British History 1945–1989 by Kenneth O. Morgan (Oxford University Press, 1990).

Sex, Class and Realism. British Cinema 1956–1963 by John Hill (British Film Institute, 1986).

Nicholas Ray, An American Journey by Bernard Eisenschitz (Faber & Faber, 1993).

Seeing Is Believing: How Hollywood Taught Us to Stop Worrying and Love the Fifties by Peter Biskind (Pantheon Books, 1983).

The Celluloid Closet: Homosexuality in the Movies by Vito Russo (Harper & Row, 1981).

BBFC Scenario Reports 1945–1975.

Chapter 10

'The Habit of Censorship: "We're paid to have dirty minds" ' by Derek Hill in *Encounter* (July, 1960).

Sexual Alienation in the Cinema by Raymond Durgnat (London, Studio Vista, 1974).

A Pictorial History of Sex in Films by Parker Tyler (Citadel Press, 1974).

Sex in the Movies by Alexander Walker (Penguin, 1968).

Chapter 11

Hollywood England: The British Film in the Sixties by Alexander Walker (Michael Joseph, 1974).

The Best of British by Jeffrey Richards and Anthony Aldgate (Oxford, 1983).

Russ Meyer. The Life and Films by David K. Frasier (1990).

Doing Rude Things. The History of the British Sex Film 1957–1981 by David McGillivray (Sun Tavern Fields, 1992).

What the Censor Saw by John Trevelyan (Michael Joseph, 1973).

Celluloid Sacrifice by Alexander Walker (Michael Joseph, 1966).

Chapter 12

Warhol by Victor Bockris (Frederick Muller, 1989).

Film Censorship by Guy Phelps (Gollancz, 1975).

Cut: The Unseen Cinema by Baxter Philips (Lorimar, 1975).

Censorship in Britain by Paul O'Higgins (Nelson, 1972).

Chapter 13

British Board of Film Censors, *Monthly Bulletins, 1975–1979*.

The Psychotronic Encyclopedia of Film by Michael Weldon (Ballantine Books, 1983).

Obscenity and Film Censorship: The Williams Report (Cambridge University Press, 1981).

Obscenity. Law in Context by Geoffrey Robertson (Weidenfeld and Nicolson 1979).

Chapter 14

The Video Nasties edited by Martin Barker (Pluto Press, 1984).

Video Violence and Children. Report from the Parlimentary Group Video Enquiry (Oasis Projects, 1983).

Nightmare Movies by Kim Newman (Bloomsbury, 1984).

Shock Xpress edited by Stefan Jaworzyn (Titan Books, 1991).

Chapter 15

Scorsese on Scorsese edited by David Thompson and Ian Christie (Faber & Faber, 1989).

Hard Core: Power, Pleasure and the 'Frenzy of the Visible' by Linda Williams (Pandora Press, 1990).

PICTURE ACKNOWLEDGEMENTS

The publishers wish to thank the following. All pictures courtesy of the Ronald Grant archive, except those listed below. The British Film Institute: 6, 8, 10, 11, 42, 43, 44, 46, 62, 69, 84, 91, 102, 105, 106, 109, 141, 178, 196 (both), 221, 224, 227. Pride Video Productions: 280. Vision Video Limited: 281. Rex Features Limited: 287. The Stills Division of the National Film Archive: 53, 100, 107. The Wisconsin Center for Film and Theater Research: 36. Duncan MacBrayne Photography: 216. The photos on page 37 and page 55 are from *Behind the Mask of Innocence* by Kevin Brownlow (Knopf, 1990). The photo on page 64 is from the *Collected Screen Plays of Bernard Shaw* (George Prior, 1980).

INDEX

Page numbers in italics refer to illustrations.